Practical Studies in E-Government

Saïd Assar · Imed Boughzala
Isabelle Boydens
Editors

Practical Studies
in E-Government

Best Practices from Around the World

 Springer

Editors
Saïd Assar
Institut Télécom
Telecom Business School
Evry, France
said.assar@it-sudparis.eu

Imed Boughzala
Institut Télécom
Telecom Business School
Evry, France
imed.boughzala@it-sudparis.eu

Isabelle Boydens
Free University of Brussels (ULB)
Information and Communication Science
Brussels, Belgium
iboydens@ulb.ac.be

ISBN 978-1-4899-8189-9   ISBN 978-1-4419-7533-1 (eBook)
DOI 10.1007/978-1-4419-7533-1
Springer New York Dordrecht Heidelberg London

Printed on acid-free paper

Springer is part of Springer Science+Business Media (www.springer.com)

Contents

Contributors

Christine Aïdonidis
Centre des Technologies de l'Information, State of Geneva,
64, 66 Rue du Grand Pré, 1211 Geneva 3, Switzerland
christine.aidonidis@etat.ge.ch

Dimitris Askounis
National Technical University of Athens,
Iroon Polytechniou 9, Athens,15780, Greece
askous@epu.ntua.gr

Saïd Assar
Insitut Télécom, Telecom Business School, 9, rue Ch. Fourier, 91011 Evry, France
said.assar@it-sudparis.eu

Godefroy Beauvallet
Institut Télécom, Télécom ParisTech,
46, Rue Barrault, 75013 Paris, France
godefroy.beauvallet@telecom-paristech.fr

William Bland
Department of Systems Engineering (MADN-SE), United States Military
Academy, 646 Swift Road, West Point, NY 10996, USA
william.bland@us.army.mil

Geert Bouckaert
Public Management Institute, Katholieke Universiteit Leuven,
Parkstraat 45, B-3000, Leuven, Belgium
geert.bouckaert@soc.kuleuven.be

Imed Boughzala
Institut Télécom, Telecom Business School,
9, Rue Ch. Fourier 91011, Evry, France
imed.boughzala@it-sudparis.eu

Younès Boughzala
Université de Savoie, Institut de Recherche en Économie et Gestion (IREGE),
4 Chemin de Bellevue, BP 80439, 74944 Annecy le Vieux Cedex, France
younes.boughzala@univ-savoie.fr

Isabelle Boydens
Département Sciences de l'Information et de la Communication – CP 123,
Université Libre de Bruxelles, Faculté de Philosophie et Lettres,
Avenue F.D. Roosevelt, 50, B-1050, Bruxelles, Belgium
iboydens@ulb.ac.be

Gaëlle Calvary
Université de Grenoble, CNRS, LIG, 385, Rue de la Bibliothèque, BP 53,
38041 Grenoble Cedex 9, France
Gaelle.Calvary@imag.fr

Yannis Charalabidis
Department of Information and Communication Systems Engineering, University
of the Aegean, School of Sciences, Karlovassi, Samos, 83200, Greece
yannisx@aegean.gr

Joëlle Coutaz
Université de Grenoble, CNRS, LIG, 385, Rue de la Bibliothèque, BP 53,
38041 Grenoble Cedex 9, France
Joelle.Coutaz@imag.fr

Joep Crompvoets
Public Management Institute, Katholieke Universiteit Leuven,
Parkstraat 45, B-3000, Leuven, Belgium
joep.crompvoets@soc.kuleuven.be

Rowena Cullen
School of Information Management, Victoria University of Wellington,
PO Box 600, Wellington, New Zealand
rowena.cullen@vuw.ac.nz

J. Ramon Gil-Garcia
Centro de Investigación y Docencia Económicas, Carretera México-Toluca 3655,
Col. Lomas de Santa Fe, CP, México 01210, DF, Mexico
joseramon.gil@cide.edu

Simon R. Goerger
Department of Systems Engineering (MADN-SE), United States Military
Academy, 646 Swift Road, West Point, NY 10996, USA
simon.goerger@us.army.mil

Dale L. Henderson
Department of Systems Engineering (MADN-SE), United States Military
Academy, 646 Swift Road, West Point, NY 10996, USA
dale.henderson@usma.edu

Lizbeth Herrera
Centro de Investigación y Docencia Económicas, Carretera México-Toluca 3655,
Col. Lomas de Santa Fe, CP México 01210, DF, Mexico
lizbeth.herrera@gmail.com

Marijn Janssen
Delft University of Technology, Jaffalaan 5, 2628 BX, Delft, The Netherlands
m.f.w.h.a.janssen@tudelft.nl

Abdelaziz Khadraoui
Department of Information Systems, University of Geneva,
Battelle, CUI, 7 Route de Drize, CH-1227 Carouge, Geneva, Switzerland
abdelaziz.khadraoui@unige.ch

Fenareti Lampathaki
National Technical University of Athens, Iroon Polytechniou 9, Athens,15780, Greece
flamp@epu.ntua.gr

Lucie Langer
Technische Universität Darmstadt, Department of Computer Science,
Cryptography and Computer Algebra Group, Hochschulstraße 10,
64289, Darmstadt, Germany
langer@cdc.informatik.tu-darmstadt.de

Michel Léonard
Department of Information Systems, University of Geneva,
Battelle, CUI, 7 Route de Drize, CH-1227 Carouge, Geneva, Switzerland
michel.leonard@unige.ch

Fabrice Mattatia
Secrétariat d'Etat chargé de la prospective et du développement de l'économie
numérique, 35 rue St-Dominique, 75007 Paris, France
fabrice.mattatia@pm.gouv.fr

Wanda Opprecht
Department of Information Systems, University of Geneva,
Battelle, CUI, 7 Route de Drize, CH-1227 Carouge, Geneva, Switzerland
wanda.opprecht@unige.ch

Florence Pontico
Région Midi-Pyrénées, DSI – Service Etudes et Solutions, 22 Boulevard du
Maréchal Juin, 31406 Toulouse, France
Florence.PONTICO@cr-mip.fr

Dominique Scapin
INRIA Paris – Rocquencourt Research Centre, Domaine de
Voluceau-Rocquencourt, BP 105, Le Chesnay 78153, France
Dominique.Scapin@inria.fr

Audrey Serna
Université de Grenoble, CNRS, LIG, 385, Rue de la Bibliothèque, BP 53,
38041 Grenoble Cedex 9, France
Audrey.Serna@imag.fr

Brian K. Sperling
Department of Systems Engineering (MADN-SE), United States Military
Academy, 646 Swift Road, West Point, NY 10996, USA
brian.sperling@us.army.mil

Glenn Vancauwenberghe
Public Management Institute, Katholieke Universiteit Leuven,
Parkstraat 45, B-3000, Leuven, Belgium
glenn.vancauwenberghe@soc.kuleuven.be

Danny Vandenbroucke
Spatial Applications Division, Katholieke Universiteit Leuven, GEO-instituut
Campus Arenberg, Celestijnenlaan 200E, BE-3001, Leuven, Belgium
danny.vandenbroucke@sadl.kuleuven.be

Anne Fleur van Veenstra
Delft University of Technology, Jaffalaan 5, 2628 BX, Delft, The Netherlands
a.f.e.vanveenstra@tudelft.nl

Marco Winckler
IRIT – University Paul Sabatier, 118, route de Narbonne,
31062 Toulouse Cedex 9, France
winckler@irit.fr

Ernest Y. Wong
Department of Systems Engineering (MADN-SE), United States Military
Academy, 646 Swift Road, West Point, NY 10996, USA
ernest.wong@us.army.mil

Chapter 1
Back to Practice, a Decade of Research in E-Government

Saïd Assar, Imed Boughzala, and Isabelle Boydens

Abstract E-government is a multidisciplinary field of research based initially on empirical insights from practice. Efforts to theoretically found the field have opened perspectives from multiple research domains. The goal of this chapter is to review evolution of the e-government field from an institutional and an academic point of view. Our position is that e-government is an emergent multidisciplinary field of research in which focus on practice is a prominent characteristic. Each chapter of the book is then briefly presented and is positioned according to a vision of the e-government domain of research.

1.1 E-Government Definition and Evolution

Information and communication technologies (ICT) have been used in governmental organizations since the beginning of the computer era. For example, one of the first large-scale applications of computers was during the presidential election in the United States in 1954. Since then, governmental information systems have evolved in parallel with those of organizations in the private sector. When Internet technologies and the e-business phenomena hit the market a decade ago, the terms *e-government* and *digital government* were introduced and many definitions have emerged in the research literature [GRÖ04b, YIL07]. For the sake of this chapter, we retain the following characteristics: (1) the usage of Internet technologies to deliver services online and to rationalize, redesign, and significantly improve public administrative processes; (2) the reorganization of public institutions in order to reduce cost and to enhance the quality and efficiency of services offered to citizens, companies, and other governmental partners; (3) the development of new democratic spaces in which relations among public institutions, citizens, and enterprises are redefined according to a participatory perspective. The ultimate goal is to leverage technology for creating a new generation of cost-efficient, transparent, interactive, and ubiquitous ICT-enabled public services.

S. Assar (✉)
Insitut Télécom, Telecom Business School, 9, rue Ch. Fourier, 91011 Evry, France
e-mail: said.assar@it-sudparis.eu

S. Assar et al. (eds.), *Practical Studies in E-Government: Best Practices from Around the World*, DOI 10.1007/978-1-4419-7533-1_1,
© Springer Science+Business Media, LLC 2011

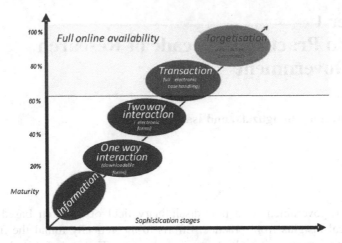

Fig. 1.1 E-government evolution framework (extracted from [EUC09])

E-government is constantly evolving all around the world. This evolution is regularly measured and tracked by public institutions, private agencies, and researchers alike. At the European level, since 2001 the European Commission has conducted a benchmarking project that measures the availability and sophistication of 20 basic public services for citizens and businesses. This benchmark establishes the foundations for the progressive and planned modernization of pan-EU e-government comparison. For businesses, the services being monitored include social security contributions for employees, corporate tax and VAT (Value Added Taxes) declaration and payment, and public procurement. For citizens, the services being tracked include income tax declaration and payment, change of address notification, job search, and requests for car registration and building permits. The development of e-services is measured with two indicators: the degree of "sophistication" of the public services that are offered online, and the number of services that are fully available online [EUC09]. Figure 1.1 presents the five-stage maturity model for benchmarking e-services sophistication. Stages 1–3 correspond to the increasing levels of sophistication which are one-way interactive and two-way interactive. Stage 4 corresponds to the "transactional" stage – also called full electronic case handling – where the user applies for and receives the service online, without any additional paperwork. The fifth level, "targetization" (or "personalization"), provides an indication of the extent by which front- and back-offices are integrated, data are reused, and services are delivered proactively (users do not have to submit a request to take advantage of the service).

According to the 2009 edition of the European Commission benchmark [EUC09], the leading six nations with full online availability of the basic 20 services are: Austria, Malta, Portugal, the United Kingdom, Sweden, and Slovenia. With regard to the online sophistication of the 20 basic services, the leading six nations are Malta, Portugal, Sweden, Austria, Slovenia, and Estonia.

At the international level, the United Nations department of Economic and Social Affairs (UNDESA) has regularly published reports that rank the United

Table 1.1 Top 20 countries in e-government development (extracted from [UN10])

Rank	Country	E-government development index value
1	Republic of Korea	0.8785
2	United States	0.8510
3	Canada	0.8448
4	United Kingdom	0.8147
5	Netherlands	0.8097
6	Norway	0.8020
7	Denmark	0.7872
8	Australia	0.7863
9	Spain	0.7516
10	France	0.7510
11	Singapore	0.7476
12	Sweden	0.7474
13	Bahrain	0.7363
14	New Zealand	0.7311
15	Germany	0.7309
16	Belgium	0.7225
17	Japan	0.7152
18	Switzerland	0.7136
19	Finland	0.6967
20	Estonia	0.6965

Nations' member states according to a quantitative composite index of e-readiness based initially on website assessment, telecommunication infrastructure, and human resource endowment [UN05, UN08].[1] In its 2010 edition, significant changes to the survey instrument were introduced, focusing more on how governments are using websites and Web portals to deliver public services and expand opportunities for citizens to participate in decision-making [UN10]. According to this latest report, Table 1.1 presents the top 20 countries in e-government development. For the E-Participation Index, Republic of Korea, Australia, and Spain hold the first three positions in the top 20 countries.

At the academic level as well, many models have been proposed to understand the maturity of e-government and to capture different stages of e-services development. Initial stages in these models are very similar in their concentration on the availability of governmental information, on the possibility of downloading forms for initiating an administrative process (e.g., identity card renewal), and on the possibility of handling this process partly or fully online in a transactional bi-directional mode; however, later stages differ slightly. In [LAY01], later stages concentrate on the vertical integration (local systems linked to higher-level systems within similar functions) and horizontal integration (systems integrated across different functions, real one-stop function for citizens and enterprises). In [SIA04], later stages concentrate on public services transformation through their integration in a homogeneous network of governmental services. This last stage is characterized by political transformations as it requires the reorganization of public agencies. In [EBR04] and the integration of public services (with each other and with private sector services and systems) is also the main issue for the latest stages of the maturity proposed frameworks. Finally, in [AND06], an extension to the initial model of [LAY01] is proposed based on an empirical investigation in Denmark. The latest stage of this extended model is called "Revolution" and highlights fundamental change in governmental practices and processes characterized by data mobility and sharing across public and private organizations, application mobility across public employees and services, and ownership of data transferred to final users. The authors recognize, however, that there are cases where direct application of their model is less appealing and where specific contextual elements should be taken into account (e.g., back-office intelligence units or homicide investigations in police departments).

To conclude this first section, the question of measuring e-government performance and evolution is an important issue for all stakeholders. Although significant and relevant data are gathered annually about the subject by international institutions (United Nations, European Commission), and although many research models have been proposed to characterize the underlying evolution process, the topic is still being investigated by the research community (e.g., [BER09, KOH08).

1.2   E-Government as a Field of Research

E-government started as a practitioner field of investigation, basically convening practitioners trying to meet the new challenges of the Internet medium by implementing new systems and offering new services creatively [GRÖ04b]. Based initially on empirical insights from practice, the first e-government conferences were practitioner-oriented with some invited academic keynotes. Rapidly, more academia-oriented conferences emerged, and the body of e-government-related knowledge grew rapidly. The maturity of the emerging research field was already questioned in 2004 [GRÖ04a]. It was criticized then as lacking theoretical foundation with insufficient levels of rigor and relevance in applying investigation methods, in establishing results, and in claiming their applicability to more general cases.

Significant efforts have been made since then to improve e-government research quality [GRÖ06], and to define e-government more rigorously as a domain of investigation and as a field of research [HEE07, HOV07]. In these studies, a large number of research papers published in prominent conferences and journals were analyzed according to multiple criteria:

* Research type: Descriptive, theoretical, theory testing, theory generating, philosophical
* Research method: Product description, survey, questionnaire, experiment, ethnography, grounded theory, document analysis, reflection on project experiment, Web content evaluation, literature review
* Researcher's home department: Business, computer science, political science, information systems, library and information studies, government agency, nonacademic research institution
* Literature used: Public administration, management, computer science, e-government, information systems, e-business, political science

Findings confirm what other researchers have suggested [SCH07]. E-government is an emergent multidisciplinary field of research in which focus on practice and on practical recommendations is a prominent characteristic. Although theoretical ground is still under construction, it certainly qualifies as a legitimate emerging scientific discipline. As technological innovations are continuously hitting the market, the frontiers of the e-government discipline are moving and its multidisciplinary nature confirmed. With the emergence of Web 2.0 as an essential dimension in Internet usage, e-government is shifting towards Government 2.0. Huge opportunities are becoming available for extending e-participation; for accelerating online public service implementation, evaluation, and adoption; and ultimately for introducing in the public sphere, open innovation and collaborative knowledge creation and diffusion [BAU09].

1.3   Presentation of the Book

The material presented in this book is a collective contribution to the e-government domain. Contributors come from nine different countries and are either practitioners in e-government or researchers who have been directly or indirectly implicated in e-government projects. Each chapter is a specific field study in which different investigation methods have been applied and combined according to the case study methodological approach [YIN03]. The primary audience for this book is scholars and practitioners in the area of e-government. It is also of interest to MSc-level students in curricula related to ICT in public administration, information systems, and e-business, and who seek practical cases in online services design, implementation, and evaluation.

To present the research topics that are covered by the book chapters, we rely on future research themes identified by the road mapping e-government research project eGovRTD 2020 [COD07, DAW08]. This project, funded by the European Community within the sixth framework program (FP6), aims to identify and characterize the key research challenges, required constituencies, and possible implementation models for holistic and dynamic governments in Europe and around the world in 2020 and beyond. This project identified 13 interrelated research themes, out of which 11 are of concern for the research work presented here. A mapping between these research themes and the chapters of this book is presented in Table 1.2, together with a mapping to the investigation methods used in the chapter's case study.

Chapter 2, entitled "E-Procurement, from Project to Practice: Empirical Evidence from the French Public Sector" by Godefroy Beauvallet, Younès Boughzala, and Saïd Assar, is an analysis of public e-procurement adoption in France. Electronic platforms for supporting public transactions are an important application of e-government. In France, new regulations since 2005 are pushing public and private actors to adopt electronic means for handling all steps of the purchase process in public organizations. Based on two different quantitative surveys made in 2005 and in 2008, the authors analyze the public and private users' perception of the virtualization of the procurement process. Between 2005 and 2008, significant progress is noticed in adopting electronic means for public

Table 1.2 Mapping among chapter content (columns), investigation methods, and research themes (lines)

	Chapter n°	02	03	04	05	06	07	08	09	10	11	12	13
Investigation method	Quantitative (surveys)	■				■							
	Qualitative (interviews)					■				■			
	Experiment								■	■	■		
	Legal document / web site analysis	■						■					■
	Project report		■	■			■				■	■	
	State of the art / review of the domain					■							■
	Design science approach			■			■		■	■	■	■	
E-government roadmap themes	Trust in e-government				■	■		■					
	Semantic and cultural interoperability of public services								■	■	■		
	Information quality						■						
	Assessing the value of government ICT investment	■	■										
	E-participation, citizen engagement and democratic process							■					
	Mission oriented goals and performance management	■	■	■									
	Cyber infrastructures for e-government			■			■			■	■	■	■
	Ontologies and intelligent information and knowledge management								■				
	Governance of public-private-civic sector relationship	■	■										
	Government's role in the virtual world				■			■					■
	Data privacy and personal identity				■	■							

agencies to publish a call for tender, for enterprises to upload a proposal using an electronic signature, and to a much less extent, for public managers to process the submitted proposals and make a decision concerning the choice of the product and of the provider. Many enterprises are still reluctant to submit proposals online because there is a lack of confidence in the digital system. And, unfortunately, there is a visible digital divide between public agencies (e.g., ministries, main governmental institutions) that have enough resources to master the technology and those, mainly local authorities in rural parts of the country who are struggling to digitalize their procurement processes.

In Chap. 3, Lizbeth Herrera and J. Ramon Gil-Garcia analyze a successful strategy involving three ICT projects through a case study of a Mexican federal agency. Entitled "Implementation of e-government in Mexico: The Case of INFONAVIT," this chapter uses a technology enactment framework composed of institutional, organizational, and managerial factors. Overall, the results of this study show that having a strategic plan that aligns the ICT project objectives with the overarching organizational goals leads to successful implementation because the technical, organizational, and institutional resources are managed in an integrated fashion. The chapter also reports specific factors that had an impact on the characteristics and success of the three ICT projects.

The context of the case study analyzed in Chap. 4 is the US Army Services. In the Chapter entitled "The Casualty Assistance Readiness Enhancement System (CARES): A Case Study in Rapid Prototyping and Design for Flexibility," Simon R. Goerger, Ernest Y. Wong, Dale L. Henderson, Brian K. Sperling, and William Bland describe and evaluate a system implemented to help in processing the benefits that are due to the surviving family of fallen US military service members. Most of these entitlements require a considerable amount of paperwork and necessitate a great deal of patience, attention to detail, and composure from families at a time when their grief is raw. Even though the US Army appoints a Casualty Assistance Officer (CAO) to help surviving family members through this process, the soldiers serving as CAOs tend to be inexperienced and oftentimes find themselves challenged to provide accurate and thorough assistance. Consequently, some families do not receive all benefits in a timely manner, and some entitlements may be overlooked entirely.

The Casualty Assistance Readiness Enhancement System (CARES) is an information system designed to improve how the Department of the Army cares for military families. The tool and associated process reduced the time required to complete forms, reduced the potential for errors on repetitive information, assisted CAOs through the process, and provided electronic copies of completed forms. The approach in the design of CARES (the process) demonstrates a viable methodology for the rapid development of a software solution to support an administrative process that is often performed by inexperienced users under the guidance and review of mid-level managers.

Chapter 5 is dedicated to electronic identification. As online services are now widely used, and as the exchanges of personal data become more and more widespread, electronic identification is becoming a key function for the security of the process and for the protection of privacy. In France and throughout Europe, e-government services, as well as private services already use different means of electronic identification. Fabrice Mattatia, in his chapter entitled "An Overview of Some Electronic Identification Use Cases in Europe" presents problems concerning identification in the digital space, and reviews the different technical solutions that are actually implemented in Europe for issuing electronic identity cards (e-ID). He discusses as well the question of e-ID interoperability, which is the main issue when it comes to giving access to all European citizens to e-services of any member state.

Chapter 6, by Rowena Cullen, is entitled "Privacy and Personal Information Held by Government: A Comparative Study, Japan and New Zealand." This chapter reports on the concepts of information privacy and trust in government among citizens in Japan and New Zealand in a transnational, cross-cultural study. Data from both countries are presented, and cultural and other factors are sought that might explain differences in attitudes shown. Hofstede's dimensions of culture are used as the theoretical background for the analysis of cultural differences. In both countries, citizens display a range of views, not related to age or gender.

New Zealand citizens express concern about information privacy in relation to information held by government, but show a higher level of trust in government overall. Japanese citizens interviewed also indicated that they had major concerns about information privacy, and had considerably less trust in government than New Zealand respondents showed. They were more inclined to attribute breaches of privacy to lax behavior in individuals than to government systems. In both countries citizens showed an awareness of the tradeoffs necessary between personal privacy and the needs of the state to hold information for the benefits of all citizens, but knew little about the protection offered by privacy legislation, and expressed overall concern about privacy practices in the modern state.

The main theme of Chap. 7 is information quality. Data quality is a strategic matter in the context of e-government as the integration of services requires authentic, coherent, and reliable data. However, establishing databases that are devoid of duplication, redundancy, or ambiguity isn't simple, neither in theory nor in practice, although administrative databases are often regarded wrongly as "simple." In her chapter entitled "Strategic Issues Relating to Data Quality for e-government: Learning from an Approach Adopted in Belgium," Isabelle Boydens demonstrates that this is not the case, in particular because of the questions of interpretation that they raise. This chapter is based on case studies stemming from the Belgian federal administration (social security, business directories, federal authentic sources, etc.). Contrary to the assertions of common theories postulating a permanent bijective relationship between data and the corresponding reality, she argues that an empirical information system evolves over time along with the interpretation of the values that it allows us to determine. To address data quality, she proposes a temporal framework that provides new operational strategies to improve administrative data quality (mainly, new ways to define quality indicators for continuous monitoring and re-engineering strategies). This framework demonstrates how the approach is generally applicable in the context of empirical information systems.

Chapter 8, by Lucie Langer and entitled "Long-Term Verifiability of Remote Electronic Elections" is directly related to the e-participation theme of research. Retention of election documents is essential for verifying the proper conduct of an election ex post. The documents retained provide for later review in case an election contest is filed. In the context of German Basic Law, the principle of public elections implies the need for public verifiability. This applies to remote electronic voting in particular as physical observation is not achievable in this case. Although the retention obligations on paper-based elections are governed by electoral law, according specifications for e-voting are still an open issue. The chapter therefore addresses the following questions. With which existing legal obligations on retention of election data is compliance needed? How can they be transferred to the scenario of remote electronic elections? Based on an analysis of the retention obligations specified in German electoral law, the author identifies the conditions that must be documented and are thus subject to long-term verifiability. She then investigates how they can be adapted to the scenario of remote electronic elections. Her work contributes to -establishing the basis for legally binding e-voting in Germany. As electoral law in Europe is rather consistent, this contribution might be useful to other countries as well.

Chapter 9 is entitled "Law-Based Ontology for e-government Services Construction: Case Study: The Specification of Services in Relationship with the Venture Creation in Switzerland," and is written by Abdelaziz Khadraoui, Wanda Opprecht, Michel Léonard, and Christine Aïdonidis. The compliance of e-government services with legal aspects is a crucial issue for administrations. This issue becomes more difficult with the fast-evolving dynamics of laws. This chapter presents an approach to describe and establish the link between e-government services and legal sources. This link is established by an ontology called "Law-Based Ontology." This ontology is used as means to define and to construct e-government services. It may not be exhaustive, but it is nonetheless based upon an unquestionable source of information, the laws themselves. The proposed approach is illustrated with one case study: the specification of services in relationship with the venture creation in Switzerland and in the State of Geneva. The authors have selected the Commercial Register area which mainly encompasses the registration of a new company and the modification of its registration.

The theme of Chap. 10 by Anne Fleur Van Veenstra and Marijn Janssen is service integration and interoperation on the Web, and it is entitled "Architectural Principles for Orchestration of Cross-Organizational Service Delivery: Case Studies from the Netherlands." Realizing Integrated Service Delivery (ISD) requires government agencies to collaborate across their organizational boundaries. Orchestration of services is one way of achieving coordination of processes across multiple organizations. In this chapter, authors identify architectural principles for orchestration by looking at three case studies of cross-organizational service delivery chain formation in the Netherlands (preparation module for joint permit requests, information system for importation of veterinary products, and information system supporting the asbestos removal process). In total, six generic principles were formulated and were subsequently validated in two workshops with experts: (1) build an intelligent front office, (2) give processes a clear starting point and end, (3) build a central workflow application keeping track of the process, (4) differentiate between simple and complex processes, (5) ensure that the decision-making responsibility and the overview of the process are not performed by the same process role, and (6) create a central point where risk profiles are maintained.

Chapter 11 is entitled "Achieving Interoperability Through Base Registries for Governmental Services and Document Management," and it is written by Yannis Charalabidis, Fenareti Lampathaki, and Dimitris Askounis. As digital infrastructures increase their presence worldwide and citizens and businesses are provided with high-quality one-stop services, there is a growing need for the systematic management of those newly defined processes and electronic documents. An Interoperability Registry is a system devoted to the formal description, composition, and publishing of traditional or electronic services, together with the relevant document and process descriptions in an integrated schema. Through such a repository, the discovery of services by users or systems can be automated, resulting in an important tool for achieving interoperability. This chapter describes the architecture, components, and underlying ontology of an interoperability regitry platform that has been developed in Greece, in the context of the new Greek Digital Strategy plan. The chapter illustrates the applicability of the approach through experimentations with the VAT process, which is, by nature, a process spanning multiple organizations.

The theme of Chap. 12 is human–computer interface. Entitled "Envisioning Advanced User Interfaces for e-government Applications: A Case Study," it is written by Gaëlle Calvary, Audrey Serna, Joëlle Coutaz, Dominique Scapin, Florence Pontico, and Marco Winckler. The adoption of e-government services provided to citizens depends upon how such applications comply with the users' needs. Unfortunately, building an e-government website doesn't guarantee that all citizens who come to use it can access its contents. These services need to be accessible to all citizens/customers equally to ensure wider reach and subsequent adoption of the e-government services. User disabilities, computer or language illiteracy (e.g., foreign language), flexibility on information access (e.g., users remotely located in rural areas, homeless, mobile users), ensuring user privacy on sensible data are some of the barriers that must be taken into account when designing the User Interface (UI) of e-government applications. Several initiatives (such as the W3C WAI) focus on how to promote usability and accessibility of content provided by e-government. And many governments are enhancing their technology to make their services compatible with new communication channels available through multiple devices including interactive digital TVs (iTV), personal digital assistants (PDAs), and mobile phones. In this chapter, the authors focus on this latter issue, which means the development of multitarget government services available across several platforms. They discuss the major constraints underlining the importance of investing in the UI's design for e-government applications. They propose a framework for envisioning advanced UIs where the adaptation to the user's capabilities, available devices, as well as physical and social environment will play a major role. This approach is illustrated through an experimental system developed for handling scholarship requests in a regional French administration.

Chapter 13 is entitled "Practices to Develop Spatial Data Infrastructures: Exploring the Contribution to e-government," and is written by Joep Crompvoets, Glenn Vancauwenberghe, Geert Bouckaert, and Danny Vandenbroucke. The main objectives of this chapter are to introduce Spatial Data Infrastructures (SDIs), and to explore their potential contribution to e-government. In order to understand the possible strengths of SDIs for e-government, the concept, components, governance, and the cost–benefit analyses regarding the implementation of these infrastructures are first explained and presented followed by a short presentation of four existing SDIs in practice (Europe, Catalonia, Flanders, and Leiedal). These practices show clearly the dynamic, integrated, and multiple natures of SDIs. The main reason to invest in SDIs is that they facilitate the sharing of spatial data so that the management and use of these spatial resources is more efficient and effective. Although sharing resources from multiple sources is still not common practice in e-government implementation, it will be very likely that ICTs will play a key role in improving the sharing of public resources. Lessons learnt from the existing SDI practices and understanding of the nature of SDIs could therefore be useful support to develop efficient and high-quality e-government systems.

Note

¹ All survey data since 2002 have been compiled by the UNDESA into an "e-government Readiness Knowledge Base" available online at http://www.unpan.org/egovkb/, retrieved July 2nd, 2010.

References

AND06   Andersen, K.V., Henriksen, H.Z., "E-government maturity models: Extension of the Layne and Lee model," Government Information Quarterly, vol. 23, pp. 236–248, 2006.

BAU09   Baumgarten, J., Chui, M., "E-government 2.0", McKinsey Quarterly, no. 4, 2009. Available online at http://www.mckinseyquarterly.com/Business_Technology/E-government_20_2408, retrieved July 2nd, 2010.

BER09   Berntzen, L., Olsen, M.G., "Benchmarking e-government: A comparative review of three international benchmarking studies", Third International Conference on Digital Society, Cancun, Mexico, pp. 77–82, February 1–7, 2009.

COD07   Codagnone, C., Wimmers, M.A., (Editors), Road mapping e-Government Research, eGovRTD2020 Project consortium, 2007. Available online at http://www.egovrtd2020.org/, retrieved Oct. 26th, 2009.

DAW08   Dawes S., "An exploratory framework for future e-government research investments," 41st Hawaii International Conference on System Sciences, HICSS 2008.

EBR04   Ebrahim, Z., Irani Z., Al Shawi S., "A Strategic Framework for E-government Adoption in Public Sector Organisations," Americas Conference on Information Systems (AMCIS), New York, August 6–8, 2004.

EURC09 European Commission, e-Government Benchmarking Reports, "eGovernment Benchmark Survey 2009: Smarter, Faster, Better eGovernment," Available online at http://ec.europa.eu/information_society/eeurope/i2010/benchmarking/index_en.htm, retrieved July 2nd, 2010.

GRÖ04a Grönlund A., "State of the art in e-gov research – A survey," Proceedings EGOV 2004, LNCS 3183, pp. 178–185, Springer, 2004.

GRÖ04b Grönlund A., Horan T.A., "Introducing e-gov: History, definitions and issues," Communication of the AIS, vol. 15, pp. 713–729, 2004.

GRÖ06   Grönlund A., Andersson, A., "E-gov research quality improvements since 2003: More rigor, but research (perhaps) redefined," Proceedings EGOV 2006, LNCS 4084, pp. 1–12, Springer, 2006.

HEE07   Heeks, R., Bailur, S., "Analyzing e-government research: Perspectives, philosophies, theories, methods, and practice", Government Information Quarterly, vol. 24, pp. 243–265, 2007.

HOV07   Hovy, E., "Chapter 3: An outline for the foundations of digital government research", In H. Chen et al. (Eds), Digital Government: Advanced Research and Case Studies, pp. 43–59, Springer, Berlin, 2007.

KOH08   Koh, C.E., Prybutok, V.R., Zhang, X., "Measuring e-government readiness", Information & Management, vol. 45, no. 8, pp. 540–546, 2008.

LAY01   Layne, K., Lee, J., "Developing fully functional E-government: A four stage model", Government Information Quarterly, vol. 18, no. 2, pp. 122–136, 2001.

SCH07   Scholl, H.J., "Chapter 2: Discipline or interdisciplinary study domain? Challenges and promises in electronic government research", In H. Chen et al. (eds), Digital government: Advanced research and case studies, pp. 21–41, Springer, Berlin, 2007.

SIA04   Siau K., Long Y., "Factors impacting e-government development," International Conference on Information Systems 2004, Washington DC, USA, Dec. 11–15, 2004.

UN05   United Nations' Global E-Government Development Report 2005. Available online at
        http://www2.unpan.org/egovkb/global_reports/05report.htm, retrieved Jul. 2nd, 2010.
UN08   United Nations' Global E-Government Development Report 2008. Available online at
        http://www2.unpan.org/egovkb/global_reports/08report.htm, retrieved Jul. 2nd, 2010.
UN10   United Nations' Global E-Government Development Report 2010. Available online at
        http://www2.unpan.org/egovkb/global_reports/10report.htm, retrieved Jul. 2nd, 2010.
YIL07   Yildiz, M., "E-government research: Reviewing the literature, limitations and ways
        forward," Government Information Quarterly, vol. 24, pp. 646–665, 2007.

Chapter 2
E-Procurement, from Project to Practice: Empirical Evidence from the French Public Sector

Godefroy Beauvallet, Younès Boughzala, and Saïd Assar

Abstract Public procurement constitutes a significant portion of national PIB in all countries and electronic platforms for supporting public transactions are an important application of e-government. In France, new regulations since 2005 are pushing public and private actors to adopt electronic means for handling all steps of the purchase process in public organisations. Based on quantitative and qualitative surveys made between 2005 and 2008, this chapter presents the general topic of e-procurement and specifically discusses the problem of e-procurement adoption in public institutions in France. The conclusions of these investigations spanning a three years period, are that public e-procurement is constantly progressing, although difficulties related to insufficient technical skills and the complexity of the juridical context hinder seriously its full adoption. They also show that a digital and an organisational divide is appearing between big administrations which have the adequate resources and skills to fully adopt e-procurement, and small administration (i.e. local authorities) which are still reluctant or unable to conduct a purchase in a digital manner.

2.1 Introduction

Since 1 January 2005, all public entities that are subject to the public procurement code in France, such as administrations, local authorities, hospitals, and public institutions, have been required in accordance with Article 56 of the French law,[1] to accept electronic tenders from vendors. That date was fixed following the overhaul of the public procurement law published in September 2001; it was one of the 140 measures in the government's electronic administration program (ADELE)

S. Assar (✉)
Institut Télécom, Telecom Business School,
9, rue Ch. Fourier, 91011 Evry, France
e-mail: said.assar@it-sudparis.eu

S. Assar et al. (eds.), *Practical Studies in E-Government: Best Practices from Around the World*, DOI 10.1007/978-1-4419-7533-1_2,
© Springer Science+Business Media, LLC 2011

published in 2004.[2] The gradual virtualisation of public procurement, in which Article 56 represents one of the first stages, is therefore at the heart of the policy implemented in France by successive governments since the end of the 1990s to improve efficiency in public procurement. "Article 56," which is part of the general policy for public services modernisation and administrative procedures simplification, is regularly presented as "the" solution to the problems encountered with regard to public procurement contracts. These problems are related to the complexity of managing public contracts, the unavailability of information on current contracts, and the high level of direct and indirect costs. In particular, e-procurement is supposed to make public procurement more efficient: lower costs, time savings, and improved productivity [GAR01, EME02, LAJ04, JUB05].

What does the public e-procurement involve? It entails implementing electronic means to process publish exchange and store information concerning public procurement without a paper medium. In concrete terms, it consists of publishing public calls for tenders (AAPC) on the Internet, sending out documents and specifications (consultation files for companies, binding tender forms, etc.) in digital form, receiving tenders electronically, and so on, with a view to ensuring greater efficiency in managing procedures for awarding public procurement contracts.

2.2 The Initial Survey in 2005

One year after the fateful deadline of 1 January 2005, although e-procurement was clearly being implemented, the results as yet have been timid, leading numerous observers to regret the excessive prudence, even conservatism, of both public sector entities awarding public procurement contracts and companies. If this hesitancy was not completely unexpected, the determining factors still needed to be defined. The prevalent tender approach in e-procurement, the top-down character of the model used to deploy this innovation, the use of technical intermediaries ("virtualisation platforms") supposed to mask the IT complexity, all these factors have played a part in these phenomena.

Factors relating to the dynamics of the project may also have played a part. Does the "official" virtualisation, that of the technical platforms where vendors submit date- and time-stamped tenders and exchange secured by asymmetric cryptography, supplement "unofficial" virtualisation, that of e-mails exchanged between parties to the contract and deliverables sent in the form of computer office documents and printed by the customer? Is it destined to replace it in the same way as industrialisation replaced traditional craft industries? Or, on the contrary, has it ridden roughshod over work practices that were beginning to be put in place using the new media, at the risk of fewer gains than losses in terms of productivity and quality? Moreover, once the official tools have been put in place, will there be any room left for innovation and ongoing improvement, or will buyers and sellers find themselves confined to purchasing practices that are imposed to such an extent by IT tools that they can only develop in line with the development of their tools?

Furthermore, do they have no real control over such developments because they are dictated by private mediators aggregating numerous customers?

To assess in concrete terms the use of public e-procurement in practice, the Institut Télécom (formerly GET)[3] carried out a survey in 2005 among public administrations in the context of the ProAdmin research project [PRO05]. Our objectives were to gain a better understanding of the e-procurement process, to assess the problems encountered by public buyers when using these systems and to determine to what extent the available tools satisfy their expectations, and so on.

From a methodological point of view our survey was based on an online questionnaire for public administrations. An electronic mail requesting the participation of "buyers" was sent to officials of procurement services, accounting officers, and financial controllers of a sample of 500 public administrations (ministries, public institutions, local authorities, etc.). After the initial electronic mailing at the beginning of October 2005, followed by reminders sent out at the beginning of December and in January 2006, 90 questionnaires were completed in an exploitable way. The overall response rate was satisfactory (18%) and the large proportion of respondents who asked to receive the results of the survey (73%) seems to demonstrate the interest that it aroused.

In this section of the chapter we attempt, using the results of this initial survey, to determine the impact of e-procurement on public administrations after 1 year's experience with the new system. On the basis of this assessment, we then attempt to clarify the benefits of e-procurement for public sector entities, as well as their representations of the desired transformation of practices. Before addressing these points, we revisit the initial objectives of the virtualisation of procurement contracts, as initially expressed by the governmental instances.

2.2.1   The Virtualisation of Public Procurement Ab Initio: Numerous Opportunities and Guaranteed Gains

2.2.1.1   Political Proactivity Requires Exogenous Change

When the idea was first mooted within the framework of the electronic administration, in the mid-1990s, virtualisation was described as a *triple challenge*: to simplify the life of companies, to initiate them into electronic commerce, and at the same time to encourage the public institutions to modernise, organise, and increase their efficiency and make savings. From that point of view, virtualisation is a relatively easy way of promoting changes in procurement procedures, saving time, making public procurement more transparent and attractive again, and developing the European market. The views expressed at that time were proactive and very optimistic. For example, the report entitled "The State and Information Technologies: Towards an Administration with Plural Access" [LAS00, p. 129] considered that *"putting in place online tendering but above all making it possible for companies to consult files online and to submit completed tenders online should be considered as priority projects. This is an area where progress can be achieved rapidly while respecting the principle of equality among companies."*

Considered therefore as a "necessity," virtualisation is one of the tools of the "administration's modernisation." Figures were quoted, for example, in terms of cost savings. Thus, several studies at that time agreed that the virtualisation of public procurement could generate real savings of between 5 and 10% a year in a sector that represents approximately 10% of French GDP.[4]

The political proactivity behind the virtualisation of public procurement – like the reasons underlying numerous projects of the French electronic administration of the 1990s [RAL05, BEA05] – explains the extremely centralised and global initial positioning of the project. It was launched exogenously to public entities and was included in the revision of the public procurement code published in 2001, in Article 56 which made it compulsory. One year later, it is possible, if not to draw up a full appraisal, to identify a trend: namely the low level of adoption of e-procurement by public administrations and companies.

2.2.1.2 Low Utilisation Rate

In accordance with Article 56, public buyers were legally required, with effect from 1 January 2005, to virtualise their procurement procedures, failing which the legal certainty of contracts concluded after that date could be called into question.[5] Without any effort to raise awareness or consensus formation a priori, either with regard to the proposed solution (the virtualisation obligation) or with regard to the problems encountered in public procurement, even less with regard to the causal chain of events linking the solution to the problems, the virtualisation management strategy was clearly proactive, but also and above all brutal. The resultant chain of events was then typical of the implementation of political decisions imposed on the administration. Faced with what is seen at the central level as resistance to change by buyers at the local level, the project management has given an increasingly structuring role to specialised central entities charged with implementing Article 56. The MINEFI[6] and the ADAE[7] thus put in place, at the beginning of 2005, a joint ministerial platform – www.marches-publics.gouv.fr – enabling them to publish information on current contracts and receive tenders from companies. The project management is thus largely exogenous to buyers. In particular, the existence of a centralised offering has reduced the use by ministries of e-procurement. For other administrations, the widespread use of platforms has transformed the project. What happened?

With the entry into applicability of Article 56, public buyers felt trapped by an additional legal constraint which simply amplified the complexity of their tasks. This lack of understanding encouraged the referents to adopt "ready-to-use" solutions (private platforms) and quickly resulted in a limited use of this new possibility and a very instrumental vision of e-procurement. Public buyers perceived virtualisation not as a fundamental factor destined to transform the future of the public procurement process, but as a simple instrument for data and information exchange. This does not mean that e-procurement has a poor image or that it is rejected by buyers. According to our initial survey[8], buyers see it as a source of simplicity (40% (B9)), efficiency (49% (B9)), transparency (45% (B9)), and traceability (62% (B9)); however, they also see it as a source of problems of confidentiality (65% (B9)) and security (56% (B9)). This image of e-procurement is not very different from the overall image of the Internet.

In fact, the Internet has a good image among the general public, which sees it as useful and versatile. Some 50% of the people interviewed in 2005 declared that it helps them to save time by simplifying and speeding up tasks.[9] However, the majority of the people interviewed had fears regarding confidentiality and security.[10] This tends to demonstrate that public e-procurement is not, for its main stakeholders, a project with an autonomous image

For the time being, the results of our initial survey showed a gap between the usefulness, perception, and acceptance of public e-procurement, regarding both its underlying principles and its expected benefits. These first results were mixed and the situation was disappointing.

2.2.2 E-Procurement In Situ: A Deceptive Situation

The results of the first survey reveal, via several key figures (as well as via the comments of the respondents in the open questions), the state of play regarding progress in implementing public e-procurement. Although at first sight the overall objectives have been attained, utilisation has not lived up to expectations. First, from a technological point of view, the system put in place remains incomplete and marked, among other things, by problems such as a lack of user-friendliness and confidence. Secondly, virtualisation has not led to changes in practices and has resulted simply in a change of medium.

2.2.2.1 An Apparent Success Which Conceals, However, a Problem of Underutilisation

One year after 1 January 2005, the results remain mixed. Overall the administrations have complied with their virtualisation obligations by putting in place the necessary means (96% of the administrations interviewed claim to have done so). Likewise the majority of public calls for tenders (AAPC) and tender files for consultation by companies (DCE) are published on the Internet. Details of current public contracts are available and listed on the websites of the administrations and/or on the sites of the e-procurement platforms. Companies can access them very easily by simply downloading the documents.

However, the number of tenders submitted electronically by companies and the level of experimentation with virtualisation by administrations for managing and awarding public procurement contracts remains, 1 year after the initial deadline, extremely timid. E-procurement has not gone beyond the invitation to tender phase (publication of AAPC and DCE). Some 82% (B4) of respondents have tested e-procurement in this first phase, whereas only 32% (B4) have received a virtualised tender. Some 8% (B4) have experimented with the virtualised selection of tenders and only 4% (B4) of the administrations interviewed have concluded a contract based on a virtualised tender. By way of example, on www.marches-publics.gouv.fr, the platform which groups together all the contracts of the ministries (7,500 calls for tender launched online in 2005), only 5%[11] of the DCE downloaded resulted in an electronic tender being submitted electronically in 2005.[12] After 1 year, therefore, the investments and complexity of the systems put in place do not seem to be in phase with the actual use of such systems: if it involves almost exclusively putting public documents online, a simple documentary site management system would have sufficed instead of complex platforms managing authentication, date- and time-stamping, submitting tenders, and so on.

What is the cause of this discrepancy? The main limit to e-procurement according to its supporters is that companies are not playing the game. As Jean-Séverin Lair of the ADAE[13] emphasises, "*We cannot impose e-procurement on companies*." However, this bottleneck still needs to be explained. Very down-to-earth factors have contributed to holding back virtualisation. Thus, technical failings and a lack of confidence as regards confidentiality have resulted in a very low number of electronic replies to invitations to tender have been downloaded electronically. According to the survey, 67% (B13) of the problems encountered by public buyers are of a technical nature. The security issues and the fear of complications using electronic documents that need to be certified manually are strong limitations when it comes to submit a tender electronically [MEFI04, MEFI05].

2.2.2.2 The Incomplete Technological Development of the Virtualisation Platforms

The technological development of the "e-procurement platforms" has taken far longer than initially planned. The current situation in 2006 is the result of an unexpected slowness in developments and, on the other hand, a more complex functional target than planned. According to our survey, this slowness is the result of a series of fears among public buyers and companies. IT solutions are expensive for administrations, and naturally even more so for the e-procurement pioneers that have had to pay more than their share of platform development costs. Furthermore, the platforms are still deemed to be immature. They are seen as not being user-friendly and insufficiently compatible with the information systems of the parties involved. The case of a respondent operating in the construction and civil engineering sector is worth studying extensively. For these companies e-procurement procedures for public contracts have resulted in additional date-entering needs. The company's table of cost evaluation is carried out using professional software, which generates a "ready-to-print" document in a format that is not accepted by the main platforms put in place. To be able to tender online, the company therefore needed to re-enter manually the elements produced by its business software program in the input mask of the platform.

Although the platforms have been criticised by companies, public buyers are not entirely satisfied either, inasmuch as one respondent explained: "*E-procurement solutions are not really user-friendly and require a certain number of checks.*" These fears and problems are related in the majority of cases to a lack of computer skills and even in office automation processes. Hence, the lack of confidence in the new electronic systems is largely systemic. It is therefore hardly surprising that the majority of public buyers consider that e-procurement is a source of risks (60% (B24)).

2.2.2.3   E-Procurement Reduced to a Change of Medium

As they have not made many changes to their procedures, public buyers have not seen the gains that they imagined would result automatically from e-procurement in terms of cost savings, simplicity, transparency, and the like. On the other hand, they find themselves with new costs and new problems. According to our survey, the main benefit apparent at this stage is the improvement in procurement timescales (55% of the administrations interviewed declared that this was the case for the pre-tender phase, 67% for the call for tender phase, 53% for the submission of tenders, and 53% for subsequent relations) (B8). E-procurement has not stimulated competition (for 56% (B20) of the respondents) and the amounts of company tenders are more or less similar to those that existed before the entry into e-procurement. Only 25% (B11) of respondents considered the return on investment to be significant.

Therefore, for the time being, in any event, the simple change of medium is not sufficient to generate either material gains nor a return on investment. The situation will perhaps improve in the coming years, but that will no doubt depend on the implementation of a true overhaul of processes. For example, one respondent declared that the return on investment "*will tend to improve over time, but that will be more as a result of an overhaul of procurement processes than of the introduction of IT resources.*"

These observations confirm that it is naive to expect public procurement to improve simply by changing the medium used. The use of IT and electronic means for public procurement operations will never lead to improved efficiency without a policy of change and organisation. The causal chain of events is far more complex – and fragile – than the vision of e-procurement generating automatic gains. In an optimistic hypothesis, in order to make the e-procurement process more efficient, the introduction of electronic means requires organisational improvements. The introduction of ICT would then become a marker of good organisational processes and the change of medium would be an opportunity to improve procurement practices.

2.2.3 Virtualisation of Public Procurement Ex Post: A Change of Medium, an Opportunity for Improvement?

2.2.3.1 The Future of E-Procurement: The Hopes and Confidence of the Stakeholders

Disillusionment is setting in with the initial vision of an automatic improvement in public procurement as a simple result of a change of medium. However, this does not mean that virtualisation cannot have a positive impact on the efficiency and quality of public procurement, but in accordance with a more complex causal mechanism. The change in medium can in fact make it easier to call into question sedimentary practices, to modify roles, tasks, and decision-making criteria, among others. It is important not to ignore the symbolic force of changing not only working documents but also their changing nature. The semiotic force of the changeover from a paper format to digitised hypertexts is inevitably reflected in the organisation of work. Moreover, it is undoubtedly this symbolic force that explains the belief of public procurement stakeholders in the positive effects of virtualisation. Despite the problems encountered, the lack of confidence, and insufficient use made of e-procurement, the survey confirms that the majority of respondents have confidence in the future of e-procurement. Public buyers consider that, although the transformation process has not been successfully accomplished, e-procurement will eventually lead to greater efficiency. Thus, 89% of respondents (B16) consider that e-procurement will improve the procurement process. In the same way, 56% believe that e-procurement will contribute positively to good public procurement management practices, and 22% consider that it is indispensable (B3). However, these respondents associate far more than a simple change of medium with e-procurement. It is described as a "complete overhaul" of public procurement by 39% (B1) of respondents, a "slight reorganisation" by 31% (B1), and seen as "simple automation" by 30% (B1).

Therefore, the current difficulties have not eroded the capital of long-term confidence in e-procurement. This process is typical of the use of ICT, where we are used to waiting a long time after deployment for positive effects that can be quantified in terms of efficiency and quality.[14] This fatalism is explicit in certain replies to the open questions in the questionnaire [PRO05], for example, the view that e-procurement is an *"inescapable expression of technological progress which facilitates access and a more modern management of public procurement"* or the view that *"the benefits are expected not over the short term but in the long term, when all companies including small structures take an interest in it."*

What is the basis of this general optimism? In terms of impact, and among the multiple challenges of public procurement, the stakeholders gave priority to the potential effects of e-procurement on the complexity and fairness of public procurement. Public buyers believe it will ensure that procedures are simpler (68% (B17)) and fairer (72% (B17)). More precisely, 70% of public buyers consider that e-procurement is a source of simplicity for public entities, 73% for companies, and 63% for public procurement auditors and paymasters (B18). In terms of organisation, with different logistics and a reorganisation of the process, public buyers consider that the benefits are mainly to be found in reduced timescales and the possibility to accomplish the related tasks more rapidly. Some 56% (B10) of public buyers see e-procurement as a means of saving time rather than money, which in no way detracts from its importance, because it helps to increase productivity by making it possible to improve preparations for public procurement contracts, launch others, rationalise expenses, implement management controls, and so on.

The reality is therefore disappointing in relation to the initial ambitions, but confidence remains high. The key success factor seems to lie in the capacity to transform the organisation of the process and make "technical" virtualisation contribute to the attainment of the "managerial" ambition. Is it possible to define more accurately representations and expectations at this specific level?

2.2.3.2   A New Focus for Public Procurement Management

For public procurement stakeholders, the initial difficulties of e-procurement lie in the teething troubles of the tools and the lack of sufficient incentives to motivate them to make the efforts to transform practices. Nevertheless, they do not seem to translate a more fundamental discrepancy between e-procurement as it is currently implemented and the routines of the stakeholders. This optimism gives rise to a new formulation of the advantage of e-procurement. Public buyers consider that it is necessary to grasp the opportunity of the change in medium to improve practices and processes. As one procurement manager emphasised in an answer to an open question in the questionnaire [PRO05], *"We have reached the limits of our traditional administrative way of thinking. E-procurement makes it possible to go beyond those limits by implementing new models with a new open-mindedness."* Consequently, despite the technical, organisational, and legal problems, e-procurement is seen as a means to perceive e-procurement in a new light based on increasing efficiency accompanied by an overhaul of procedures.

Public buyers support the general injunction to "rationalise" public procurement and see virtualisation as an opportunity for accomplishing such a transformation. Can this representation be refined as a possible overhaul of processes to achieve greater efficiency? It is depicted as a change of culture, the current approach being marked by a legal conformist culture which needs to be replaced by an economic approach focused on innovation. One procurement manager declared in an answer to an open question in the questionnaire [PRO05] that e-procurement *"will in time make it possible to accelerate the validation at the different levels of the procedure, simplify administrative tasks, reorganise working methods, etc."* In the same way, e-procurement will help to improve relations with audit, accounting, and payment services. Some 51% (B15) of respondents consider that eventually e-procurement will lead to a change in relations between procurement services and audit and payment services.

2.2.4   Public E-Procurement: Triggering a Dynamic of Improvement?

Our survey has helped us to fine-tune our understanding of the interest of public buyers and companies in e-procurement at its initial stages of development. The initial paradox concerned stakeholders who, although seeming to be convinced of the benefit of e-procurement, consider at the same time that a simple change of medium will never lead to an improvement in the process. Public buyers want a far-reaching transformation of the whole system, including a legal and organisational overhaul. Whereas 36% of respondents believe that technical improvements are above all necessary to make public procurement more efficient, 23% believe that organisational improvements are more important and 35% would give priority to legal improvements (B12). The only problem is that buyers do not know how to launch this overall project, moreover, according to our survey, they doubt whether this falls within the scope of their responsibilities. From this point of view, e-procurement seems to offer a perfect opportunity to overhaul completely existing practices and processes in place and initiate a dynamic of gradual improvement.[15]

Is this transformation model compatible with what we currently know about e-procurement? In other words, does the latter really facilitate the expected organisational change, or, on the contrary, does it contribute to making systems rigid and inflexible? The inescapable fact is that, to the date of the initial survey, the effects of e-procurement have been limited: the procurement function is switching to a new medium while adapting to a minimal extent to the newly available technological tools. This adaptation has not changed much as regards the fundamental causes of the problems facing buyers; in certain cases, it has served to expose their difficulties to a wider audience (e.g., by facilitating access to contract documents and exposing therefore, on occasions, their mediocrity). Far from initiating a virtuous cycle of transformation, e-procurement is seen in practice as a troublesome but short transition from a "paper-based" equilibrium to another "computer-based" medium, motivated by the need to comply with their legal obligations with regard to e-procurement. Once this objective has been attained, they can move on to other things; adoption remains limited.

2.3   The 2007 and 2008 Surveys

As the adoption of e-procurement did not attain its initial expectations, the governmental authorities appointed a group of experts to observe and measure e-procurement. This group of experts was also charged with the mission of disseminating good practices and gathering knowledge about the implementation of e-procurement. The procurement expert group regularly organised practitioners' workshops and created an online library of documents in which were stored and made available presentations, discussions, and recommendations issued by the group.[16] As part of the expert group activities, quantitative and qualitative surveys were made regularly to assess different aspects of the ongoing e-procurement adoption and diffusion process. Two important surveys have been conducted in 2007 and in 2008 to evaluate the reality of e-procurement practices, to assess the perception of stakeholders, and to gather recommendations concerning the future evolution of e-procurement.

The first survey was made by the TNS-SOFRES survey organisation in July to October 2007 [MEFI07]. This survey was qualitative using 1h30 interview. It concerned 15 persons from the buy side (procurement managers in different public administrations) and 18 persons from the sell side (marketing managers in enterprises of different size and domain of activity). The main results are the following:

- There are different practices according to the size and nature of the procurement contract: for formalised contracts, usage of e-procurement is generalised and the public actors feel confident about it, but for adaptable contracts[17] where the public entity has a large choice of alternatives, actors in public institutions fear juridical complications as many bidding contracts have been cancelled by the administrative jurisdiction due to procedural errors.
- Small public structures have big difficulties in handling procurement processes electronically, and it is often the managers' secretaries who are responsible for sourcing and procurement, and who are adequately trained for such a mission.
- The juridical risk is so important for public actors (fear of cancellation and/or juridical complications) that some institutions have introduced specific constraints on procurement processes which go beyond the initial constraints defined by the general law.
- Most sell-side actors (private enterprises) are rather critical: they are facing many different electronic platforms depending on the public institution with which they deal, and for small-sized companies, they consider that they did not get the sufficient level of training nor do they have the adequate human resources to deal with the complexity of answering electronically to a public call for tenders.
- Actors in public institutions continue, however, to believe in the potential of e-procurement to modernise the public sector and to enhance its efficiency.

The second survey was made in the April–May 2008 period for the *Direction des Journaux Officiels* [DJO08], a governmental organisation responsible for managing juridical information and who plays an important role in publishing data and information concerning e-procurement processes. This survey was quantitative with online questionnaires, and concerned 747 persons on the buy side, and 851 persons on the sell side. Some of the most significant results are the following:

- Actors (public and private) are aware of e-procurement potential and possibilities; there is a high level of satisfaction concerning the diffusion of general information about e-procurement.
- A significant portion (60–80%) of public actors use electronic means to publish calls for tenders and give the possibilities to bidding companies to respond electronically. However, only a small portion (22%) effectively handles offers electronically through an e-procurement platform.

- In a similar pattern, a large number of enterprises download documents concerning calls for tenders, however, only a small portion take the opportunity of using the e-procurement platform to respond.
- 30% of surveyed actors have fully virtualised calls for tender processes, the reasons invoked are related to the oncoming mandatory aspect of e-procurement, the perception of time and money gains, and the desire to participate in what is perceived as a modernisation process.
- 13% of surveyed actors have never used electronic means to handle procurement processes, the reasons invoked are related to the ongoing optional aspect of e-procurement, to the insufficient level of training and knowledge about the e-procurement tools and processes, and to the fear of juridical complications if these tools are not used adequately.

2.4 Conclusion

The first survey that we carried out reveals that 1 year after the legal obligation introduced with effect from 1 January 2005, the utilisation of e-procurement by the public sector remains limited. The administrations have clearly complied with their obligations by acquiring the necessary means; however, e-procurement is used only to a limited extent and has not really been grasped as an opportunity to reorganise the procurement processes. The volume of tenders submitted electronically by companies is almost negligible and e-procurement has not gone beyond the phase of consulting calls for tender online.

In addition, various technical, organisational, and legal problems still exist. The optimistic assumption of an improvement in practices as a result of a change of medium must give way to a more pragmatic vision. This revision supposes a modification of the project management, which to date has focused more on selection aids, making available technical solutions and a move towards accounting for "opening marketplaces" rather than towards uses and enhanced performance. The e-procurement managers must modify their actions to improve the project's implementation at the operational level, using an organisational approach based on observing/modifying practices. That is, in any event, the view expressed by the majority of public procurement practitioners interviewed in year 2006.

The two surveys conducted in 2007 and in 2008 confirmed the main conclusions of our initial survey. Although e-procurement diffusion has progressed constantly, there is a visible digital and organisational divide. Small-size companies and local public authorities suffer from insufficient technical skills and resources. Juridical and organisational context for conducting online business is still insufficient for handling the sophisticated parts of the procurement process (submitting offers, analysing offers, and decision making). It is also insufficient for dealing with specific purchasing processes where the responsibility of the public actor is deeply engaged (MAPA category of calls for tenders), and where the fear of juridical complication (or even cancellation) hinders the full electronic support of underlying process. The stated objectives of 100% of public procurement contracts online and at least 50% of contracts concluded electronically by 2010 seem to be far from the current concerns of practitioners.

How could improvements be made on the basis of the lessons learned from these surveys? To encourage the adoption of e-procurement, doesn't the solution lie in an approach based on reorganising the procurement process in a participative spirit? We have explored in previous research works the collaborative dimension of e-procurement [ASS06, ASS08], and certain official declarations point in that direction: the adoption of common principles for e-procurement platform user interfaces, the standardisation of data and information relating to purchase orders and invoices, the standardisation at the European level of corporate identification elements, cross-border recognition of electronic signatures, and so on. We are aware, however, that a lot still remains to be done in this area, notably as regards improving "platform" offerings: alert systems, monitoring functions, virtualised solutions for documents (company registration certificates, binding tender forms, qualifying bid documents, etc.).

Notes

[1] The virtualisation of public procurement is based on Article 56 of the Public Procurement Code and on its two implementing decrees; the decree of September 18th, 2001 specifying the procedure for electronic tendering and the decree of April 30th, 2002 stipulating the conditions applying to electronic exchanges.

[2] ADELE 2004–2007 government program "Action Plan of the Electronic Administration," Ministry for the Civil Service, Reform and Territorial Development, Junior Ministry charged with State Reform, launched on 9 February, 2004.

[3] The Institut Télécom is a public administration under the supervision of the Ministry of the Economy, Finance and Industry, which is charged with organising higher education and research in ICT.

[4] See [GAR01] for example. Several press articles even referred to savings of 15% thanks to public e-procurement virtualisation. See "Achatpublic.com passe les marchés publics en ligne", *Journal du net* (July 21, 2003), or "Les nouvelles technologies font baisser les coûts des achats publics," *Le Monde de l'économie* (May 14, 2002, p.14).

[5] A competitor excluded from the contract could use the argument that it was impossible to consult the tender documents online or to tender online to claim that there was not a level playing field between competing vendors. Although the threat is theoretical at this stage – to the best of our knowledge no litigation has yet arisen on this point – the legalistic approach of the public administrations is such that they have all endeavoured to put in place a form of virtualisation, if not within the prescribed time, at least in the months following the deadline.

[6] Ministry of the Economy, Finance and Industry.

[7] Agency for the Development of the Electronic Administration.

[8] For ease of reference regarding the results of the survey, the figures (Bxx) correspond to question number xx in the "buyer" questionnaire and figures (Snn) to question number nn in the "seller" questionnaire. Accordingly, by way of example, "51% (B15)" means that 51% of the respondents replied "yes" to question 15 of the "buyer" questionnaire and "52% (S7)" means that 52% of the respondents replied "yes" to question 7 of the "seller" questionnaire [PRO05].

[9] Ipsos/Club Internet survey (June 2005).

[10] TNS Sofres/Cap Gemini survey (August 2005).

[11] 46,452 invitations to tender files were downloaded from this platform with an average of more than seven consultation files downloaded per contract.

[12] "Marchés publics: l'Etat doit convaincre les entreprises," *Le Journal du Net*, 26 January 2006.

[13] *Idem.*

[14] One can consider that this observation is the intrafirm equivalent of the Solow paradox globally: "Computers can be found everywhere except in productivity statistics." Although the Solow paradox now seems to have been resolved through the acceleration of productivity growth since 1995, the underlying causal relations remain obscure.

[15] This belief is firmly rooted – although badly established – in the power of an exogenous crisis to transform practices and organisation, and views very similar to those expressed regarding the Year 2000 effect on information systems, or regarding the changeover to the euro on the transformation of companies' accounting and financial systems.

[16] Available online at http://www.telecom.gouv.fr/rubriques-menu/entreprises-economie-numerique/dematerialisation-marches-publics/28.html, retrieved July 12th, 2010.

[17] MAPA: *Marché à Procédure Adapté*, a procurement contract in which the public actor has a certain autonomy in defining the purchasing process.

References

ASS06 S. Assar, I. Boughzala, Y. Boughzala (2006) "Collaborative features in French public e-procurement" in F. Feltz, B. Otjacques, A. Oberweis, N. Poussing (editors): "AIM 2006: Information Systems and Collaboration: State of the Art and Perspectives", Lecture Notes in Informatics, vol. p–92, pp. 83–103.

ASS08 S. Assar, I. Boughzala (2008) "Empirical evaluation of public e-procurement platforms in France" International Journal of Value Chain Management, 2(1):90–108, Inderscience Enterprises Ltd.

BEA05 G. Beauvallet, M-C. Le Garff, A-L. Negri and F. Cara (2005) "Apprentissages individuels et collectifs de l'utilisation d'Internet pour la recherche d'emploi", Revue de l'IRES, n° 52 – 2006/3, special issue "Internet, recrutement et recherche d'emploi", available online at http://www.ires-fr.org/images/files/Revues/r523.pdf, retrieved July 12th, 2010.

DJO08 Direction des Journaux Officiels – IFOP Institute (2008), "Etude sur la dematerialisation dans les marchés publics", available online at http://www.journal-office.gouv.fr/documents/resultats_etude_quantitative_dematerialisation_mp.pdf, retrieved July 12th, 2010.

EME02 C. Emery (2002) "Passer un marché public: principes, procédures, contentieux", Delmas Editions, Paris, France.

GAR01 E. Garandeau (2001) "Les procédures électroniques de gestion des achats publics", research report, General Inspectorate of Finance, available online at http://www.telecom.gouv.fr/fonds_documentaire/men/adm/rapport7_2.pdf, retrieved July 12th, 2010.

JUB05 F. Jubert, E. Montfort, R. Stakowski (2005) "La e-administration; Levier de la réforme de l'Etat", Dunod Editions, Paris, France.

LAJ04 T. Lajoie., L. Hislaire (2004) "Les marchés publics dematerialisés", Eyrolles Editions, Paris, France.

LAS00 B. Lasserre (2000) "L'Etat et les technologies d'information et de la communication: vers une administration à accès pluriel", French National Plan, available online at http://www.ladocumentationfrancaise.fr/rapports-publics/004000954/index.shtml, retrieved July 12th, 2010.

LOR98 F. Lorenz (1998) "Le commerce électronique: une nouvelle donne pour les consommateurs, les entreprises, les citoyens et les pouvoirs publics", Ministry of the Economy,

Finance and Industry, available online at http://www.ladocumentationfrancaise.fr/rapports-publics/984000049, retrieved July 12th, 2010.

MEFI04   Ministry of the Economy, Finance and Industry (2004) "Vade-mecum juridique sur la dématérialisation des marchés publics", report of the Legal Affairs Directorate, available online at http://www.minefe.gouv.fr/directions_services/daj/marches_publics/vademecum/vmdemat.htm, retrieved July 12th, 2010.

MEFI05   Ministry of the Economy, Finance and Industry (2005), "Guide technique pour la sécurité de la dématérialisation des achats public", report of the Digital Economy Agency, available online at http://www.telecom.gouv.fr/fonds_documentaire/men/adm/recommandations.pdf, retrieved July 12th, 2010.

MEFI07   Ministry of the Economy, Finance and Industry - TNS Sofres Institute (2007), "La perception de la dématérialisation", qualitative study report, available online at http://www.telecom.gouv.fr/doc/achpub/rap-dematerialisation1007.pdf, retrieved July 12th, 2010.

PRO05   The ProAdmin research project, available online at http://www-public.it-sudparis.eu/~assar/proadmin, retrieved July 12th, 2010.

RAL05   P. Rallet, M. Lesteven (2005) "La dématérialisation des achats publics; de l'incantation au pilotage", colloquium of the French-language association of electronic management, June 24, 2005.

Chapter 3
Implementation of E-Government in Mexico: The Case of Infonavit

Lizbeth Herrera and J. Ramon Gil-Garcia

Abstract The implementation of information and communication technologies (ICTs) in the public sector is a strategy for administrative reform that has grown in importance in recent years. The use of ICT in government can help to improve the efficiency, quality, and transparency of public services and reduce the operating costs of bureaucracy. ICTs have also opened a new communication channel for government to provide public services to citizens without intermediaries. However, the implementation of an ICT initiative is not a simple process. Organizations frequently invest a great amount of resources into ICT initiatives, but the results they obtain often do not meet expectations. This observation is particularly true in some developing countries. Based on a case study of a Mexican federal agency, this chapter analyzes a successful strategy involving three ICT projects, taking into consideration institutional, organizational, and managerial aspects. Overall, the results of this study show that having a strategic plan that aligns the ICT project objectives with the overarching organizational goals leads to successful implementation because the technical, organizational, and institutional resources are managed in an integrated fashion. The chapter also reports on specific factors that had an impact on the characteristics and success of the three ICT projects.

3.1 Introduction

The concept of electronic government (e-government) does not have a single definition, but in general it is associated with the use of ICT in government to deliver public services, improve the effectiveness of the bureaucracy, and promote democratic values through citizen participation [GIL03]. However, the adoption, implementation, and use of ICTs are heavily influenced by individual and organizational acceptance of them [RIV03]. This governmental change not only depends

J. Ramon Gil-Garcia (✉)
Centro de Investigación y Docencia Económicas, Carretera México-Toluca 3655,
Col. Lomas de Santa Fe, CP, México 01210, DF, Mexico
e-mail: josermon.gil@cide.edu

S. Assar et al. (eds.), *Practical Studies in E-Government: Best Practices from Around the World*, DOI 10.1007/978-1-4419-7533-1_3,
© Springer Science+Business Media, LLC 2011

on investments in infrastructure, but upon more integral changes at the intersection of people, processes, and rules [RIV04]. The introduction of ICT in an organization does not produce change by itself; to take advantage of the technologies and deliver a better service, the organization needs to introduce a strategy that pursues institutional and organizational change by means of a shift in the routines and cultural values of the public servants [RAM05, YAN07].

According to Heeks [HEE03], the potential benefits of e-government projects have contributed to the development of ICT initiatives in developing countries. However, the reality is that the majority of these projects fail. The rate of success and failure of e-government in developing countries is not well known because there are not enough data. However, it is estimated that the success rate for ICT initiatives in these countries could be as low as 15% [HEE03]. In the case of Mexico, the use of ICT began at the end of the 1990s. ICTs were used sporadically in public programs and there was no national strategy for developing e-government [SOT06]. In 2001, a national e-government program was created as a strategy to improve transparency, quality, and efficiency within the federal government [OEC05]. Similar to other Latin American countries, Mexico has problems with corruption, lacks a well-established civil service, and has not created a governmentwide citizen-centric strategy, among other issues. These factors make the implementation of e-government particularly challenging, but at the same time, they are strong incentives for governments to initiate ICT projects.

There were some additional contextual conditions that triggered the implementation of e-government in Mexico. For more than a 100 years, Mexico had a presidential system similar to the one in the United States, but it was only in 2000 that Mexico initiated a real system of checks-and-balances [WEL02]. At that time, an opposition political party won the presidential election, but did not obtain enough votes to control the legislature. The political change and the divided government allowed for the introduction of new reforms with the purpose of improving transparency and efficiency in government. Public organizations began exploring ICTs to change the way they delivered services to citizens and to become more efficient and transparent. As a result, there were many government ICT projects, but not all of them were successful.

An example of a successful e-government implementation in Mexico was the strategy called Alternative Service Delivery Channels (ASDC), developed and deployed by the Institute of the National Fund for Workers' Housing (Infonavit), which was given an Innova Award in 2002 and a National Innova Award in 2003 [PRE07]. The Innova award is given to public organizations that implement innovative practices to improve the delivery of public services and add value to citizens. The impact of the ASDC strategy was measured through the number of workers that Infonavit could help. The strategy considered a minimum of 12 million users. During 2001, Infonavit carried out a series of reforms focused on strengthening the financial stability of the Institute, which included strategies for modernization aimed at greater efficiency, transparency, and rendering of accounts in its operations. A key tool in this reform process was the use of ICT. The purpose of this chapter is to examine the strategies that allowed for successful implementation of ICT in Infonavit.

This document is divided into five sections including this introduction. In the second section we review institutional theory in general and the technology enactment framework in particular. In addition, we describe a comprehensive e-government model based on Fountain's theory [FOU01], but with additional factors cited in recent literature. In the third section we describe the research design and methods used in this study. In the fourth section we present the analysis and the main results of the case study in light of each theoretical construct and their respective variables. Finally, in the fifth section we present some final remarks.

3.2 Institutions and the Technology Enactment Framework

In general, there are two dominant approaches to analyzing e-government. The first concerns the impact of ICT on the structure and performance of an organization. This approach generally assumes that ICT has a positive effect on organizational processes, accountability, transparency, and citizen participation. The second approach focuses on how to evaluate the diverse factors that affect the success or failure of e-government initiatives. There is no single answer about which factors are the most important for e-government initiatives [GIL07]. From the perspective of Yildz [YIL07], the second approach is called process. This approach analyzes the implementation of e-government through observation, review of documents, and interviews with participants. The difference between the two approaches is that the first is related to output, such as the benefits of the application of ICT, whereas the second recognizes that ICT implementation influences both technical and organizational elements, among other factors. Fountain's technology enactment framework [FOU01] is based on the process approach and proposes the use of institutional theory to understand the selection, design, implementation, and use of ICT in organizations. In the following we briefly describe institutional theory in general and the technology enactment framework in particular, including their main concepts and propositions.

3.2.1 Institutional Theory

There are several approaches to the study of institutions as a way to explain social and organizational processes. According to Castillo [CAS97], the existence of diverse institutional theories arises from the diverse definitions of institutions. Therefore, the specific definition of an institution depends on the approach taken. In general terms, an institution is a system of rules that give meaning to social life. Rules can be normative, organizational, informal arrangements, regulatory, or constitutional, among others. Likewise, the notion of institution is used to refer to acts that are not sanctioned by any formal authority, but instead are embedded in everyday life, such as having a coffee every morning at work or speaking to the boss when she or he is walking down the hall. Peters [PET03] says that institutions restrict human behavior according to the values, routines, symbols, regulations, decrees, and resources of individuals.

According to North [NOR93], institutions are rules that limit the behavior of individuals, which are created by the individuals themselves in order to give form to human interaction. One of the characteristics of institutions is to provide certainty, which is why they act as reference guides for day-to-day activities. But the stability and certainty that institutions provide for human life do not necessarily produce efficiency. In addition, institutions are different in each country, therefore, each individual will behave in a different way depending on the institutions established in his social context. For this reason, carrying out a procedure or operation in one country may be very different from doing the same thing in another. Institutional theory has been used to understand e-government phenomena and one of the most refined institutional approaches is the technology enactment framework.

3.2.2　Technology Enactment Framework

Fountain [FOU01] created the technology enactment framework based on her research of government IT projects. Although the framework could be used to understand any IT project, it is designed for the government context. In the following, we briefly explain the basics of this framework. According to Fountain, information technology can modify the structures and processes of organizations, which can then affect the use and implementation of technology. Fountain's model posits that organizational or institutional structures – such as norms, regulations, and hierarchies, as well as informal rules, beliefs, routines, and values – exercise influence on the development of ICT due to the way they modify the individuals' perceptions and behaviors about how to use or implement these technologies.

The technology enactment framework consists of five main constructs. The first refers to technology factors, which are the physical components and information that enable data processing, the Internet connection, and the software, hardware, and telecommunications devices. Fountain uses the term objective technology, which could be conceptualized as all the possible characteristics and features that a system could have in contrast to the enacted technology, which encompass the characteristics and features that the organization selected for the system or IT initiative. The second construct, organizational form, includes elements of bureaucracy and organizational networks such as hierarchy, jurisdiction, and social capital, among others. The third construct is institutional arrangements, such as cultural, formal, and legal elements, as well as cognitive and sociostructural components. The fourth construct, the enacted technology, is the result of the interaction among objective technology, organizational forms, and institutional arrangements. Finally, the results are the outcomes of the enactment process and they are indeterminate, multiple, and many times influenced by a political logic.

In this document we propose a comprehensive model for studying e-government, which stems from Fountain's technology enactment framework, but also addresses its criticism and recent additions to this theory. This model was formulated by taking into account the pre-existing relationships in Fountain's model, as well as those suggested in recent documents related to the development and implementation of e-government. This model proposes specific variables in order to bring its components to light and enable its application to a practical case. Finally, the comprehensive model shows the relationship between different organizational, institutional, contextual, managerial, and technological factors that influence the implementation of ICT in organizations. In the following, we briefly describe the variables included in the proposed model.

Contextual factors affect both organizational forms and institutional arrangements (see Fig. 3.1). Context is formed by the external conditions that affect processes and organizational structures. In this case, they refer to the economic environment, the demand for public policy, and the competition with other organizations from the same sector. Organizational factors refer to the size of the organization, its personnel, structure, and networks. Institutional factors refer to written and unwritten rules that affect organizations: regulations, laws, budgets, and culture. Managerial factors focus on the way public administrators manage e-government strategies, such as the use of methodologies, process re-engineering, and leadership, among others. The objective technology consists of the physical characteristics of the hardware, software, or

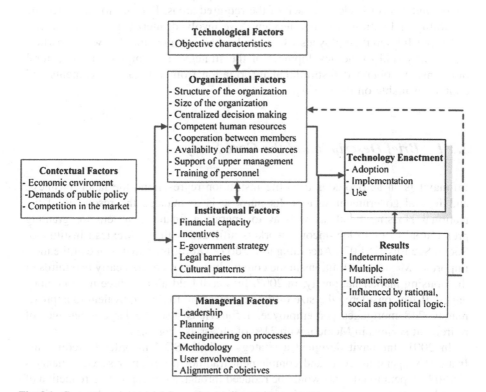

Fig. 3.1 Comprehensive model for understanding e-government

networks that members of the organization use in their work or to communicate with each other. The technology enactment is the selection, implementation, and use of the ICT inside the organization; it also includes how the individuals perceive and understand the technology in the organization. Lastly, the results of technology enactment can be indeterminate, multiple, and/or unanticipated because each organization has its own rules, context, values, and skill sets. The results of an e-government project will depend on how organizations apply the strategies in a variable environment.

3.3   Research Design and Methods

This study adopts a case study research strategy. The case is the ASDC strategy of Infonavit. We used semistructured interviews and document analysis. The questions were related to the five general constructs from the technology enactment framework: contextual, institutional, organizational, managerial, and technological factors. For the interviews, we selected eight key individuals who participated in the ASDC strategy and possessed a broad knowledge of the organization, the organizational culture, and the institutional environment. The interviewees were personnel at the level of deputy directors, coordinators, managers, and project leaders in each of the required areas. In order to guarantee the reliability and validity of the interviews, we involved internal personnel as well as former Infonavit employees who have left the organization, but whose participation was vital to the development of the strategy. To complement the actors' opinions, we obtained institutional information from Infonavit documents and content available on its website.

3.3.1   Brief Description of the Case Study

Infonavit is an autonomous tripartite institution representing the labor, business, and federal government sectors. Its purpose is to manage the resources of the National Housing Fund, as well as to operate a financial system for granting preferential loans to low-income workers affiliated with the Mexican Institute of Social Security [INF07]. According to Pardo [PAR06], Infonavit is one of the most important Mexican institutions in the country because it covers nearly two thirds of the housing market nationally. In 2007, Infonavit held almost three million mortgages. If we considered the size of the organization, that is equivalent to approximately 748 mortgages per employee. Infonavit is also the largest manager of retirement savings in Mexico, with 31% of all assets (Fig. 3.2).

In 2001, Infonavit designed a strategy called ASDC in order to reduce the Institute's operating costs and complement traditional customer service channels [INF07]. Operational costs would be reduced through a corresponding reduction of the workforce necessary to receive information or services at the Infonavit offices.

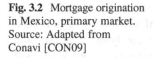
Fig. 3.2 Mortgage origination
in Mexico, primary market.
Source: Adapted from
Conavi [CON09]

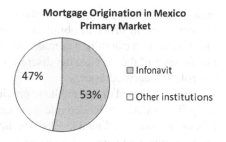

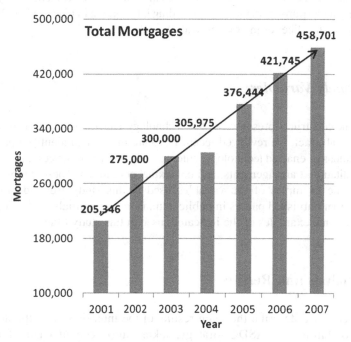

Fig. 3.3 Total mortgages. Source: Adapted from Conavi [CON09]

The use of ICTs was a key element of that strategy. The idea was to serve a large volume of requests via electronic media and to use service centers to manage customer requirements. Infonavit has been able to double the number of mortgages given to workers since 2001 (Fig. 3.3).

Infonavit provides services to about 12 million workers, a million businesses, and also collaborates with banks, notaries, constructors, and other companies. Prior to 2001, the process for obtaining a mortgage was very complex because of bureaucratic processes and the existence of intermediaries. When the workers wanted to ask questions about their account balance or whether they had met all the loan requirements, they waited in long lines outside Infonavit and had to pay the intermediates for the information. As a result, an illegal market of services was created to provide public information about account statements (money and points workers need in order to obtain a mortgage) [INF07]. Infonavit wanted to reduce three issues that combined to make the application process costly to the worker: the inefficiency of the service, the discretionary nature of the application processes, and the role of intermediaries.

The ASDC used digital media to provide Infonavit services efficiently and transparently. The ASDC are divided into three large components: the Internet portal, Infonatel (phone access), and digital kiosks. The Internet portal is where individuals can consult their accounts and carry out transactions. Infonatel is a call center designed to provide solutions and advice and promote the services that Infonavit offers. And lastly, digital kiosks are general-purpose devices for providing information in places where Infonavit does not have an office for interacting with the public.

3.3.2   Study Variables

Because the constructs presented in the technology enactment framework are very general and abstract, we reviewed recent literature in order to identify operationalized definitions of enacted technology, outcomes, managerial practices, organizational forms, institutional arrangements, and contextual conditions. These definitions and more specific examples of the variables used in this study were identified and extracted from published papers in public administration journals. In the following, we present some examples of the indicators used in this study (Table 3.1).

3.4   Analysis and Results

In this section we describe the main results of the interviews and the document analysis of Infonavit's ASDC strategy, taking into account each of the five constructs: technological factors, managerial practices, organizational forms, institutional arrangements, and contextual conditions. To evaluate whether the variable had an impact, we took into consideration the participant answers. We also compared the results with official information and documents published by others about the Infonavit experience.

3.4.1   Technological Factors

According to the activity report of the Department of Innovation and Quality for 2001, Web technology was defined as the technological platform Infonavit would use, because of its potential benefits. For example, the Web provides access from any computer, at any time, 365 days a year. In this case, the availability of Web

Table 3.1 Constructs and variables in recent literature

Construct	Variables	References
Technological	Characteristics of the technology in terms of platforms, languages, databases, security, and access, among others.	[PEL07, STR06]
Managerial	Leadership Internal planning User involvement strategy Development and implementation methodology Alignment of technology objectives with those of the organization	[BRO99, DET02, GIL07, GAG01]
Organizational	Structure of the organization Number of levels in hierarchy Size of the organization Decision-making processes Competent human resources Cooperation and communication between members Availability of human resources Political support and support of senior management Training	[DET02, GIL05a, LEE02, MEL03, TAT01, VON07, WES01]
Institutional	Financial capacity External incentives The existence of a governmentwide electronic government strategy Legal barriers Cultural patterns	[GIL07, MOO02, TAT01, WEA99, WES01]
Contextual	Economic conditions Demand for government services and goods Competition in the market	[CLA07, GIL05, NOR05, WEL07]

technology led Infonavit to opt for the development of a Web portal as the first ASDC to help thousands of eligible individuals avoid applying for loans in person at the Institute's offices.

A technician said, With respect to the portal, the use of Internet was a rising trend at that moment with applications like Flash or programming languages such as Java. For the kiosks, we searched many models and we decided on an IBM model because this technology was already working [for] a number of companies in the country. The machine was tested, it was easy to use and it had fast transaction response rates. Finally, Infonatel had a very innovative design and it looked modern and functional. In general, the technological platform was thought to be the most appropriate at that time for solving the problems with efficiency and transparency of Infonavit's services. Regarding technical characteristics, the Web was considered the best delivery option as it supported a great volume of transactions in real-time.

Although the first version of the portal was simple and not very well designed, the most important thing was that workers could consult the account statement of their housing subaccount and their current balance. Within Infonatel, the technology was not considered state of the art, however, it was certainly robust because of the fact that it continues to function well after 7 years. Kiosks, however, were considered to be the best service option based on a study of equipment in service in other organizations at the time, in addition to the fact that they are simple and user friendly.

According to a 2002 activity report from the Department of Innovation, the Internet portal helps Infonavit to provide virtual information and services to thousands of users. For example, in January 2001 the portal was accessed fewer than one million times, whereas by December of that year this access number had increased to eight million. Over the period of 2001–2002, there were at least 15 million inquiries about the loan prequalification process. Infonatel, on the other hand, received nearly 2.5 million phone calls in 1 year. It would have been difficult to achieve these service delivery figures offline, but by using ICT as an operational tool, Infonavit was able to respond to millions of questions without the use of intermediaries.

3.4.2   Managerial Factors

One of the reasons why the administrative reform of Infonavit moved forward successfully was the ability of the managing director to listen to all employees in the organization and to encourage them to participate. As Cerdán and colleagues [CER06] mention, the leadership exercised by Infonavit's managing director helped to bridge the differences among the organization's members and to use the planning process as an instrument for cooperation and discussion within the organization. The project leader for the ASDC strategy played a fundamental role in seeing the three projects through to completion. The people who participated in the portal, kiosks, and Infonatel believe that without the leader's efforts, the project would not have achieved the results it did. In general, they recognize that the leader always knew what was happening in the projects. Furthermore, this leader had a personal style that motivated people to get results. The leader of the strategy was an enthusiastic and committed person who played an important role in achieving the objectives because he motivated people to finish their tasks on time.

Regarding the planning process, three types of projects were defined: short-, medium-, and long-term. Short-term projects were made up of activities that had to be carried out so that systems would keep functioning. Systems that had previously undergone diagnostics and situation analysis were projected in the medium-term, leaving system improvements to be considered in the long-term. The Innovation and Quality department established an internal policy that projects must have deliverables and that projects should not exceed 9 months given that they could face greater changes in technology, suppliers, and personnel. The underlying strategy of the ASDC called for clearly defined phases in each project, including deliverables for both internal participants and suppliers, which created an incentive for the strategy to be completed within the set timeframe.

Related to delivery of the projects, user participation significantly contributed to the development of the ASDC. Each channel had a defined user area; for example, the user of the portal was the social communication department, whereas the loan department was the user of Infonatel. Users contributed actively to project requirements and control. One Infonavit analyst mentioned that one element that ensured the system would be usable was that the users groups participated in the development of the projects together with the IT staff.

The coestablishment of a technical leader and a leader from the user area had a positive effect on the overall strategy. Each project had at least two people responsible for it, each with different viewpoints, but with a shared objective. The projects grew according to the business requirements, but took into consideration the potential of ICTs. The result was a well-defined project with the best available technological characteristics of the market. Having partners from the user and technical areas enabled systems development that incorporated the necessary characteristics within the required timeframes. Furthermore, once implementation was complete, the systems were used by some of the same people who had acted as testers.

Lastly, the alignment of objectives for the innovation department with those of the business area was an easy fit because every line of operation had been defined in the strategic program, which led to the creation of the ASDC strategy. According to Infonavit's internal documents, the ASDC strategy was created based on the institutional mission; specifically, objective number four, which is related to efficiency and simplification of processes to make them transparent through the use of ICTs. Figure 3.4 shows how Infonavit aligned its substantive and technical objectives by following the National Development Plan. The innovation team and those who participated in the ASDC believed that the most important objective was fulfilling the needs of the Institute and converting those needs into a solution through the intensive use of ICT.

Infonatel was created to assist workers via telephone and to reduce the number of people who have to physically go to Infonavit service centers. It also has the potential to call people who have a mortgage with information about payment. Finally, the kiosks were designed to bring services closer to the workers and to reduce the waiting time at the service centers. The convergence of the objectives in the business and innovation areas helped the ASDC strategy gain acceptance from users and management because technology was not seen as foreign to Infonavit, but as a primary component for carrying out processes. This view at least partially explains why the alignment of objectives had a positive effect on the development of ASDC.

3.4.3   Organizational Factors

In July 2001, the organization's structure was modified in order to meet the objectives of the 2001–2006 Strategic Program so that it largely became a financial institution. According to Cerdán et al. [CER06], this change in organizational

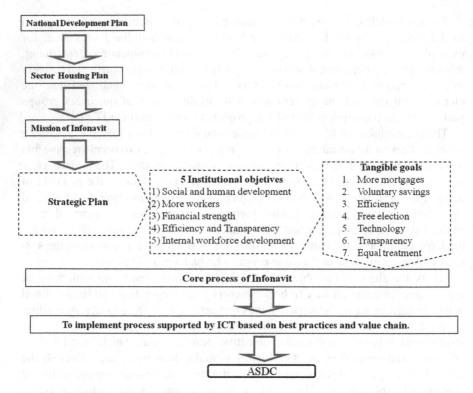

Fig. 3.4 Alignment of objectives [INF07]

structure was clearly justified in the new mission and planning strategy of the Institute, as well as its main functions as a financial organization. The changes that took place were as follows: from the five departments that existed in 2000 (finance, legal, taxation, technical, and administration and planning), seven were created in 2001 (mortgages, portfolio administration, tax collection, legal, technical, innovation and quality, and finance and planning). This new structure makes Infonavit a network-type organization that achieves its results through cooperation.

This new structure allowed the Institute to concentrate on its core activity of granting housing loans to achieve financial sustainability better and focus on improving its processes through technology. From 2001 forward, the innovation and quality department would take part in the Institute's decision-making processes because it no longer depended hierarchically on another area, but instead had the authority to participate directly and actively in the process of administrative reform. The development of ASDC became positively associated with the modification of the Institute's structure because the innovation and quality department would have the same weight in decision-making processes as other departments and would be well informed of changes in the organization. Finally, Méndez [MEN06] indicates that the structure of Infonavit is somewhat different from classical government structures inasmuch as it is comprised of three different sectors (federal government, private sector, and workers).

The projects also had the support of the organization's senior management; Infonavit's working team considered that to be a determining factor in the development of the ASDC strategies, from its adoption through to its implementation and use. The support of senior management translated into approval and support for each of the three initiatives (the portal, kiosks, and Infonatel) from the board of directors. This board was made up of labor unions, private sector employers, and the federal government. The managing director gave his full commitment to supporting the ASDC strategy. This support was provided in the form of granting financial and human resources to the three projects, punctual follow-up at each phase of the ASDC strategies, resolution of conflicts, and the transfer of unionized personnel to the Infonatel offices, located in Rosario in the State of Mexico.

The combined support of management and the board of directors facilitated Infonavit's administrative reform and helped it to meet its goal of granting the most mortgages in its history during a 6-year period. To some, the managing director is looked upon as a leader who had the vision for transforming Infonavit into a transparent and efficient institution. However, worth mentioning is the support of the labor union, which helped to achieve the necessary changes among the personnel to use ICT intensively within Infonavit. The union was able to get the employees to change their processes and routines, which created a positive environment for the ASDC.

Regarding the skills and abilities of the ASDC working team, the data collected about their professional competency indicated that they were highly trained in their fields. Every member profile consisted of at least one profession directly related to the position and more than 5 years experience performing those duties in the private sector. According to the interviews, the technical staff was formed by engineers of telecommunications, informatics, or systems. The manager of innovation had a bachelor's degree in computer systems and a master's degree in business administration. The team also had experience in information technology consulting. However, for the majority of them, it was their first experience in the public sector, which made administrative procedures complicated at first. Over time, the language, physical environment, communication channels, attitudes toward service, orientation toward results, and commitment to the work were positively modified. In addition, there was adequate access to human resources and each project in the strategy had the necessary personnel.

These two variables positively influenced the ASDC strategy because Infonavit had the necessary personnel with the required technical and business backgrounds to undertake the three projects and implement them. At the beginning of the ASDC initiative, there was no clear and formalized methodology to manage the projects, but the team knew how to develop a project and used their experience to put some standards and controls into practice. When the project kicked off, team members already knew how to manage an information technology project and they were trained in methodologies for developing systems and information management. In addition, there were external staff members (through outsourcing) to deal with certain processes for the project, which could be helped and overseen by internal staff. Overall, the ASDC had professional human resources with the capacity to manage the entire strategy.

3.4.4 Institutional Factors

From the point of view of those who took part in the ASDC strategy, the availability of financial resources was a positive and significant element in the development of the three projects, but was most important to Infonatel because its technical requirements demanded a much larger initial economic investment. Infonatel needed resources from the very beginning with the rehabilitation of the facilities (including cleaning, network and telephone cabling, and renovating them) up until it began operations, which required purchasing specialized equipment for receiving calls, as well as training and hiring new staff members. Infonavit could deliver the required financial resources because it has financial autonomy and independence. One part of Infonavit's income comes from federal government subsidies and the other portion comes from revenue from the provision of financial services. Because the ASCD was an institutional strategy with the objective of improving the core services of Infonavit, it always had the necessary resources available.

Regarding the legal framework, in particular the existence of a policy, plan, or regulations for electronic government that would encourage the use of ICT, Infonavit defined its 2001 mission in the following way, "Fulfill our constitutional mandate of granting loans to workers so that they may acquire, freely and transparently, a home that is most appropriate to their needs in respect to price, quality and location" ([CON05]: 101). To undertake this mission, Infonavit established its Strategic Plan 2001–2006, which focused extensively on the use of information technology [INF07]. The strategic program had four main objectives. The first was to contribute to the social and human development of workers through free choice of housing and informing workers about their rights. The second objective was to increase the number of loans via reduced intermediaries. The third objective was related to the organization's fiscal stability, which would be made possible through a reduction of debtors. The last objective was to operate in a transparent and efficient way. Infonavit's general goal was to reduce the number of procedures and to improve response time by using ICTs. This strategic plan laid the groundwork so that the ASDC strategy could take shape because it clearly articulated the actions and behaviors that the Institute wanted to cultivate. The ASDC directly applied to the fourth objective, but also contributed to the rest of the plan.

Lastly, we look at the values of the organization and those of its members. Infonavit undertook a strategy of cultural transformation during the first 3 years of the 2001 administration through employee training. Infonavit's new work logic was to be highly focused on results. The reference values were integrity and honesty, nobility and respect, strength and efficacy, optimism and audacity, cultural nationalism, continuous learning, and dedication to the user, innovation, creativity, and transparency [CER06].

The ethical values of the ASDC team reflected their desire to change the way business was performed. The common factors in achieving that goal were to work in teams and deliver the projects on time. They knew the problems within Infonavit and they were motivated to carefully proceed with their task to transform the organization. The values were important for the ASDC strategy because the team believed that each member could change the status quo of the process through his job. It was very important for them to change the organization, improve service, and eliminate unnecessary procedures. Shared values allowed the team members to design and implement new services, using technology as the medium to make them more efficient.

3.4.5   Contextual Factors

From an economic perspective, the housing sector in Mexico translates to 1.4% of the Gross Domestic Product (GDP) between 1995 and 2005. Approximately 10,000 companies formally participate at different points throughout the entire housing process, from the construction of homes through to their financing; even the raw materials used are national. In terms of employment, this sector generates around 10% of the national total. Therefore, the housing sector represents a pillar of economic and social development for the country [CON05]. Toward the end of 1998, the economic growth of the country, measured as the number of individuals registered with the Mexican Institute of Social Security (IMSS by its initials in Spanish), was approximately 12.5 million workers. By 2000, this figure had reached 15 million, an increase of approximately 20% in the number of individuals registered with IMSS. One environmental element relevant to Infonavit's performance was the rate of inflation, which was steadily decreasing and contributed to a reduction of interest rates. For example, in January 1999 the inflation rate was 19.01%, whereas in December 2000 it had decreased by half to 9.49% [GON06].

The downward trend of the inflation rate created a favorable environment for loan disbursement because the purchasing power of workers had increased, interest rates were lower than in other years, and there was stability in the prices of goods and services. Therefore, there was an opportunity to purchase a house through a loan. In this period there were more people registered as employed in formal jobs than in prior years, which implies there was more money available to Infonavit to finance the loans as well.

The original groundwork for this economic growth was laid during the presidency of Ernesto Zedillo, when there was greater economic stability and higher employment, which resulted in the growth in the number of individuals affiliated with IMSS, each with the right to apply for an Infonavit loan. Once financial stability was achieved within the country, the demand for housing increased, which had a direct impact on the transformation of Infonavit because it encouraged the establishment of strategies to meet this demand. In 2000, the housing sector in Mexico experienced a deficit of 4.6 million homes and a stagnating construction industry due to the effects of the 1994 financial crisis. The perspective of the ASDC team was that the demand for housing was very high and would require more efficient service in order to grant loans in as short a time as possible. The team was well aware that Infonavit's service capability in respect to granting loans had been inadequate. The factors that enabled Infonavit's performance after 2000, regarding the new schemes for granting mortgage loans as well as the reduction in administrative and legal regulation, were the economic, institutional, and political conditions brewing in the national context [GON06].

3.5   Final Comments

Electronic government implies much more than the simple introduction of ICTs into government processes. It is a comprehensive process affected by a broad range of factors, not just the technology itself. e-government is a useful tool for modernizing the state given that it enables government to offer higher-quality services to citizens and provide those services in a more efficient, effective, and transparent way. Previous studies on e-government have shown that the success of these initiatives depends on a great number of factors that affect their adoption, design, implementation, and use [FOU01, GIL05, LEE02, MEI06, MEL03, MOO02]. It was evident from our study of a successful example in Mexico that many of the variables studied in the literature were also important to the ASDC strategy, ranging from the institution's resources to the administration's ability to manage them.

The results of this case are also important because there are few studies on the development of e-government in Mexico in comparison to the great number of studies carried out at different levels of government in developed countries. According to Sotelo [SOT06], although the development of electronic government in Mexico has been a slow step-by-step process, it is currently expanding. One of the reasons behind this slow progress is a wide digital divide in Mexico, which needs to be tackled. Access to the Internet in urban areas reaches 32%, whereas in rural zones it stands at only 6% [MAR08]. This disparity in access to ICT and infrastructure has had an adverse impact on the growth of e-government projects in developing countries, including Mexico and similar countries in Latin America [LUN07]. We think that this case was successful because the ASDC strategy had three main communication channels with citizens. The channels were substitutes for one another and workers could perform all transactions using any of them. For instance, if a worker did not have access to the portal, she could use the call center or a digital kiosk to obtain the same service.

In 2001, Infonavit opened the Internet channel outward so that it could be accessed directly by eligible individuals. All the system users had to do was enter their social security or loan number in order to find out their balance, which in the past could only be done through a union intermediary. In respect to Infonatel, the organization's capacity to receive calls was increased; allowing them to address the problem of individuals left unattended. At the beginning of the project, approximately 52% of the total call volume was due to busy phone lines. And finally, the digital kiosk project helped to reduce the workload of delegates by taking care of minor transactions that took 5 min or less. The purpose of this equipment was to improve attention to the customers and make operations more agile, simple, and transparent to all citizens.

The study of this Mexican experience provides evidence that e-government projects need to be designed comprehensively to consider not only technology, but also external factors in the environment, human resource aspects, and the organization's regulatory framework. One of the elements that helped Infonavit to develop its ASDC strategy and achieve the desired outcomes in a timely fashion was that it established deliverables for every phase of the project. This accountability is important not just for gauging progress, but also to encourage user groups and general management to support the project because they can see tangible results and benefits in the medium term, not just the long term. In addition, as was mentioned several times throughout the chapter, the objectives of the three components of the ASDC strategy were clearly and strongly aligned to the overall goals of Infonavit as an organization.

Acknowledgments The authors would like to thank Infonavit for the assistance it provided so that we could carry out this research. This work was partially supported by the National Science Foundation under Grant No. 0131923 and 0630239. Any opinions, findings, conclusions, or recommendations expressed in this material are those of the authors and do not necessarily reflect the views of the National Science Foundation.

References

BRO99   Brown, Douglas M. "Information Systems for Improved. Performance Management. Development Approaches in U.S. Public Agencies". In: Reinventing Government in the Information Age: International practice in IT-enabled public sector reform/edited by Richard Heeks. London: Routledge, 1999.

CAS97   Castillo AD, "El nuevo institucionalismo en el análisis organizacional: Conceptos y enunciados explicativos. Documento de trabajo (Centro de Investigación y Docencia Económicas)". Administración Pública No. 44, 1997.

CER06   Cerdán Verástegui Alfonso, González A. Manuel A. and Velasco, S. Ernesto, "La reforma en Marcha, 2001-2006" en *El proceso de modernización en el INFONAVIT 2001-2006: estrategia, redes y liderazgo* por María del Carmen Pardo, Ernesto Velasco Sánchez. México: El Colegio de México, 2006.

CLA07   Clayton Thomas J, Gregory S. "The New Face of Government: Citizen-Initiated Contacts in the Era of E-Government". Journal of Public Administration Research and Theory, 13, 1, 2003, pp 83–102.

CON05   Conafovi, Fondo De Cultura Económica y Secretaría De Desarrollo Social. *Vivienda: evidencia del cambio.* México, DF. Colección Editorial del gobierno del cambio, 2005.

CON09   Conavi, Comision Nacional De Vivienda, 2009. www.conavi.gob.mx/housing/INFONAVIT. pdf, consulted 15 July 09.

DET02   Detlor B, and Finn K, "Towards a framework for government portal design: The government, citizen, and portal perspectives". In A. Gronlund (Ed.), Electronic government: Design, applications, and management. Hershey, Pennsylvania: Idea Group, pp. 99–119, 2002.

FOU01   FOUNTAIN J. E, *Building the Virtual State: Information Technology and Institutional Change*, Washington, DC: Brookings Institution Press, 2001.

GIL03   Gil-Garcia JR, and Luna-Reyes LF, "Towards a Definition of Electronic Government: A Comparative Review". In: A. Mendez Vilas et al. (Ed.), Techno-legal Aspects of the Information Society and New Economy: An Overview. Badajoz, Spain: Formatex, 2003.

GIL05   Gil-Garcia JR, Enacting State Websites: A Mixed Method Study Exploring e-government Success in Multi-Organizational Settings, Doctoral Thesis. University at Albany, State University of New York, Albany, NY, 2005.

GIL05a   Gil-Garcia JR, and Pardo T, "E-government success factors: mapping practical tools to theoretical foundations". Government Information Quarterly, 22, 2, 2005, pp 187–216.

GIL07   Gil-Garcia JR, and Helbig N, "Exploring e-government Benefits and Success Factors". In: Ari-Veikko Anttiroiko and Matti Malkia (Eds). Encyclopedia of Digital Government. Hershey, PA: Idea Group, 2007.

GAG01   Gagnon Y-C, "The Behavior of Public Managers in Adopting New Technologies". Public Performance & Management Review, 24, 4, 2001, pp 337–350.

GON06   González Arreola M, "Cambios de las políticas institucionales" en *El proceso de modernización en el INFONAVIT 2001–2006: estrategia, redes y liderazgo* por María del Carmen Pardo, Ernesto Velasco Sánchez. Mexico: El Colegio de Mexico, 2006.

HEE03   Heeks R, "Most eGovernment-for-Development Projects Fail: How Can Risks be Reduced, iGovernment." IDPM. University of Manchester, UK. Working Paper Series, Paper no. 14, 2003.

INF07   INFONAVIT, 2007, http://www.infonavit.org.mx, consulted 23.11.2007.

LEE02   Leenes RE, "The Enschede Virtual Public Counter: OLE 2000 a case study," In A. Gronlund (Ed.), Electronic government: Design, applications, and management. Hershey, Pennsylvania: Idea Group, pp 205–225. 2002.

LUN07   Luna-Reyes LF, Gil-García JR, and Cruz CB, "Collaborative Digital Government in Mexico: Some Lessons from Federal Web-Based Interorganizational Information Integration Initiatives". Government Information Quarterly, 24, 2007, pp 808–826.

MAR08   Mariscal J, and Ramirez F, "Retos para desarrollo del sector de las telecomunicaciones en México, Documento de trabajo (Centro de Investigación y Docencia Económicas)". Administración Pública No. 218, 2008.

MEI06   MEIJER, A.J. "ICTs and Political Accountability: An Assessment of the Impact of Digitization in Government on Political Accountability in Connecticut, Massachusetts and New York State". NCDG Working Paper # 06-002, 2006.

MEL03   Melitski J, "Capacity and E-Government Performance: An analysis Based on Early. Adopters of Internet Technologies in New Jersey". Public Performance and Management Review, 26, 4, 2003, pp 376–390.

MEN06   MÉNDEZ "I. Marco Analítico" en *El proceso de modernización en el INFONAVIT 2001-2006: estrategia, redes y liderazgo* por María del Carmen Pardo, Ernesto Velasco Sánchez. Mexico: El Colegio de Mexico, 2006.

MOO02   Moon MJ, "The Evolution of E Government among Municipalities: Rhetoric or Reality?" Public Administration Review, 62, 4, 2002, pp 424–433.

NOR93   North DC *"Instituciones, Cambio Institucional y Desempeño Económico"*. México: FCE, 1993.

NOR05   Norris DF, Moon MJ. "Advancing E-Government at the Grass Roots: Tortoise or Hare?" Public Administration Review, 65, 1, 2005, pp 64–73.

OEC05   OECD, E-Government Studies Mexico Organization for Economic Co-operation and Development. México: OECD Press, 2005.

PAR06   Pardo María Del Carmen, "Introducción", in: El proceso de modernización en el INFONAVIT 2001–2006: estrategia, redes y liderazgo por María del Carmen Pardo, Ernesto Velasco Sánchez. México: El Colegio de México, 2006.

PET03   Peters BG, *"El nuevo institucionalismo: la teoría institucional en ciencia política"*. Barcelona: Gedisa, 2003.

PEL07   Peled A, "The Electronic Mountain: A Tale of Two Tels". The American Review of Public Administration, 37, 2007, p 458.

PRE07   Presidency of the Republic, 2007, http://innova.fox.presidencia.gob.mx/ciudadanos/ practicas, 18.10.2007.

RAM05   Ramió C, and Salvador M, "*Instituciones y nueva gestión pública en América Latina*". Barcelona: Fundación CIDOB, 2005.

RIV03   Rivera Urrutia E, "*La nueva economía, gobierno electrónico y reforma del estado: Chile a la luz de la experiencia internacional*". Santiago, Chile: FLACSO-Chile Editorial Universitaria, 2003.

RIV04   Rivera Urrutia E, La construcción del gobierno digital como un problema de innovación institucional. Documento de trabajo (Centro de Investigación y Docencia Económicas). Administración Pública No. 144, 2004.

SOT06   Sotelo Nava A, "*México: un gobierno digital en expansión*," México DF, Editorial Abraham Sotelo, 2006.

STR06   Streib G, and Navarro I, "Citizen Demand for Interactive E-Government: The Case of Georgia Consumer Services". The American Review of Public Administration, 36, 2006, 288.

TAT01   Ho, AT-K, and Smith JF, "Information Technology Planning and the Y2K. Problem in Local Governments". American Review of Public Administration, 31, 2, 2001, pp 158–180.

VON07   Vonk G, Geertman S, and Schot P, "New Technologies Stuck in Old Hierarchies: The Diffusion of Geo-Information Technologies in Dutch Public Organizations". Public Administration Review, 67, 4, 2007, pp 745–756.

WEA99   Weare C, Musso JA, and Hale ML, "Electronic Democracy and the Diffusion of Municipal Web Pages in California". Administration & Society, 31, 1, 1999, pp 3–27.

WEL02   Weldon J, "Las fuentes políticas del presidencialismo en México" en Shugart Matthew y Mainwairing Scott, Presidencialismo y Democracias en América Latina. Buenos Aires: Paidós, 2002, pp 175–253.

WEL07   Welch E, and Pandey SK, "E-Government and Bureaucracy: Toward a Better Understanding of Intranet Implementation and Its Effect on Red Tape". Journal of Public Administration Research and Theory, 17, 3, 2007, pp 379–404.

WES01   West JP, and Berman EM, "The impact of revitalized management practices on the Adoption of Information Technology: A National Survey of Local Governments". Public Performance & Management Review, 24, 3, 2001, pp 233–253.

YAN07   Yang K, and Rho S-Y, "E-Government for Better Performance: Promises, Realities, and Challenges". International Journal of Public Administration, 30, 11, 2007, pp 1197–1217.

YIL07   Yildiz M, "E-Government Research: Reviewing the Literature, Limitations, and Ways Forward". Government Information Quarterly, 24, 3, 2007, pp 646–665.

Chapter 4
The Casualty Assistance Readiness Enhancement System: A Case Study in Rapid Prototyping and Design for Flexibility

Simon R. Goerger, Ernest Y. Wong, Dale L. Henderson, Brian K. Sperling, and William Bland

Abstract Numerous government benefits are available to the surviving family of fallen U.S. military service members. Unfortunately, most of these entitlements require a considerable amount of paperwork to process correctly, necessitating a great deal of patience, attention to detail, and composure from families at a time when their grief is raw. Even though the U.S. Army appoints a Casualty Assistance Officer (CAO) to help surviving family members through this process, the soldiers serving as CAOs tend to be inexperienced and oftentimes find themselves challenged to provide accurate and thorough assistance. Consequently, some families do not receive all benefits in a timely manner, and some entitlements may be overlooked entirely. To help with the military's Casualty Program, we have developed the Casualty Assistance Readiness Enhancement System (CARES), an information system that improves how the Department of the Army cares for military families in arguably their greatest time of need. The tool and associated process reduced the time required to complete forms, reduced the potential for errors on repetitive information, assisted CAOs through the process, and provided electronic copies of completed forms.

4.1 Introduction

> *A good programmer is someone who always looks both ways*
> *before crossing a one-way street.*
> ~Doug Linder

Today's world often seeks software solutions to procedural problems. Many methodologies exist to assist organizing the development of software products to meet the large needs of large-scale issues. However, many of these methodologies fail to address rapidly the need of an organization with limited resources that

S.R. Goerger (✉)
Department of Systems Engineering (MADN-SE), United States
Military Academy, 646 Swift Road, West Point, NY 10996, USA
e-mail: simon.goerger@us.army.mil

S. Assar et al. (eds.), *Practical Studies in E-Government: Best Practices from Around the World*, DOI 10.1007/978-1-4419-7533-1_4,
© Springer Science+Business Media, LLC 2011

requires a solution to assist them with the development of a product to guide one-time users through the bureaucratic complexities associated with a process. The basic design of the business process management (BPM) software tool must easily accommodate unpredictable product modifications while maintaining data security and standalone functionality.

The Systems Decision Process (SDP)[1] meets many of these requirements due to its focus on the problem development phase and the stakeholder focus during reassessment of solution design, decision-making, and implementation phases. This chapter briefly discusses the methodology and demonstrates its effectiveness in meeting the needs of the organizational clients, product users, and product beneficiaries. The demonstration is made through the review of the exemplar of the development of the Casualty Assistance Readiness Enhancement System (CARES).

This chapter reviews some current software development methodologies. It introduces an issue that requires a possible software solution that cannot be adequately met by some of the current software development methodologies and introduces a systems design methodology, the SDP, to address the shortfalls of rapid development of software. Next, the SDP methodology is applied to assist the development of one-time users in completing a complex task. The chapter steps through two iterations of the development of CARES using the SDP methodology. The chapter concludes with a discussion of lessons learned from the experience of applying the systems design methodology to this type of software development product.

4.2 Background

Software development teams can create a BPM software tool using one of many software development methodologies. This section addresses the strengths and weaknesses of some of the industry standard software development methodologies. Next, the section outlines some of the specific issues initially identified with CARES that necessitated an alternate methodology for the development of this product.

4.2.1 Literature Review

The Project Management Institute provides many viable products, training and education, and professional collaborative environments for the management of programs. Products address issues such as financing, resource management, stakeholder management, product development, and many other industry standards. For product development, such as software development, there are many methods used for the development of software products. Two of these are Rapid Application Development (RAD) and Extreme Programming.

RAD is an agile methodology for software development that minimizes initial planning in favor of rapid prototyping and testing. A British software engineer named James Martin in 1991 developed RAD in response to the less flexible methods such as the Structured Systems Analysis and Design Method and other waterfall-based models. Waterfall models proved limited for software development due to their systematic approach that made it difficult to integrate changes to requirements while ensuring the completion of one phase of software development before moving into a subsequent phase. The RAD methodology addressed the difficulties of integrating client and system requirements by the use of an iterative development process and product prototypes. In the initial development stages, software engineers create data and business process models of the business requirements in order to help identify the basic requirements of the system. After these theoretical models are developed, initial prototypes help the software developer and users verify the validity of the theoretical models. With user input, a series of product validations, model refinements, and software modifications is cycled through until the desired product is produced.

A variant of RAD is Extreme Programming. Extreme Programming is a style of software development that integrates the customer closely into the cyclic development of prototypes using a disciplined approach to the tracking of software requirements modifications and product prototypes. It has shown itself to be viable for the development of products that require a small team of coders working with clients and project managers. Developers use the methodology for short or longer duration projects. Although usable for surge production, project managers normally use Extreme Programming for use in more sustained projects. Extreme Programming is not as applicable for programs developed for one-time users of a process-driven tool. When the user base is small enough that a dedicated team of clients working hand in hand with developers is not viable, Extreme Programming can have difficulties maintaining the required relationships between developers and clients/ users. The same holds true if there are few subject matter experts of the process and a predominance of future one-time users of the process being automated.

The strength of RAD and Extreme Programming is also one of its major limitations. This limitation is the breadth of their initial assessment of requirements. For a well-known process executed by many users, the review of baseline documentation and processing rules can be augmented with subject matter experts to gain a sound understanding of the system. Armed with this knowledge, software developers can design and produce a viable prototype for rapid production cycles. This process is not as effective when dealing with systems that are not stable, do not have predictable requirements modification schedules, and have a majority of users who may only use the system once.

4.2.2   Issue

Numerous government benefits are available to the surviving family of fallen U.S. military service members. Unfortunately, most of these entitlements require a considerable amount of paperwork to correctly process, necessitating a great deal of patience, attention to detail, and composure from families at a time when their grief is raw. Even though the U.S. Army appoints a Casualty Assistance Officer (CAO) to help surviving family members through this process, the soldiers serving as CAOs tend to be inexperienced and oftentimes find themselves challenged to provide accurate and thorough assistance. Consequently, in the past, some families did not receive all benefits in a timely manner, with some entitlements being overlooked entirely. To help with the military's Casualty Program, we have developed the CARES, an information system[2] that improves how the Department of the Army cares for military families in arguably their greatest time of need. The tool and associated process reduced the time required to complete forms, reduced the potential for errors on repetitive information, assisted CAOs through the process, and provided electronic copies of completed forms.

From 2005 to 2008, with heightened media attention on U.S. military casualties in our nation's ongoing war against terrorism, the Department of Defense made a concerted effort to enhance the way it administers and conducts its Casualty Program. Although the numerous government benefits and entitlements serve as means to help ease the anguish families endure after the loss of a loved one serving in the Armed Forces, the process of applying for such assistance requires considerable patience and persistence. Moreover, because new legislation and regulations periodically change many of these entitlements – typically enacted to further enhance the benefits provided for surviving family members – a considerable amount of knowledge is required to accurately and thoroughly process requests for such benefits [HEA06].

To help the families of those who have died in service to our nation, the U.S. Army appoints a soldier to serve as the Casualty Assistance Officer (CAO) responsible for assisting surviving families and loved ones in the aftermath of their loss. These soldiers serve as representatives of the Secretary of the Army and the Army itself, and their performance as CAOs helps to shape the family's lasting impression of the Army as an institution that cares for its own. CAOs assist eligible next of kin in making arrangements for the funeral or memorial service, settling claims, and paying survivor benefits. The length of the CAO assignment typically lasts 3–6 months, however, there have been certain circumstances necessitating assignments lasting upwards of 2 years. Casualty assistance concludes when all claims have been completed, payment of survivor benefits has begun to flow to the next of kin, all paperwork has been prepared and properly filed with the appropriate agencies, and the Casualty Assistance Center (CAC) overseeing the case releases the CAO from his duties [USA05a].

Casualty Assistance Officers, however, tend not to be very experienced at this somber task, usually serving in this capacity for the very first and only time. Despite ongoing efforts to improve their readiness, training, and preparedness, CAOs continue to be challenged in their ability to provide accurate and thorough assistance. Not only must they negotiate through such emotionally demanding circumstances, they must also convey a sense of authority on all matters pertaining to the benefits and entitlements process. CAOs are required to interact with numerous organizations including legal aid, the chaplain's office, finance, and retirement services. Additionally, they must help to prepare claims, benefits, and entitlements to a variety of government agencies, including the Department of Defense, Department of Veterans Administration, Internal Revenue Service, and Social Security Administration. Therefore, to expect CAOs to be experts at all these tasks, regardless of the amount of training they receive and regardless of the level of dedication they demonstrate, is overly optimistic.

In August 2005, the Casualty and Memorial Affairs Operations Center (CMAOC) of the U.S. Army Human Resources Command (HRC) contacted the Operations Research Center of Excellence (ORCEN) in the Department of Systems Engineering at the United States Military Academy (USMA) to see if it could help introduce an BPM system that would make it easier for CAOs to fulfill CMAOC's mission. Specifically, the CMAOC requested that the ORCEN design a system that automated the paperwork completion process for claims, benefits, and entitlements related to service member casualties. Required was a CARES design that provided a simple system to guide CAOs through the bureaucratic complexities associated with the requests for claims, benefits, and entitlements. More important, CARES needed to provide an accommodating electronic forms completion tool that the government could quickly alter as new laws, regulations, and entitlements arose pertaining to the military's Casualty Program. Its basic design also needed to provide data security and standalone functionality while allowing one-time use by individuals unfamiliar with the bureaucratic complexities of the BPM system.

4.3 Methodology

To effectively accomplish this task, developers need to deal with a number of issues, including the ongoing debate of whether all government agencies involved could effectively implement a paperless system,[3] what additional resources CAOs would need with an automated system, how to link to CMAOC and other relevant databases, and how best to integrate such a system so CAOs could best leverage its capabilities. In addition, the design of the system would have to be flexible enough to account for new legislation, changing benefit amounts, and the potential obsolescence of existing forms and documents.

Using the SDP[4] taught to cadets attending USMA – a structured problem-solving process useful in the design of multidisciplinary, large-scale, and complex problems graphically portrayed in Fig. 4.1 – one can create a BPM software tool that would help to improve the military's Casualty Program [UNI04]. By focusing on whether the government would be able to implement a coherent paperless standard, the immediate task and overriding concern was to deploy a system that CAOs could utilize as part of the existing processes and standards. Being aware that ongoing changes to the Casualty Assistance program are likely (especially with respect to amended forms, new options and benefits, and revised entitlements) one must make sure the design of the system is robust enough to accommodate periodic updates. Accordingly, the appropriate approach is to frame the project as a design for flexibility. In order to maximize the likelihood that the system would actually accomplish its intended purpose and be implemented by HRC, the design of the system had to be scalable, easily modified, and simple enough for both CAOs to use and CACs to administer.

The key to the methodology is the emphasis on the problem definition phase with its in-depth stakeholder analysis and functional analysis. Unlike the RAD

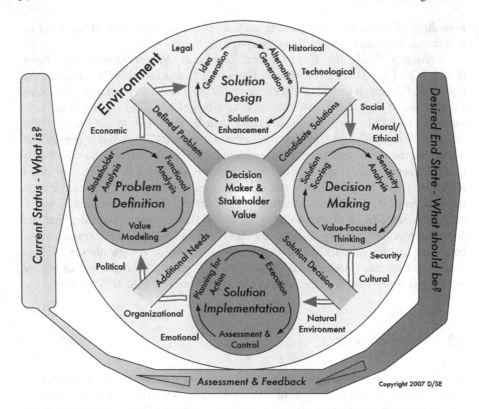

Fig. 4.1 The Systems Decision Process (SDP) framework (from Systems Decision Making in Systems Engineering and Management)

and Extreme Programming which do a more cursory problem definition phase in the attempt to quickly understand and develop potential products for assessment by the client, the SDP spends from 33 to 50% of its time looking at and revisiting the problem definition. This is to ensure the CARES design takes into account as many of the stakeholder initial requirements and subsequent needs as possible.

As with Extreme Programming, SDP continues to incorporate the clients in the solution design and decision-making phases with rapid prototype assessment. During these phases, developers continuously reassess and validate the problem statement to account for changes in entitlements, claims process, and laws. New and modified requirements are rapidly integrating them into the base design and coded into CARES.

The solution implementation phase also emphasizes the continuous reassessment of the problem statement as client and user feedback during the initial software training sessions and beta testing (discussed later) the process was used to refine the BPM software tool and subsequent training package.

For one to understand better the importance of the problem definition phase, the next section reviews the stakeholder analysis of the CARES development process.

4.3.1   Stakeholder Analysis

"Usability of interactive computer systems is at the very core of the computer, communications, and information revolution, which is moving our society into the post-industrial era," writes James Foley in a text on designing user interfaces [HIX93]. To help ensure that CARES developed into a usable system, the ORCEN conducted a stakeholder analysis that allowed it to better scope the project requirements and gain more information and insights into the problem areas. Specifically, the stakeholder analysis enabled developers to [MAN06].

– Leverage the opinions, recommendations, and perceptions of leaders and experts in the Casualty Program.
– Generate support from the stakeholders on the direction of the design for CARES.
– Gain the support and resources of stakeholders in helping to construct, test, and evaluate CARES.
– Foster open lines of communication with stakeholders to ensure they understand the intent and goals of CARES.
– Anticipate stakeholder reaction to CARES and progressively modify the system in a way that is most likely to gain stakeholder support and approval.

The stakeholders who comprised the system consisted not only of the client, but also the users and potential beneficiaries of the CARES. Such stakeholders included representatives of the U.S. Army Casualty and Memorial Affairs Operations Center and the Casualty Advisory Board. Likely beneficiaries include the family of service members, soldiers assigned the responsibility of being CAOs, CACs, and associated organizations that will have increased confidence in the military's casualty assistance system.

System designers interviewed stakeholders regarding system and family requirements, current casualty assistance processes, perceived needs and issues with the Casualty Program, and suggestions for moving forward with the CARES. These interviews helped to inform the problem definition phase of the project and grounded the development team with better insights into how it could best design and implement CARES on behalf of HRC and CMAOC.

The development team continued to conduct stakeholder analysis throughout the process to identify changing requirements and policies. Between 2005 and 2007 the number of entitlements and associated documents increased by five. Understanding these constraints and other characteristics of the system led to the eventual redefining and clarification of the problem statement during our initial iteration through the SDP.

4.3.2   Redefining the Problem Statement

After conducting our stakeholder analysis, designers were able to generate a set of criteria that helped them evaluate potential alternative designs and ultimately proceed with the best course of action. A hierarchical listing of the criteria from most important to least is as follows:

- Speed of implementation (How soon to field?)
- System flexibility (Can it be modified to changes?)
- System reliability (Does it function as intended?)
- Ease of use (Does it have an intuitive interface?)
- Process transparency (Does it make it clearer for the CAO and family members?)
- Implementation costs (Will it require additional equipment, training, or infrastructure?)
- Impacts of personnel turnover (Will change in key decision makers result in problem statement modification or possible project cancellation?)

These criteria helped to redefine the initial project statement presented to the ORCEN by the client to ensure it was working to address the correct problem.

4.3.2.1 Initial Problem Statement

In an Unfinanced Requirement Statement dated 13 May 2005, HRC initiated the following request [USA05b]: We want a "Casualty Assistance Wizard [that] would simplify and streamline the laborious task of completing all paperwork required when assisting surviving family members apply for all eligible benefits and entitlements from the Army, DoD, Department of Veterans' Affairs, and the Social Security Administration after losing their loved one on active duty. The wizard application would function much like TurboTax or other wizard applications in that it would access relevant personal information from [various military personnel databases] to auto-populate the family member's benefits application record, analyze that case record, and then use that analysis to ask a series of simple questions to determine automatically what benefits and entitlements the family member is eligible to receive and which forms must be completed for that purpose. The wizard should reside behind a secure web portal and include capability for digital or electronic signature and secure electronic transfer of record content to the agencies listed above. For those Casualty Assistance Officers and families without Internet access, the wizard must also be available with more limited capability in a CD or DVD format for use with a laptop computer. Once developed, a minor annual funding [is required] to maintain and update the wizard application."

This initial problem statement failed to capture the nuances required to meet the client's needs. Some examples include: one-time use, limited long-term software support, and unscheduled modifications to policies and entitlements. A revised problem statement was required.

4.3.2.2 Revised Problem Statement

Based upon our stakeholder analysis and the value criteria we developed, the ORCEN drafted the following revised problem statement. The overall objective is to help to enhance the military's Casualty Program under the assumption that the Armed Forces will continue to conduct the Casualty Program in accordance with current regulations and existing paradigms (e.g., no outsourcing of functions to third parties, no major overhaul of training, and no permanent CAOs). To do so effectively, [the ORCEN] intends to develop CARES as a tool that:

- Automates, simplifies, and streamlines the paperwork requirements for entitlements and benefits.
- Equips CAOs with the capability to provide reliable information and valued service to surviving family members, and helps educate, train, and guide CAOs in the execution of their duties.
- Contributes in providing timely, accurate, responsive, and transparent assistance to surviving family members in the trying times they must endure.
- Provides the CMOAC and CACs with greater visibility on the progress of individual cases so that they can proactively manage and better assist CAOs for the benefit of surviving family members.

Successful implementation of this information system required that designers consider the needs of the three primary stakeholders within the military Casualty Program: the surviving family members who are the intended beneficiaries of the system, the CAOs who are the end-users of the system, and the casualty program administrators who have arguably the greatest influence and impact on how the system will be employed. Figure 4.2 shows the ideal bridging function that CARES can provide to these three primary stakeholders. The design for the system, therefore, had to be flexible enough to take into account the various tradeoffs generated by oftentimes competing interests and goals.

Similar to RAD, the process would require rapid prototyping. However, understanding that quick prototyping would need to include unscheduled modifications to incorporate changes to processes and entitlements reinforced the need to continual revisiting of the problem definition phase.

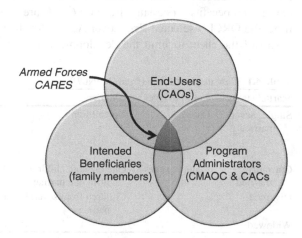

Fig. 4.2 Linking stakeholders with CARES (based on [WON07])

4.3.3 Rapid Prototyping to Overcome Inertia

In order to ensure our design for CARES was continually progressing in the proper direction, the ORCEN built the system as a series of rapid prototypes [ISE95]. Doing so allowed it to develop working models that it could promptly change and refine based on the feedback and insights of its expert stakeholders. Furthermore, the ORCEN believed rapid prototyping helped it to overcome much of the institutional inertia oftentimes associated with efforts to introduce change and modernize in large bureaucratic organizations.

Prototyping started with assessment of the necessary process to meet the requirements of the key stakeholders: the family members, past CAOs, and the Army Casualty Assistance Program. To accomplish this, the ORCEN designers conducted a comprehensive review of congressional mandates, U.S. Army regulations, and Casualty Assistance Products. Augmented with information from interviews with CACs and CAOs resulted in an enhanced understanding of the needs of its clients. Due to the sensitivity of the topic, interviewing of service family members was limited to a small pool of individuals who had recently lost family members. To capture the input from the family members and to ensure confidentiality and sensitivity, CMAOC conducted a robust review of family member comments and CAC after action reviews and provided feedback to the product development team. Designers used this information to generate a case diagnostic tree (Table 4.1) and process flow graph (Fig. 4.3) that helped developers visualize viable beneficiaries and process requirements in a manner that was logical in its flow and complete in its design.

Early analysis on the project revealed that nearly all the data contained in a soldier's Department of Defense Form 93, Record of Emergency Data, provided a great deal of the information needed to automatically populate casualty benefits forms. The initial design, therefore, consisted of a very basic MS Excel spreadsheet application linked to several MS Word forms. Figure 4.4 shows a screenshot of one of the earliest design layouts for CARES. Much of the focus for the initial prototype was on its functionality, determining whether the developers could gain access to and link confidential data elements into the various forms required for casualty claims and benefits processing. Because CAOs are assigned to just one casualty at a time, the ORCEN selected Excel over Access for the initial design due to the initial desire of the client to limit the development of an additional database to support

Table 4.1 Case diagnostic tree (from [HEN07])

Marital status	# of Marriages	Children	Parents	Siblings
Single, never married	Once	No children	Both parents living and married to each other	No siblings
Currently married	Multiple times	One or more children from one partner	Mother deceased	One or more siblings
Divorced		Children from several partners	Father deceased	Half and step siblings
Widowed			Parents divorced	

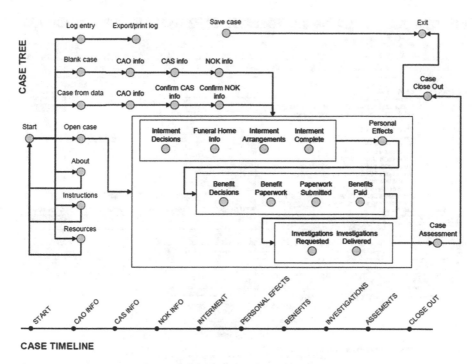

CASE TIMELINE

Fig. 4.3 Casualty process flow and case timeline (from [HEN07])

CARES. Limiting privacy and security concerns over personal data also influenced the ORCEN's decision to choose Excel over Access. A standalone Excel workbook for each casualty limited access to and possible cross-file corruption of data.

After the initial acceptance of the Excel prototype, development of the product was done in C# to provide additional functionality, platform independence, and data security. Figure 4.5 is a snapshot of the resulting C# layout based on client feedback on the Excel prototype.

Although the initial prototype demonstrated a satisfactory design of CARES for stakeholder requirements, the ORCEN wished to develop a more user-friendly system interface. Based on its belief that most of today's soldiers are familiar with the Internet and Web interfaces, the ORCEN decided to develop CARES as an Internet service tool that would be hosted on HRC's existing website [USA09]. It developed prototype CARES websites using Active Server Pages (ASP), Structured Query Language (SQL), and Visual Basic (VB). The ORCEN envisioned CAOs interacting with CARES via the Internet on the front end, whereas data linkages for automatically populating forms would continue to be linked between MS Excel and Word on the back end. Figure 4.6 shows a screenshot of the Web-based layout it designed for CARES.

The ORCEN eventually concluded, however, that CAOs would not have guaranteed access to the Internet, especially during their time directly assisting family members in their homes. Therefore, designers returned to the initial prototype and refurbished it with a Web-like user interface. By combining the attributes they

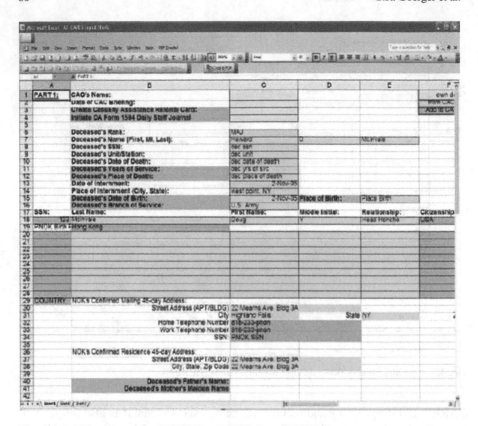

Fig. 4.4 Initial prototype for CARES Excel–2006 (from [WON07])

found to be most attractive in the initial prototype and the Web portal, developers were able to quickly continue on their path forward with the design for CARES. Figures 4.7 and 4.8 provide screenshots of the CARES Excel Version 1.0 and CARES C# Version 1.0 layouts, respectively.

Thus not only did rapid prototyping help to give the key stakeholders a means to actually visualize the system as the ORCEN continually improved upon it, rapid prototyping also helped to improve its ability to communicate how best to modify the system to ensure it would meet the requirements defined in the revised problem statement. Rapid prototyping also provided the following benefits.

- Provided stakeholders a way to tangibly evaluate CARES.
- Empowered stakeholders with the realization that their input would actually play a critical role in the development and refinement of the system.
- Allowed us to develop the system without being deterred or fearful that it was simply a working model (imperfect by design).
- Provided us with the ability to swiftly introduce changes to the system based on stakeholder feedback.
- Offered an accurate way to gauge progress and project success.

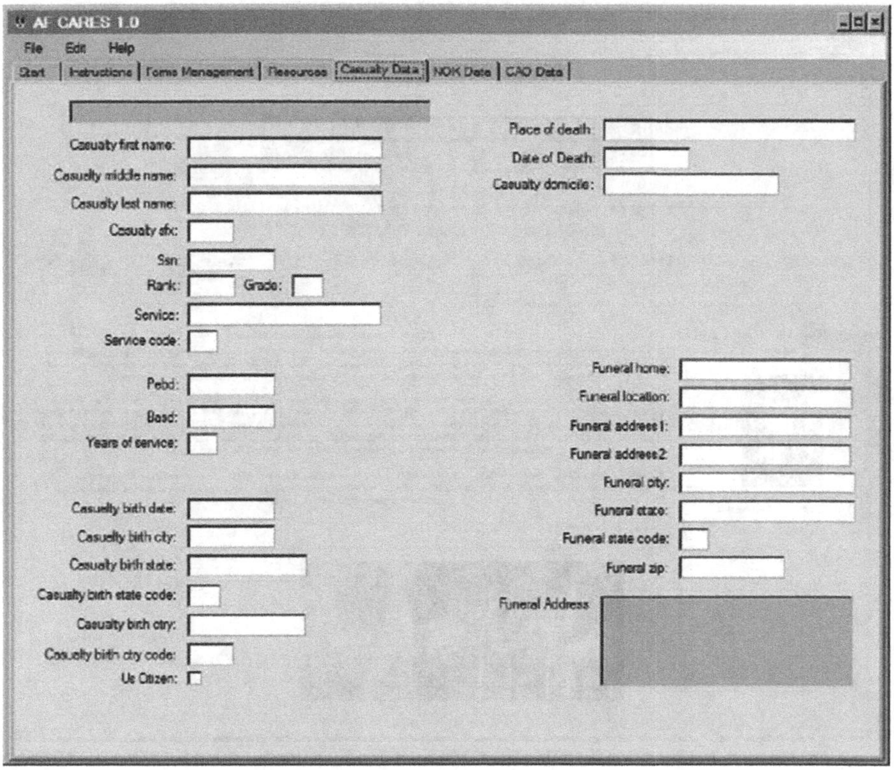

Fig. 4.5 Coded prototype for CARES C# – 2007 (from [HEN07])

– Presented us with the means to actually build changes into the system without being encumbered by much of the technical complexity associated with linking data elements into forms.
– Permitted us to capitalize on and further develop those ideas that showed promise and quickly abandon those that held little potential.

4.3.4   Greater Alignment of Product and Process

In order for CARES to serve its purpose of being a usable information system that helps to better link CAOs, family members, and program administrators with one another and better align stakeholder interests, the designers realized that the system had to have the following attributes.

– Easily updates and accommodates changes
– Intuitive to use
– Portable

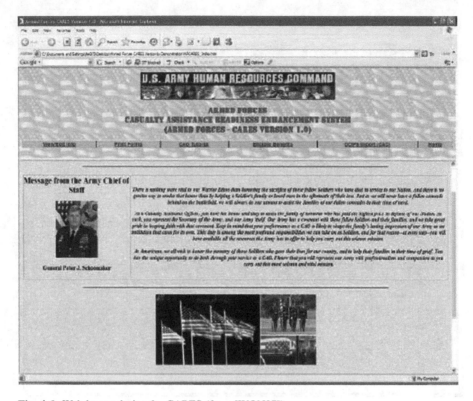

Fig. 4.6 Web layout design for CARES (from [WON07])

- Requires no unique resources
- Requires limited additional training
- Gives CAOs the power to override data errors maintained within government electronic records
- Gives both CAOs and family members a more detailed explanation of their various options
- Gives CMAOC and CACs near real-time visibility on the progress of individual cases
- Automates the burdensome emotional process of filling out casualty claims and benefits forms

Although some of these attributes are at odds with one another and tradeoffs are apparent, designers used a balanced approach in their design of CARES, one that simultaneously satisfied the needs of CAOs, family members, and program administrators. Deborah Hix and H. R. Hartson advise, "Ensuring usability in an interface requires attention to two main components: the product and the process by which the product is developed" [HIX93]. For this project, CARES and the data stored within it represent the product; and the activities associated with the military's Casualty Program represent the process. Linking the two together in a harmonious and synergistic manner was one of the designers' key goals. Figure 4.9 illustrates our goal of attempting to balance and create greater

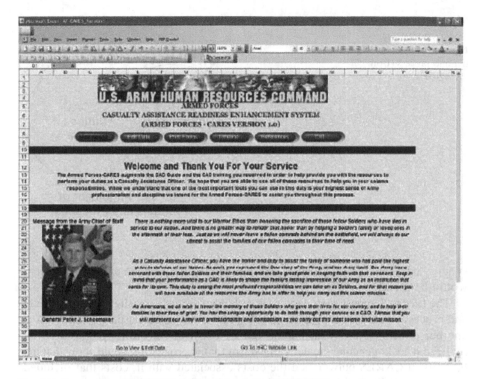

Fig. 4.7 Screenshot of CARES Excel Version 1.0 (from [WON07])

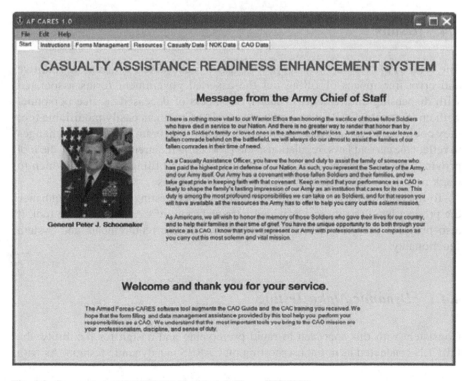

Fig. 4.8 Screenshot of CARES C# Version 1.0 (From [HEN07])

Fig. 4.9 Alignment of product and process (from
[WON07])

synergy between the system itself and the functions required to ensure the system would be useful.

The need to demonstrate to various stakeholders that a better alignment of product and process would help ensure greater success for the entire Casualty Program was another critical objective in our design of CARES. Accordingly, the ORCEN realized it could generate greater enthusiasm for the project if it could show that the benefits of CARES outweighed the costs associated with it, costs that included the time needed to develop, test, evaluate, and implement the system.

4.4 Results

The final BPM software product provided CAOs and CACs with a more intuitive and error-free means of filling out the assorted government forms associated with dispensing entitlements to family members of deceased service personnel with entitlements. CARES also provided CMAOC with an easily modifiable tool they could use to rapidly insert new entitlement forms or modify process changes to reflect the current laws, regulations, and procedural requirements. Finally, the tool provided the systems with an automated tracking and filing system by which to track and store the entitlement documents for each case.

To fine-tune CARES, we conducted alpha and beta testing. This helped enhance the product functionality and provided a trained cadre of CACs to field the tool. It also provided user feedback for the client to validate requirements and system functionality.

4.4.1 Dynamic Alpha Testing

Consistent with this approach to rapid prototyping and design for flexibility, the ORCEN conducted its initial user testing on CARES in a dynamic fashion. As with most traditional alpha tests, it solicited feedback primarily from members of our systems engineering department for internal assessment. However, unlike many typical alpha tests, the ORCEN staggered its test releases instead of soliciting user input all at once and from a single version of the prototype. This not only allowed designers and developers to continuously modify the program based on user feedback, but more important, dynamic alpha testing provided testers with the most up-to-date version of the prototype. Additional benefits of conducting alpha testing in this manner include:

- Allowing testers to concentrate on their areas of expertise (e.g., design layout, human–computer interface, data linkages, and casualty assistance functions), and leveraging their focused feedback.
- Not putting undue pressure on alpha testers to meet an arbitrary short deadline or suspense, but instead, permitting them greater flexibility in their own timetable for progressively providing their feedback.
- Giving system developers more time to react to constructive feedback and comments, thereby improving the prospects for an even better version of the program in its subsequent release.

4.4.2 Dynamic Beta Testing

CARES Excel Version 1.0 and CARES C# Version 1.0 beta testing was conducted in December 2006 with the CMAOC, various CACs, and a select number of CAOs. With CARES Excel Version 1.0, there were 38 potential claims and benefits forms that CARES helped to automatically populate. A series of questions in the program prompted CAOs into identifying which of the 38 forms were required for their particular circumstances. Figure 4.10 shows a small section of CARES Excel Version 1.0 that helped CAOs determine which forms were required and linked the CAOs to prefilled forms customized with data pertaining to their cases. In CARES C# Version 1.0, 34 forms had been transferred into the Portable Document Format (PDF) and used the Portable Document Format for Microsoft.Net Framework (PDF4NET) adopted by the U.S. Army in 2007. This enhanced the cross-platform capabilities of the forms and aligned the system for the future use of digital signatures.

CARES saved Word and PDF forms with case data in an electronic folder for use in quick updates. Once completed, the folder provided CMAOC with an electronic case history.

Developers and clients discovered several procedural and policy issues in this preliminary deployment of CARES Excel Version 1.0.

- The software had rigid working directory management.
- The users were not authorized to perform the installation.
- Local policies among the regional CACs varied with respect to installing software applications built by an Army agency.

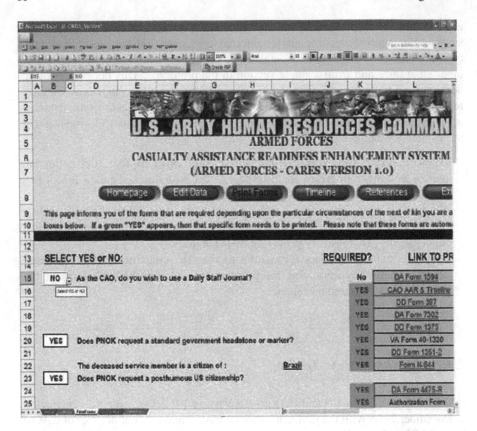

Fig. 4.10 Helping to ascertain required forms (from [WON07])

- The installation instructions were in a readme.txt file embedded in the zipped deployment archive. Users who did not know how to open this archive could not access the installation instructions.
- The software did not handle less than perfect datasets; it would break on a missing casualty social security number or badly formed Excel spreadsheet tab label in the DCIPS extract.

Using lessons learned from this deployment, minor upgrades were incorporated into the software, and a larger scale deployment, using the DCIPS and AKO portals was conducted during February of 2007. A more thorough installation and users' guide was also made available through the AKO portal. The CACs using CARES C# Version 1.0 provided feedback through the AKO portal and through surveys administered by the Operations Research Center, and through informal communications with the development team.

To facilitate tracking CAO progress, an electronic logbook helped CAOs keep track of their activities and required actions, which can be e-mailed to CACs so there is improved situation awareness on the status of individual cases. Figure 4.11

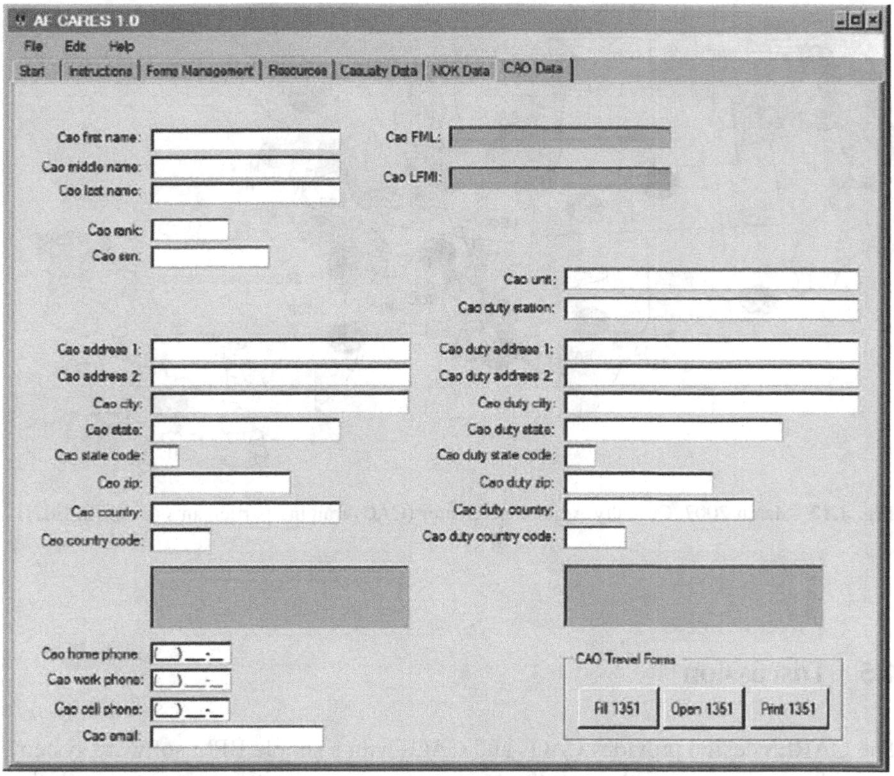

Fig. 4.11 CARES C# Version 1.0 CAO data tab (from [HEN07])

shows how CARES permits CAOs to keep track of their critical actions electronically and how it helps guide CAOs sequentially through the process. The release date for CARES C# Version 1.0 was January 2007.

CARES does not entirely auto-fill forms. The system prompts additional questions through the interface to complete this process, especially on forms that create the most errors and problems for CAOs and CACs. By March 2007, CARES C# Version 1.0 had been deployed to all 35 CACs with 76 users participating in an Army Knowledge Online (AKO) knowledge center implemented to facilitate deployment, support, and the identification of capability gaps against an objective software assistance capability.

On 18 September 2007, the ORCEN conducted additional training in its facilities at the United States Military Academy. Figure 4.12 shows the CAC locations from which trainees were assigned. During this beta testing session, we used CARES C# Version 1.0 and a software package to provide a simulation training and product development session with Casualty Assistance professionals.

The dual effort proved to be the timeliest feedback and gave CAC users the opportunity to learn the system while providing immediate input into product development. By the end of the 8-hour training and development session, the project had sound input from experienced users and product buy-in from first-line supervisors.

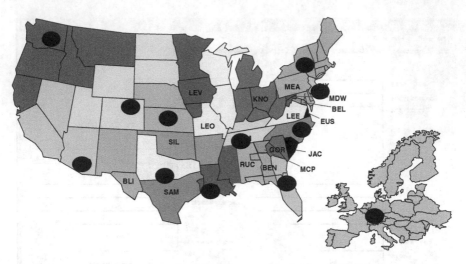

Fig. 4.12 March 2007, Casualty Assistance Center (CAC) training participants (from [SPE07])

4.5 Discussion

The CARES design provides CAOs and CACs with a simple BPM software system to guide one-time users through the bureaucratic complexities associated with the requests for claims, benefits, and entitlements. Simultaneously, the CARES design provided an accommodating tool simplistic in design but easily modified to accommodate new laws, regulations, and entitlements enacted to enhance the military's Casualty Program.

Even though CARES is tailored for the U.S. Army, we also assessed whether to make the next version of CARES into a joint product customized for rapid use by the other service components. It is important to note that CARES Excel Version 1.0 and CARES C# Version 1.0 merely facilitated the paper-driven process that is currently in place. A subsequent version of the program incorporating digital signatures will help expedite a shift to a paperless paradigm. Fortunately, the flexible design the ORCEN adopted for CARES made such advancements in the system relatively easy to implement.

The combined method of beta testing and training is applicable for a product designed for use by an assortment of onetime users with little to no former knowledge of the process and a small group of subject matter experts. It helped to provide rapid user-generated modifications, facilitated training of the power user cadre, and generated buy-in from mid-level managers and users.

4.6   Conclusions

According to Foley, "The means of production is less and less the sweat of our brow, or the leveraging of our muscle power with steam or water or electric power, or mindless repetition of work on the assembly line. Rather, the means of production increasingly is the leveraging of our intellectual power with computers" [HIX93]. It is our belief that the work on this project and the development of the Army CARES allowed the U.S. Army to leverage information technology to enhance its military's Casualty Program. Although originally focused on enhancing the Army's program, the CARES design allows for further enhancements to meet the Casualty Program requirements of the Department of Defense with minimal effort. The flexible design incorporated into CARES can be customized to suit the particular needs of each of the other service components – Air Force, Coast Guard, Marines, and Navy – and will allow future developers to modify it in conformance with new laws and updated regulations. The approach in the design of CARES (the process) demonstrates a viable methodology for the rapid development of a BPM software solution to enhance the process for a complex and nonstable specialized program that is executed by inexperienced users under the guidance and review of mid-level managers.

Acknowledgments This project was originally funded under the vision and leadership of Colonel Mary Torgersen, Director, U.S. Army Casualty and Memorial Affairs Operations Center. The authors would like to gratefully acknowledge the enduring impact and immense contributions that Mr. Daniel Ruiz and Captain Sonya Alexander of HRC have made on the development of CARES. The authors would also like to thank the following individuals for their feedback, suggestions, and recommendations for improvements on the initial test versions of CARES: Major Gregory Boylan, Major Terry Barron, Major Deidre Aramanda, and Ms. Gail Reynolds. The authors are indebted to Ms. Kriste McTamaney, Mr. Tom Rumple, Lieutenant Colonel Grant Dewey, and Lieutenant Colonel Bob Amico for their valued assistance and support on the project. Finally, we wish to thank the CACs and family members whose experiences and insight into the process provided the foundation of facts that allowed us to develop a tool to meet the needs of a real-world issue.

Notes

[1] Originally known as Systems Engineering and Management Process (SEMP), SDP is discussed in detail in the ref. [PAR08].

[2] The information system developed in this chapter is synonymous with automating a business process management (BPM) system.

[3] The original BPM had the ability for CAOs to complete forms by hand or by using electronically generated forms, however, many organizations would only process hard copies of the forms signed in ink.

[4] Systems Decision Process (SDP) is discussed in detail on pages 243–419 of ref. [PAR08].

References

GRE08   Gregory S. Parnell, Patrick J. Driscoll, Dale L. Henderson, eds. *Systems Decision Making in Systems Engineering and Management*. Hoboken, New Jersey: Wiley, 2008, pp. 243–419.

HEA06   Headquarters, Department of the Army, *Army Regulation 600-8-1, Army Casualty Program*, Washington, DC, April 7, 2006.

HEN07   Henderson DL, "The Armed Forces Casualty Assistance Readiness Enhancement System (AF-CARES), Version 1.0," Technical Report, Operations Research Center, United States Military Academy, West Point, NY, June 8, 2007.

HIX93   Hix D and Hartson HR, *Developing User Interfaces: Ensuring Usability Through Product & Process*. Wiley, New York, 1993, p. v.

ISE95   Isensee S. *The Art of Rapid Prototyping*. International Thomson Computer Press, London, 1995.

MAN06   Manktelow R, "Stakeholder Analysis and Stakeholder Management – Winning Support for your Projects," Mind Tools Website, accessed April 4, 2006 at www.mindtools.com/pages/article/newPPM_07.htm.

SPE07   Sperling BK, Henderson DL, and Cook J, "The Army Casualty Assistance Readiness Enhancement System (Army CARES) Field Test," Presentation, Department of Systems Engineering, United States Military Academy, West Point, NY, September 18, 2007, p, 4.

UNI04   United States Military Academy, Department of Systems Engineering (Eds.), Readings for Systems Engineering & Engineering Management, Thomas Custom Publishing, Mason, OH, 2004, p. 2.

USA05a   U.S. Army Casualty and Memorial Affairs Operations Center, "Casualty Assistance Officer Guide – What You Should Know and Do to Fulfill Your CAO Duties," 2nd Ed., U.S. Army Human Resources Command, Alexandria, VA, July 2005, pp. 6–7.

USA05b   U.S. Army Human Resources Command, "Unfinanced Requirement (UFR) – Casualty Assistance Wizard for Survivor Benefits," dated 13 May 2005, Alexandria, VA.

USA09   U.S. Army Human Resources Command, "CMAOC," dated 18 June 2009, Alexandria, VA. https://www.hrc.army.mil/site/Active/TAGD/CMAOC/cmaoc.htm (visited 28 July 2009).

WON07   Wong EY, Bland W, and Goerger SR, "The Armed Forces Casualty Assistance Readiness Enhancement System (CARES) A Case Study in Rapid Prototyping and Design for Flexibility," Proceedings of the 40th Annual Hawaii International Conference on System Sciences (HICSS 2007), IEEE Computer Society, January 2007, p. 4.

Chapter 5
An Overview of Some Electronic Identification Use Cases in Europe

Fabrice Mattatia

Abstract As online services become more and more widely used, and as the exchanges of personal data become more and more widespread, electronic identification appears to be a key function for the security of the process and for the protection of privacy. It is the sole means of ensuring only authorized people have access to the data. In France and throughout Europe, e-government services, as well as private services, already use different means of electronic identification. Among the different technical solutions stand the electronic identity card: around 20 million eID cards have already been issued in Europe. The question of their interoperability is now open, in order that all European citizens may access the e-services of any Member State. With the development of electronic administration comes the need for the citizen to be able to prove his or her identity. This is essential if the citizen wants access to her personal data or administrative files, or if he wants to claim a right attached to his very identity. On the other hand, administrations have the obligation to ensure the personal data they store are not displayed to people who are not entitled to see them. They also have the need to detect fraudsters. Electronic identification, which is the ability to prove someone's identity on the Internet, thus becomes a central matter.

5.1 Electronic Administration and Identity

Basically, identity is a personal and human matter, and not one that is either technical or administrative. We are ourselves first and foremost because we are born as ourselves, one might say. Personal identity and social identity are nevertheless matters which we need in certain circumstances to protect and to authenticate. Such authentication has hitherto been provided by official documents in paper or plastic such as identity cards. In cyberspace, Internet users can produce

F. Mattatia (✉)
Secrétariat d'Etat chargé de la prospective et du développement de l'économie numérique,
35 rue St-Dominique, 75007 Paris, France
e-mail: fabrice.mattatia@pm.gouv.fr

S. Assar et al. (eds.), *Practical Studies in E-Government: Best Practices from Around the World*, DOI 10.1007/978-1-4419-7533-1_5,
© Springer Science+Business Media, LLC 2011

pseudonyms and aliases at will, but for certain procedures it is still essential to be able to authenticate one's identity by electronic means.

The nature of electronic identification, sometimes termed, improperly, "electronic identity," makes it a central focus for electronic administration. This is so because the dematerialisation of human contact, with the elimination of face-to-face contact, makes it imperative in the case of sensitive transactions to verify the identity of those involved, who may be private citizens (e.g., for access to personal data), public officials (e.g., for official administrative documents), elected representatives (e.g., signatures on statutory documents), or professionals (e.g., VAT returns or employee hiring declarations).

Among the media for electronic identification is the electronic identity card. Other media exist in some contexts: other public or private-sector cards, for example, as well as electronic certificates or knowledge of a security code, to name but a few. Some countries make a distinction between electronic identification and the electronic identity card, accepting the portability of electronic identity certificates on mobile telephones, bank cards, private cards, employee identity cards, and so on.

So what exactly is an electronic identity card? Although there are variations from country to country, one can say that it is an identity card of traditional type whose hardcopy information is repeated on a chip for the purposes of verification by law enforcement personnel (according to the country concerned, a photograph and fingerprints may or may not be on the chip); the chip will also contain keys and electronic certificates for access to online services. The electronic identity card is thus firstly an official administrative document in electronic form, and secondly a key for access to other electronic administration services.

At this point, it can be observed that in several European countries,[1] but not in France, the basis of individual electronic identification, and of identity itself, is a set of exhaustive national population records made available to the departments and agencies charged with the task of managing and verifying identities, in conjunction with a personal identification number available for use by all official departments and agencies.

For a better understanding of the issues involved in electronic identification, we begin here with a general overview of the electronic administration services and identification solutions that exist both in France and in some other European countries, along with the types of fraud of which individual identity can be a target. We then go on to describe the broad lines of the projected French electronic identity card that was made a subject of public debate in 2005. This enables us to look at the range of reactions aroused by the project.

5.2 Electronic Administration in France and the Need for Identity

A very large number of electronic administration services exist in France, and it is not relevant to our purposes here to provide an exhaustive list of them. We can, however, look at a few of them to illustrate the relationship between such services and electronic identification.

For the general public, there are numerous electronic services that provide better alternatives to traditional procedures. Among the most familiar is the online filing of income tax returns ("TéléIR"), but there are others: service employment vouchers (*"chèques emploi-service"*), monthly updates to the personal situation of jobseekers, and so on. All these services have a common feature: they require only authentication of the citizen's identity,[2] in addition to which the authentication is low-grade, being based on a software certificate in the case of TéléIR[3] and on a password in the other two examples. This is so because there is no need to seek an absolute guarantee of the user's identity for three reasons: these procedures generate an acknowledgement of receipt which would alert users if an impostor were to carry them out under his or her name; the outcome is reversible (i.e., it is always possible to rectify the records later if there is a problem); and identity fraud on these services is rare because there is no gain for a fraudster.

In 2004, the French national family allowance fund began to install terminals on its public premises enabling individuals to access their records online. The sign-on identifier used is the welfare beneficiary's identification number. The same portal can be used to access the national pensions fund, social security, the national unemployment service (ANPE), the social security contributions organisation (URSSAF), the unemployment benefit fund (ASSEDIC), and so on, using a different identifier and security code in each case. In order to simplify access to all these services for the beneficiaries, a move towards the use of the same social security number for all these teleservices is currently envisaged, for the sake of user-friendliness.

The situation is somewhat different in the case of the electronic medical care form (*feuille de soins électronique* or FSE) in the "Sesam" national health insurance system. This electronic service requires identification not only of the beneficiary who is to be reimbursed but also of the healthcare professional (doctor, pharmacist, nurse, etc.) certifying that the healthcare involved has actually been provided. Given that an FSE triggers monetary payments, it is essential to ensure that it originates with an authorised person. It is for this reason that healthcare professionals are identified with a high degree of security on the basis of their Health Professional Identity Card (*Carte de Professionnel de Santé* – CPS), which has a chip containing the electronic keys to enable the professional to authenticate her identity for the system and to sign documents. As for patients, they have their "Carte Vitale 1," which contains neither key nor security code and is used solely to provide the contact details of the insured. It has no capability for individual identification.[4] Handling approximately one billion FSEs every year, Sesam can be said without fear of contradiction to be one of the major achievements in the field of electronic administration anywhere in the world.

In the wider context, cards in the CPS category are of benefit to the entire health sector (public-sector hospitals as well as private practice). All health professionals can use them to provide an online guarantee not only of their identity but also their status or professional details, which obviously has advantages for accessing medical records online, exchanging confidential information, signing electronic prescriptions,[5] sending on medical test results, monitoring waiting lists for transplants, participating in electronic public health alert networks, and so on.[6] By the end of 2008, around 650,000 professionals held CPS cards.

Electronic administration is also relevant to companies, which are obliged to comply with several official formalities (employee hiring declarations, payment of social contributions, affidavits, and the like). So it was for companies that the *"net-entreprises"* portal was created to allow them to manage their documents electronically. One or more individuals must be designated in each company for the performance of formalities online. They must be able to provide evidence both of their identity and due authorisation. Such individuals are for this reason provided with an identification tool, a password or a certificate (certificate on a workstation or on a card according to the precise circumstances).

Another example is online VAT returns and payments ("TéléTVA"), which are compulsory in France for companies above a certain size. The representatives of these companies are therefore provided with certificates (on a workstation, a card, or a USB key).

Reliable online identification of individuals authorised to enter into commitments binding on their company is also essential for submitting electronic tenders for contracts, as is now permitted by the French Code of Public Procurement Law (*Code des Marchés Publics*).

Local government bodies also feel the need for electronic identification in a number of contexts. The *Caisse des Dépôts et Consignations* (CDC) and various partners have, for example, developed the FAST project (*Fournisseur d'Accès Sécurisé Transactionnel*/secure access provider for transactions), a solution that enables public-sector actors to exchange official documents electronically in a secure manner. Concretely, FAST enables data to be date- and time-stamped and kept on record, and also enables signing and encrypting messages between official departments and agencies. It provides reliable electronic identification for all those involved. For example, FAST makes it possible to exchange official documents subject to legal verification and links local government to its general treasury body. Over 600 municipalities were using FAST by the end of 2007.

A final example is provided by a little-known application developed by GILFAM (*Groupement pour l'Informatisation du Livre Foncier d'Alsace-Moselle*/Grouping for the computerisation of the Alsace-Moselle land register). The Alsace-Moselle region inherited from German law the *Livre Foncier* (land register) which replaces the *Conservation des Hypothèques* (mortgage record office) in use elsewhere in France. For this reason, title to real estate is not proven by means of a title deed as is the case in the rest of France, but by an entry in the *Livre Foncier* under the signature of a land registry magistrate. The 40,000 volumes which make up the *Livre* have been scanned in order to allow it to be computerised. Once in place, this new electronic service will require identification of those involved at a minimum of three levels: identification of land register staff for data management purposes (based on a smartcard plus a PIN), higher-level identification of magistrates for placing electronic signatures on the documents updating land title (smartcard, PIN, and fingerprint verification), and possibly identification of applicants for access to the data (access is permitted for any individual with a legitimate interest and direct access online is planned for court bailiffs, process servers, and notaries, who will in this case need a high-level identification tool not yet defined).

The few examples provided here demonstrate that the need for identification for electronic administration purposes breaks down into a number of detailed instances:

- The personal identity of a private individual, patient, taxpayer, etc.
- The identity of public servants
- The identity of professionals and their authorisation to carry out certain procedures in the case of company employees or officers

The level of authentication provided by such identification will vary according to what is required. Whereas a low level of security (based on a password or electronic certificate) is sufficient for certain electronic services whose outcome is reversible and which do not allow access to personal data (a typical case: online returns and declarations), a higher level is essential where payments are triggered or for signing formal documents that create liabilities for individuals or companies. The smart-card has hitherto constituted the surest and most practical means of proving identity electronically.

The need for identification increases steadily, because a single individual will be at one and the same time a social security rights holder, a taxpayer, a citizen, a public servant or a company employee, the user of various electronic administration services, and so on. Then it appears to be more efficient to provide each individual with a tool that will enable her to provide proof of identity in the same way for a number of these services, if not for all of them.

The concept of an electronic identity card is therefore one that arises quite naturally in this context, and it is now a reality in several European countries, as we show below. However, due to parameters specific to France – and specifically the principle whereby data records must not be interconnected – the identity card cannot be universal, nor be used for health insurance among other applications. It would nevertheless provide a straightforward means of access to the electronic administration services of central and local government for which the user must be identified.

In order to avoid any hint of "Big Brother" for the citizen, the possibility of using more than one means of access must also be guaranteed. Therefore, the French e-government administration issued in 2010 a general security policy (*Référentiel Général de Sécurité* – RGS), which classifies the levels of security required for each service. At any given level, proof of identity of any kind compatible with that level would be accepted for electronic administration purposes. Private individuals would thus have a choice between using official methods (not only the electronic identity card, but also cards for municipal facilities and sector-specific electronic certificates) or commercial tools (inasmuch as RGS recognises private-sector tools capable of guaranteeing the same level of security).

Another possible way forward to avoid the "Big Brother" threat is provided by identity federation systems, which delegate to a trusted third party the task of identifying private individuals online and of providing them with a "token" for access to online services, without it being possible to link this token with others issued for use in relation to other services.[7]

5.3 Identity Fraud in the Context of Electronic Administration

What are the risks of identity fraud in the context of electronic administration that would justify recourse to an electronic identity card?

The password has numerous weaknesses as a method. It is possible to guess a poorly chosen password.[8] Passwords can also be stolen if revealed by indiscretion, by hacking into a computer, or if they are written down. The greatest danger lies in the fact that, unlike a smartcard, the theft of a password will go unnoticed.

For the legitimate holder of a password, forgetfulness is a formidable enemy. Users of multiple online services face a thorny problem: should they use the same password for all those services, which increases the risk of its disclosure if there is a failure in security on one of the websites concerned, or should they invent a new password for each service, which would require a feat of memory for private individuals making intensive use of electronic administration?

In the case of sensitive online services, the risk of theft by phishing is increasing year by year. Phishing involves sending out to millions of Internet users massive numbers of emails pretending to come from legitimate services and asking them to carry out an operation that will reveal their password. See Fig. 5.1. Despite a low rate of success, this type of fraud enables the passwords of a number of victims to be obtained, allowing their identity to be stolen for the purposes of the service concerned. For obvious reasons, phishing is primarily aimed at the present time at the customers of online banks with a view to emptying their accounts of funds[9] (see Fig. 5.2), rather than citizens going peaceably about their business, declaring online that they have hired a cleaning lady. However, as electronic administration makes it increasingly possible to create entitlements and access sensitive information, it will increasingly be a target for phishing (to gain access to records concerning prominent public figures, siphon off welfare payments by modifying account numbers, and so on).

Account suspended	
Dear customer,	
We are writing you this email to inform you that your ZZZZZZZZ account has been temporarily suspended for incoming and outgoing transactions due to a payment you received that is being suspected by our security team as being an exchange with another e-currency.	
In accordance with our terms and conditions, article 3.2,ZZZZZZZZ strictly forbids exchanges of any kind with other e-currencies.	
To remake your account fully operational, we would like to kindly ask you to confirm your identity by clicking the link below and filling the forms. Once this this process has been completed, your account will be reactivated.	

Reactivate your account

Feel free to contact our support team for any questions you might have.

Best regards,
the ZZZZZZZZ security department.

Fig. 5.1 Phishing mail pretending that the account is suspended and asking the customer to enter his or her login and password in order to reactivate it, July 2007

Fig. 5.2 Closure of the site of an online bank, www.lcl.fr, as a result of a phishing campaign, February 2006

Phishing hinders the development of e-services: first it undermines customers' trust, and second it forces the websites to invest heavily in e-security.

In fact, traditional official administration is already vulnerable now to identity fraud where the establishment of entitlement to benefits is concerned: it is easy to falsify[10] or to counterfeit[11] a birth certificate in order to create a false identity and the supporting documentation for ben efit entitlements (e.g., false social security contribution certificates to obtain payment of unemployment benefits, or, as in a recent case involving €8 million, false tax credit certificates). There is a risk that the generalisation of electronic administration, when associated with the disappearance of face-to-face contact, will lead to an upsurge in fraudulent benefit claims (inasmuch as industrial-scale fraud is now becoming possible) in the absence of strong authentication of the identities of applicants and the genuineness of their entitlements.

The advantage of an electronic identity card is that it counters all these risks simultaneously[12]:

- It replaces the password (eliminating the risk of forgetting it).
- It cannot be obtained by spying or copying, and the only way to get it is to steal it (but in that event the holder will notice the fact and put a stop on the card immediately).
- It is not vulnerable to phishing (because the authentication key is within the chip, remains there, and cannot be displayed).
- It authenticates the holder's identity for those dealing with him because it is possible to check online the card's authenticity and the information it contains.

5.4   Electronic Identification in Europe: National Concepts and Their Impact on Daily Experience

We provide below a rapid overview, with no pretention to exhaustiveness, of the practices and projects of some European countries with regard to electronic identification and administration. This allows a comparison with the French situation.

5.4.1   Belgium

Belgium has been issuing electronic identity cards since 2004. They are compulsory from the age of 12 and remain valid for 5 years. A fee of around 10€ is charged for issuance.

The (contact-type) chip on this card contains most notably a digitised photograph and keys for identification and electronic signature for online use. The card is based on the national population register containing all the civil status details and addresses of Belgian citizens.

It is currently used for the following.

- Customised access to websites and computer systems
- Attachment of attribute certificates for notaries (for online legal documents)
- Online filing of income tax and VAT returns
- Online vehicle registration
- Electronic voting
- Access for the individual to the national population register and details of access by public offici als to an individual's records
- Private uses: online banking, online purchases (e.g., recharging prepaid phone cards), registered electronic mail
- Access for private citizens to municipal waste collection centres, swimming pools, and libraries

Other planned uses:

- A discussion forum reserved for under-18s (to avoid paedophiles).
- The chip also has space, currently unused, for other applications (payments, healthcare, transport, etc.).

By the end of 2009, more than eight million cards have been issued.

5.4.2   Estonia

Estonia possesses an exhaustive population register (compulsory for all, including foreign residents) containing the personal identification number, the address (an up-to-date address is supposedly compulsory but is required only for making applications for certain entitlements), and a photograph.

Electronic identity cards, which have been issued since 2002, are mandatory for everybody from the age of 15 with a fee being charged for issuance. By the end of 2009, more than 1.1 million cards have been issued in a population of 1.4 million (10% should be added to this figure for foreign residents, who are also issued with cards for use as residence permits).

Presently, the chip is used to store personal data (which reproduces the hardcopy data without the photograph), protected by a security code, along with electronic identification and signature keys and certificates. Both keys are activated using two different security codes (with four digits for holder identification and five for signatures) that can be customised using management software provided free of charge.

The State guarantees only the personal data, not the certificates, the latter being issued under contracts between holders and private-sector providers. The option of certificate portability on mobile telephones (as is the case in Finland and Lithuania) is currently under consideration.

The system is designed in such a way that the identity card contains only a minimum of personal information, only details that do not change over time (no address is included, for example). The card is used as a key for access to databases managing information and benefit entitlements. The card can, for example, be used instead of a driving licence: an officer carrying out a check needs only to access the licence database using the individual's personal identification number to determine whether everything is in order. In the case of public transport, customers can use either their mobile telephone, the Internet, or go to the counter to buy an e-ticket which is then stored under the holder's name in a database. In the event of a ticket check, the inspector logs on to the database with the identity card to verify the validity of the e-ticket. The price of the ticket purchased by telephone is added to the telephone bill issued by the telecom company (this was the principle underlying Minitel billing in France in the 1980s). Nearly one million journey and season tickets were sold in this way in 2005.

The world's very first elections with e-voting were held in October 2005: using their card, 9,000 citizens were able to vote from anywhere in the world via Internet for local elections. Estonia also held the world's first national elections with Internet e-voting in March 2007 (30,000 e-voters).

Over 200 e-services are available to private individuals, including municipal portals, ranging from online banking (banks have seen the benefits of the card for secure access to accounts and they issue card readers as free gifts), to online income tax returns and payments (used by 70% of the population).

To encourage the spread of this technology, a "starter package" containing software, card reader, and documentation is offered for €20. There is a specific statute stipulating that government-purchased computers must now come equipped with a card reader.

Other services are proposed to facilitate the use of electronic administration: an email address is offered to all citizens (the template for which is *lastname.firstname@eesti.ee*) from which e-mails can be forwarded to any "real" address of the individual's choosing) for their public- and private-sector correspondents, who are thus able to contact them at any time. Likewise, each citizen has data storage space of 10 MB and can configure this to enable sharing of certain documents with other citizens; an access portal provides easy links to all official documents (driving licence, social security, form E111, etc).

5.4.3 Finland

In 1996, the Finnish government began to work on an electronic identity card containing qualified identification, encryption, and signature certificates. This work led to the launch in 1999 of an optional identity card containing a chip and a certificate. The goal was to align with the development of the new technologies and to counter the security problems generated by phishing.

The vast majority of identification documents issued in Finland are passports (3.7 million issued for a population of just over 5 million). By the end of 2009, 275,000 electronic identity cards were in circulation.

Finland has a number of interconnected sets of official records (exhaustive because they are compulsory) that provide a structure for official administrative procedures and activity. The four main databases relate to the following.

• Population, a central register managed by an agency attached to the Ministry of the Interior
• Real estate
• Companies
• Vehicles

Since 1985, updates to these data bases have replaced national censes (allowing the annual per capita cost of producing the annual per capita cost of producing the equivalent data to be cut from U.S.$6 to $0.17). This also enables income tax returns to be sent precompleted by cross-referencing employer, insurance, banking, social security, and other data.

The population register in which the details of all Finnish citizens and foreign residents are recorded is used as a database for the issuance of official documents. The register contains the following information: last name, first names, personal identification code, date and place of birth, home address (notification of address changes is obligatory), nationality, mother tongue, profession, family relations, and date of death.

The personal identification code is made up of the date of birth plus three digits and a letter. It is shown on all official documents issued and is used for many purposes in day-to-day life, including for private purposes, to provide evidence of the holder's home address.

The chip holds keys and certificates (the certificates data include the personal identification code): one set for identification and encryption and another for electronic signature. Both keys are activated by different security codes.

Additionally, private individuals can ask for the same types of certificate to be loaded on to their bank cards, mobile telephone SIM cards, cards for municipal services, work-related identity cards, and so on. Such certificates use different keys but are linked by the personal identification code.

Where mobile telephones are concerned, for example, individuals must first obtain a compatible SIM card from the telecom company and then go to a police station to request that the certificates be uploaded immediately.

In the case of electronic services, the type of identification required changes according to the applicable level of security. Some services do not need to identify the individual, whereas others (those handling personal information or legal transactions) demand a high level of authentication, hence the use of qualified certificates.

Most Finnish citizens use online banking services involving a standised system of authentication based on several code numbers (each person has a list of code numbers provided by the bank). In 99% of cases identification is based on this system, compared with 1% for the identity card.

Many people in Finland also use the Internet to buy e-tickets for the cinema. This is an example of a service that requires no identification. And indeed the law prohibits identification where it is unnecessary and where there is no doubt as to identity (the national registers and personal identification codes in fact leave little room for doubt). This means that it is even possible to file a divorce petition via the Internet without having to add an electronic signature.

The following services are just a few examples of the use of online identification in Finland:

- Enrolment in secondary education
- The national employment agency: online transmission of CVs by the unemployed
- Pension records
- Income tax returns
- For public servants: access to the network from any official workstation; teleworking.

Identification based on the banking system is also accepted by these services, and in the final analysis this system constitutes a form of identity federation. Since 2004, health insurance information can be incorporated into the ID card and used as a health card at pharmacies, medical clinics, and other service providers.

To make electronic administration easier, there is an umbrella website for all available electronic forms, plus an online public-sector directory.

5.4.4   Italy

The identity card is optional in Italy (from the age of 15), and a fee is charged for issuance.

More than one million electronic identity cards were issued in 2007 in Italy. Two of the main objectives announced are to make the current document secure and encourage development of the use of online services and electronic administration.

The chip on this electronic identity card contains a photograph, prints of the index fingers, and electronic keys and certificates for identification and signature. The dematerialised records (which include the fingerprints) are kept on a national server but can be accessed only by local official bodies in the "provinces" (counties).

Electronic identification is used in many ways:

- Proof of identity at polling stations
- Online access to information
- Online payment of taxes and national and local fines
- Online payment of school fees
- Notification of changes of address
- Electronic registration for municipal services (sports facilities)

- Hospital appointments
- Online applications for welfare benefits and the like

The Italian regions and local authorities also issue local eID cards. These cards just hold the keys and certificates for online authentication and signature, and cannot be used for traditional identification purposes (such as a travel document, for instance): the name and photograph of the holder aren't printed on them. They are Lombardy region issued nine million such regional cards.

5.4.5 Portugal

The Portuguese Agency for the Modernization of Administration launched a Citizen card project in 2007, merging in one card five former cards: identity card, health card, voter's card, taxpayer card, and social insurance card.

The identity of Portuguese citizens is authenticated using a central database containing identification details, a photograph, and fingerprints. The identity card is compulsory (and a fee is charged for issuance) from the age of 6. As the Constitution forbids the use of universal citizen numbers, a citizen is identified by different numbers in each administration and the Citizen card bears all the numbers. The Citizen cards also support authentication and electronic signature keys.

5.4.6 Spain

The identity of Spanish citizens is authenticated using a central database containing identification details, a photograph, and the right index fingerprint. The identity card is compulsory (and a fee is charged for issuance) from the age of 14. Each Spanish citizen keeps throughout his life the same identity card number, which is used by Spain's other official departments and agencies (e.g., property title deeds are drawn up using this number).

All actions relating to the database (sign-on, accessing data, modifying data, etc.) are traced with a view to ensuring the security of the application and to protect personal information. The control exercised by the Spanish data protection authority is very strict on this point (six-monthly audits).

The electronic identity card has been deployed since March 2006. More than 13 million cards were issued by the end of 2009. In addition to identification details, the chip contains a photograph and prints of both index fingers, along with keys and certificates for electronic identification and signature.

The purpose of this card is to encourage the development of electronic administration and e-commerce in Spain. The certificates used are of standard type to enable them to be used in other European Union countries.

The identification functionality is activated by simple insertion of the card in a reader, whereas use of the electronic signature requires a security code to be keyed in. The government offers an application free of charge to enable these functionalities to be used. Identification and signature certificates are valid for 30 months and private individuals are able to renew them free of charge at terminals installed in the majority of Spanish police stations and available for use around the clock. The terminals also enable the individual to verify the content of the chip, change the security code, and check certificate expiry dates.

5.4.7   Sweden

Sweden possesses a central population register. All individuals working in Sweden must be on it and are issued with a personal identification number. The register holds names and home addresses but not photographs.

The personal identification number is made up of the date of birth plus four digits. It is shown on the official documents issued and has numerous routine day-to-day uses, including private applications (bank access and linking into the bank card database). In addition, any person can review data held on the national register, including information on other individuals.

Traditionally, although the government did not issue a national identity card until October 2005, various private-sector companies and public bodies in Sweden issue identity cards compliant with a national standard, based on the central register and recognised throughout the country. The card in most widespread use is issued by the Swedish post office.

The new national (official) electronic identity card which is now issued by the police (and which is additional to the cards already mentioned) has two chips, one for travel identification of the holder and the other for online identification and signature certificates. The latter are not included when the card is produced (the new card holds only a "transitional" certificate).

The government has approved four commercial certification authorities who offer this service to individuals requesting it, and those authorities bear complete responsibility for certificate management. The certificates can be uploaded on computers (software-based certificates) or on the different kinds of eID cards. Currently two million card-based certificates and 1.5 million software certificates have been issued. In 2007 there were 40–50 million eID-transactions registered for public, banking, and private sector e-services.

The aim is to encourage the spread of the new technologies throughout the whole of society and increase the number of applications, in conjunction with a highly ambitious policy for equipping public servants for electronic administration.

Actors in the public domain (government, local authorities, public services, etc.) are indeed currently equipping very large numbers of staff with qualified certificates for identification, encryption, and electronic signatures. As an illustration of this, all members of staff of the Ministry of Finance have had a smartcard since 1995. The third version of the card, deployed since 2004, contains five certificates (two for work-related identification/encryption and signatures, two for the same applications in the private sphere, and an e-mail address authentication certificate). It is also used as a badge for access to buildings and as an identity card, with its certificates being usable for other electronic public- and private-sector services. There are two different security codes, one for authentication of identity and the other for signature. The chip also holds network passwords. Lastly, members of staff can use these certificates to sign on to the official network from their homes via a VPN (for teleworking purposes).

Another instance of the high level of mobilisation of public departments and agencies in favour of electronic services is the decision taken by the Swedish employment agency to issue all jobseekers with qualified electronic certificates to enable them to perform administrative procedures and look for jobs on the Internet.

Other electronic administration services include:

- Online filing of income tax returns: There have been numerous problems of piracy involving the electronic certificates issued hitherto by the Ministry of Finance (designed on the same lines as France's TéléIR). The move to a card-based certificate has been recommended.
- The healthcare network: A special infrastructure for the management of keys is planned, a target having been set for 100,000 identity cards to be issued to health professionals, containing a photograph, keys, and certificates, and details of the holder's employer and profession (this seems to be equivalent to the CPS system in France, described previously). There are plans for a social security card for private citizens.

The certificate on each of the aforementioned cards can be used for any purpose (e.g., a healthcare professional's card can be used to file income tax returns online). Portability of the certificate on bank payment cards and mobile telephones is currently under consideration (as in the example of Finland).

The electronic national identity card is optional and a fee is charged. Its certificates are free for private individuals and public servants. The issuer is remunerated when the cancellation list is called up via public- or private-sector e-services. The individual citizen therefore pays nothing and the service pays one Swedish crown (approximately €0.10) each time the information is called up.

Table 5.1 and Fig. 5.3 provide a broader overview of the situation in Europe.

Table 5.1 Summary of the characteristics of the electronic identity cards described

	Number of eID cards – end 2009	Database	Obligatory card	Fee	Citizen personal number	Website
Belgium	8.3 millions	Yes	Yes	Yes	Yes	www.eid.belgium.be
Estonia	1.1 million	Yes	Yes	Yes	Yes	www.id.ee
Finland	275,000	Yes	No	Yes	Yes	www.fineid.fi
Italia	1 million+10 millions regional cards	Yes	No	Yes	Yes	www.cartaidentita.it
Portugal	400,000	Yes	Yes	Yes	Several	www.cartaodecidadao.pt
Spain	13 millions	Yes	Yes	Yes	Yes	www.dnielectronico.es
Sweden	2 million private cards+65,000 officials (2007)	Yes	No	Yes	Yes	www.polisen.se/service

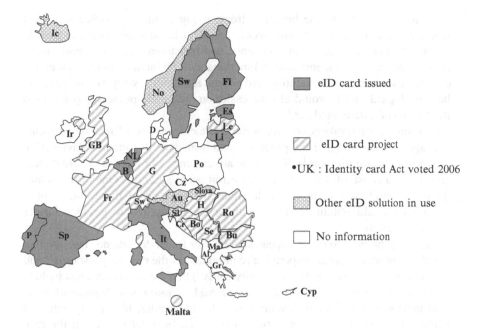

Fig. 5.3   Electronic identification in Europe

5.5   The Projected French Electronic Identity Card

5.5.1   The Broad Lines of the 2005 Project

The project designed early in 2005 by the Ministry of the Interior was aimed at providing a solution to the problems of identity fraud and identification on the Internet, within the parameters specific to France, notable among which is the prohibition on any interconnection of official records and any allocation of universal identification numbers to French citizens.

The programme, known as "INES" (*Identité Nationale Électronique Sécurisée*/ Secure national electronic identity), had defined four goals:

- To authenticate the identity of private individuals and to combat identity fraud by preventing undue issuance of official documents on the basis of stolen, counterfeited, or falsified birth certificates, by preventing issuance of official documents to the same person under more than one identity, and finally by preventing the theft and sale of authentic official documents (not forgetting of course that the card issued must also be impossible to falsify or counterfeit).
- To enable transposition onto the Internet of routine day-to-day formalities: just as it is possible for individuals to use their identity card in official contexts (competitive examinations and tests, applications for welfare benefits, recognition of entitlements, voting, applications for driving licences, and so on), at the

bank to gain access to the holder's strongbox, or at the post office to collect registered postal mail, it would seem logical to be able to access electronic administration services, online accounts, and registered electronic mail on the basis of an electronic identification functionality. The inclusion of such identification capabilities in the identity card we are all familiar with would appear to be only logical and it would also be easier on the public purse compared with the launch of a dedicated card.

- To optimise formal procedures for both private citizens and official departments and agencies by merging the processes and management functions involved in passports and identity cards. The latter are currently similar but differentiated, and this is a cause of delay, duplicated effort, and extra cost. One of the consequences would be that private individuals holding one of these two identity documents could obtain the other without being required to produce further proof of identity.

- To upgrade the card to the European standard for travel documents, because that standard stipulates (as an imperative requirement in the case of passports,[13] and on a consultation basis in that of identity cards[14]) that the document must include a contactless chip (i.e., a chip that can be read by radio at a distance of some centimetres) holding identification details for the holder, his photograph, and eventually (from 2008 to 2009) two fingerprints. In order to prevent the chip being read without the knowledge of the holder, access to this information will be possible only if a security code is entered (in addition, the fingerprints will be protected by a second code reserved for use by law enforcement personnel).

From a technical standpoint, as there is no centralized birth register in France, the elimination of fraud must necessarily involve direct communication of birth certificates from the town hall of the place of birth to the town hall issuing the identity document. In order to avoid the theft and sale of official documents, the two fingerprints stored on the chip make it possible to guarantee the link between the card and its holder. Lastly, given the lack of any national population register (which exists, as we have already seen, in Belgium, Italy, Spain, Sweden, Finland, and Estonia, with the likely addition of the United Kingdom in the future) and citizen identification numbers, a biometric database is essential if a citizen's identity is to be properly authenticated. This is the position of the Consultative Committee of the Convention for the protection of individuals with regard to automatic processing of personal data ("Convention 108") of the Council of Europe, which stated in 2005:

> The use of biometrics in the issuance of a passport, an identity card or a visa aims at establishing that the person has not already applied under another name. The feature that is to be enrolled should be compared with the data that are already in the system. This purpose of avoiding double entries entails a system of identification. [...]

And:

> In the case of identification, the presented sample is not only matched with the enrolled data of the alleged same person, but also with the biometric data of other data subjects in the same database or connected databases. This excludes the possibility of having the enrolled data solely stored on an individual storage medium. It implies a search to establish

a possible hit between the presented sample of the individual and the enrolled data of (many) other individuals. [...][15]

At this point, any biometric component (an earprint, e.g.) might be suitable for this database. The choice of fingerprints can be justified on the grounds of the long history of this technique, which has proven its worth over more than a century, its ease of use, its cost, its compatibility with choices already made internationally for compulsory application to passports, and by the fact that it is, paradoxically, anonymous and protective of privacy (this is so because a fingerprint is totally unrevealing with regard to age, sex, health, religion, or consumption of illicit substances, something which cannot be said for other methods such as photography, iris recognition, and so on). Of course, fingerprints also permit the database to be used in the judicial context for criminal investigation purposes.

In order to avoid any misuse of the database and to protect privacy, INES had defined a range of measures that were technical (data encryption, anonymous storage of fingerprints separately from individual identification details, traceability of data access by public officials), organisational (restriction of access to authorised officials performing specified tasks), and judicial (a bill was planned to strengthen sanctions in the event of misuse).

5.5.2 The 2005 Public Debate

In light of the sensitivity of the topic and its potential impact on individual privacy, the Ministry of the Interior decided at the end of 2004, as part of an innovative approach guided by good citizenship and transparency, to announce its project and seek the views of the public before reaching any final decision on the matter.

The project was presented in a number of specialist colloquia (Forum on Electronic Administration, European Forum of Trusted Third Parties, etc.), and the Internet Rights Forum (*Forum des Droits sur l'Internet* – FDI), a quasi-public body, was mandated to organise an online debate and presentations in the French regions. The outcome was a debate that was "unique on a topic of this importance [...] a fine example of electronic democracy,"[16] involving several hundred people on the Internet and at public meetings throughout France.

The press and the general public were thus able to latch on to this topic, making it possible to observe the project's impact on notions of identity both for the public and academics. Given the project's specific features, reactions related not only to technical aspects (the card, its level of security, methods for reviewing data held on it), but also to the protection of privacy (the nature of the information held on the card, and who should be entitled to see it), and even the way in which identity should be defined (with regard to biometrics most notably).

From the general standpoint, an opinion poll involving a representative sample of the population revealed that 74% of the population took a favourable view of the projected electronic identity card, that 75% approved the building of a fingerprint database, and even that 69% of the population wanted the card to be compulsory.[17]

The public debates revealed that the general public often had highly diverse expectations with regard to electronic identity cards. Some said, on grounds of ease of use, that they wanted an identity card that would provide access to all services, not only official (tax, social security, medical records) but also private (online banking, etc.). From a technical standpoint this would mean either that the card should store the whole range of numbers specific to each sector[18] (social security number, tax-payer's ID number, account number, and so on), with all the management issues this would entail (given that the numbers concerned are managed by different organisations), or that each individual citizen should be given a number for use in all contexts,[19] with the attendant risk that database interconnection would then become possible.

Others either rejected the very concept of the electronic identity card (pointing to dangers in the "Big Brother" category), or preferred a card of minimal type, containing only the holder's identification details.

Numerous "experts" then entered the debate to explain that individual identity cannot be reduced to bits of data,[20] or even that it cannot and must not be pinned down.[21] This meant that the State stood accused, paradoxically, of improperly endeavouring to "seek out possible suspects or dangerous individuals allegedly seeking to disguise themselves with false identities."[22] Moreover, "counterfeiting, falsifying and usurping the identities of others can be seen as practices that evidence a rejection of forms of identity imposed by the State."[23] From this point of view, those committing identity fraud are not confidence tricksters or criminals, the conclusion to which one might rashly have jumped, but they are militant philosophers whose activities it would undoubtedly be morally regrettable to impede.

More seriously, the debate did confirm that for some people biometrics were a source of dark imaginings and fears: the fear of giving up part of one's body, as well as the fear of error and an all-powerful machine able to decide without right of appeal, or even the fear of the unchanging unbending character of the data recorded, as opposed to the natural variability of the living organism.[24]

The Big Brother imaginings generated by electronic cards were also frequently observed: there were fears that the Ministry of the Interior would receive regular reports revealing every detail of the citizens' lives, activities, and movements. In this respect it is interesting to note that the same individuals generally have no objection to the fact that their telco provider can monitor their location around the clock by means of their cellular telephone, or that their Internet Service Provider is aware of every aspect of their personal tastes, purchases, or even their more or less legal downloads, that their bankers and their chain store can analyse their spending patterns with greatest interest. Pierre Trudel, a lecturer at Montreal University, thus wrote:

> It continues to be disturbing to observe the extent to which the risk of misuse of the data dominates the debate when the discussion concerns tools and processes for the identification of individuals. It is as if one were to look at road construction on the basis of the postulate that the combination of drink and driving and its disastrous consequences is the inevitable outcome of the act of driving a car![25]

Despite the fact that all too many of the contributions also testified to ignorance of the subject,[26] the debate essentially underscored the need for safeguards in the context of implementation of an electronic identity card. Such safeguards had in fact been included in the original project, but apparently they had not been made sufficiently clear.

5.5.3   The 2009 Update

The public debate led to a delay of the project, in order to modify it to take into account the main objections.

The balance between the security requirements and the protection of privacy led to the new proposal of a noncompulsory card, with optional electronic identification tools. A biometric database remains essential if fraud is to be countered, and access to the data held must be tightly restricted. Thus the balance follows 11 of the 12 recommendations the FDI expressed in its conclusions of the 2005 debate.

The project was then once again delayed because of the 2007 elections in France. A bill containing all these provisions is to be submitted to Parliament.

5.6   Interoperability Aspects

The use of electronic identification tools to access electronic services throughout Europe is one main goal of the European Union in its i2010 programme, in order to improve public services to the citizens. The 2005 Manchester ministerial declaration stated: "By 2010 European citizens and businesses shall be able to benefit from secure means of electronic identification that maximise user convenience while respecting data protection regulations. Such means shall be made available under the responsibility of the Member States but recognised across the EU."[27]

Since 2001, European eID project managers have met twice a year in the so-called "Porvoo Group Meetings" (from the town of Porvoo, Finland, which was the first meeting place), in order to update their knowledge of each other's projects, and to coordinate their technical specifications. The meetings are also open to non-European countries: American and Asian managers often attend the meetings. Interoperability, which is the possibility to use a national eID tool in another country, is a difficult matter inasmuch as eID tools and e-services were not coordinated throughout Europe from the initial design phase. But some cases show it is possible: Estonian or Belgian citizens can thus use their national electronic ID cards to access the municipal services of the Italian town of Grosseto.

On a more general ground, the European Commission launched in 2007 a call for a global interoperability pilot, which would enable all European citizens to access all European e-services. A consortium called STORK, with participants from 15 member states, was, in 2008, in negotiation with the Commission to propose several pilot tools.

5.7 Conclusion

This general overview makes it possible to see that the impact of electronic identification, and especially electronic identity cards, is very great both in terms of the development of electronic administration services, and of public perception of the nature of identity and the role of the state in protecting it. The situation varies widely between countries, France being typified by ambivalence in the views of the general public, who assign to the state alone the role of protector of identity, but who at the same time suspect that same state of using the information collected for improper purposes (despite the fact that it is far less exhaustive than in other countries). A balance between identity authentication and protection of privacy will be essential if the projects currently under way in this field are to succeed. A study published in January 2008 by Afnor (the French standardization body) revealed that the widespread use of an electronic identity card could lead to billions of euros of savings, productivity growth, and new services, which would bring benefit to the citizens, to the administration, and to private companies.[28]

Glossary

Certificate In the case of electronic identification, this is a public electronic document that cannot be falsified and which guarantees the identity of the holder of a tool, an electronic identity card, for example.

Electronic identification A functionality that allows an Internet user wishing to do so to authenticate his identity when logging on to the Internet, a local area network, or a computer. According to the desired level of security, proof of identity can be based on the user's personal knowledge (e.g., a security code), something she possesses (e.g., a smartcard), a personal characteristic (e.g., fingerprints), or even a combination of all three.

Electronic identity card Although there are variants in different countries, it is possible to say that it is an identity card of traditional type in which the hardcopy information has been transposed onto a chip for the purposes of verification by law enforcement personnel (depending on the country concerned, a photograph and fingerprints may or may not be stored on the chip), and which also contains electronic keys and certificates for use with online services.

Disclaimer: The views expressed in this chapter are those of the author alone.

Notes

[1] Among them Belgium, Finland, Sweden, Estonia, Italy, and Spain, in addition to the United Kingdom since the passing of the Identity Cards Act of 30 March 2006.

[2] The term "authentication" is used from a technical standpoint to indicate a procedure for proving a person's identity. However, its use is incorrect in the legal context, where the term "identification" is preferred.

[3] The French Ministry of Finance provides each taxpayer with a downloadable electronic certificate free of charge. In 2007, 7.4 million electronic income tax returns were filed, a number sharply larger than the previous year.

[4] It is shared by several rights holders in the same family and moreover, given that it has no photograph, it can easily be used fraudulently by uninsured third parties if it is stolen or as part of a scheme for illegal trafficking; in this case, its main benefit for those defrauding the system is not so much the reimbursement but the possibility of access to healthcare free of charge.

[5] This is possible not only internally in hospitals but also, as in the case of certain establishments in the United States, between a medical practitioner and the pharmacy closest to the home of the patient.

[6] For more details see [MAT03].

[7] *For more details see* [MCG06].

[8] How many people still use their name as a password, or their birthday as a security code?

[9] The first attempt at fraud of this type in France, in 2005, met with very little success: it consisted of an email *in English* addressed *simultaneously* to customers of four high-street banks ("Dear bank A/bank B/bank C/bank D customer..."), two points that naturally helped arouse suspicion in the minds of the customers concerned. In February 2006, a double phishing campaign targeting customers of the Crédit Lyonnais led to the temporary closure of this online banking service. The BNP was also targeted a few weeks later. This illustrates the negative impact phishing can have on online services.

[10] Falsification: fraudulent alteration of otherwise authentic documents.

[11] Counterfeiting: the creation of documents that are not authentic.

[12] For more details see [MAT07].

[13] European Council regulation 2252/2004 of 13 December 2004.

[14] Work done by the European Council and the Commission for the definition of minimum standards applicable in all Member States on a voluntary basis.

[15] Council of Europe, Consultative Committee of the Convention for the protection of individuals with regard to automatic processing of personal data, Progress report on the application of the principles of Convention 108 to the collection and processing of biometric data, T-PD (2005) BIOM E, 2–4 February 2005, § 23 and 21.

[16] André Santini, at the time Mayor of Issy-les-Moulineaux, and since 2007 Minister of Civil Service, in an interview given to *Acteurs Publics* no. 16 in September 2005.

[17] Similarly, an opinion poll conducted in 2002 on behalf of the FDI showed that 73% of respondents favoured the concept of an electronic identity card enabling official formalities to be carried out on the Internet.

[18] As in Portugal, for example.

[19] As in Belgium or in Estonia, for example.

[20] An example: Claudine Dardy, lecturer in sociology at the University of Paris XII: "The body becomes an object to be cut up and parcelled out in chips" [FDI05], page 73.

[21] An example: Alain Damasio, a writer: "Identity per se does not exist [...]. We do not suffer from doubt as to identity. What we do suffer from is excessive assignment of individual identity [...]. Offering each citizen the possibility of doubling, of multiplying his or her approaches to personal identity in the contexts they are led to frequent, surely this amounts ultimately to offering them an opportunity for mobility, for vitality in relationships with others that would be hobbled by an identity card?" [FDI05], page 26.

[22] Pierre Piazza, researcher at INHES [FDI05], page 6.

[23] Idem.

[24] On this topic see in particular [CDG04]: some in a secondary school where a hand-shaped reader was installed were afraid of being "eaten" by the machine.

[25] [FDI05], page 67.

[26] For example, a national daily newspaper reported that the chairman of a respectable not-for-profit French association that has existed for over a century had denounced the project, because it would, according to him, "make it compulsory to declare all changes of address." In fact, given that no such provision had ever been included, one might ask whether the journalist misreported what had been said or whether such a statement had actually been made. If the latter were true, at best the chairman concerned had manifestly not read the documentation. And one could add that such an obligation exists in many European democracies without threat to citizens' rights.

[27] U.K. Presidency of the E.U., Ministerial Declaration approved unanimously on 24 November 2005, Manchester, United Kingdom.

[28] [AFN08].

References

AFN08   AFNOR/Standarmedia, *Etude d'impact: la signature électronique et les infrastructures à clé publique dans le contexte de l'identité numérique*, [Survey on the impact of electronic signature and public key infrastructures in a digital identity context] [January 2008].

CDG04   Craipeau S., Dubey G., Guchet X.: R*apport final du projet incitatif GET 2003: La Biométrie, usages et représentations*, GET, 2004 [Final report on the GET 2003 incentive project: Biometrics – applications and perceptions].

FDI05   Forum des Droits sur l'Internet, Débat national sur la carte d'identité électronique, avis de spéc*ialistes*, Forum des Droits sur l'Internet, 2005 [National debate on the electronic identity card – experts opinion].

MAT03   Mattatia F., Panorama de l'informatisation du secteur de la santé, in *La Jaune et la Rouge*, February 2003, pp. 15–18. [Computerisation in the healthcare sector: an overview].

MAT07   Mattatia F., "The utility of electronic identity cards for a safer digital world", in *Annals of Telecommunications*, 62, no. 11–12, 2007.

MCG06   Malville E., Crom J.-M., Gourmelen G., "A survey on identity federation solutions", in *Annals of Telecommunications*, 61, no: 3–4, 2006.

Chapter 6
Privacy and Personal Information Held by Government: A Comparative Study, Japan and New Zealand

Rowena Cullen

Abstract This chapter reports on the concepts of information privacy and trust in government among citizens in Japan and New Zealand in a transnational, cross-cultural study. Data from both countries are presented, and cultural and other factors are sought that might explain differences in attitudes shown. In both countries, citizens display a range of views, not related to age or gender. New Zealand citizens express concern about information privacy in relation to information held by government, but show a higher level of trust in government overall, and most attribute breaches of privacy to incompetence, rather than deliberate malfeasance. Japanese citizens interviewed also indicated that they had major concerns about information privacy, and had considerably less trust in government than New Zealand respondents showed. They were more inclined to attribute breaches of privacy to lax behavior in individuals than government systems. In both countries citizens showed an awareness of the tradeoffs necessary between personal privacy and the needs of the state to hold information for the benefit of all citizens, but knew little about the protection offered by privacy legislation, and expressed overall concern about privacy practices in the modern state. The study also provides evidence of cultural differences that can be related to Hofstede's dimensions of culture.

6.1 Introduction

Concepts such as privacy, attitudes to personal information, and trust in government are inevitably influenced by personal experience and cultural factors, which will differ from country to country. This chapter reports on an investigation of citizens'

R. Cullen (✉)
School of Information Management, Victoria University of Wellington, PO Box 600,
Wellington, New Zealand
e-mail: rowena.cullen@vuw.ac.nz

S. Assar et al. (eds.), *Practical Studies in E-Government: Best Practices from Around the World*, DOI 10.1007/978-1-4419-7533-1_6,
© Springer Science+Business Media, LLC 2011

concerns about information privacy, and the impact of this on their trust in government in two very different countries. The New Zealand data are drawn from a study conducted in 2005 [CUL07], which was followed by an exploration of the same issues with Japanese citizens in 2007, in order to identify any differences in perceptions, concerns, and the role of cultural factors in determining these. The chapter begins with an overview of the two countries involved, and briefly discusses the concept of information privacy in relation to government, previous literature on concepts of privacy in both countries, and the state of privacy legislation in each. It then outlines the two phases of the study, and presents data from both quantitative and qualitative aspects of the study. It concludes by exploring cultural differences that become evident in these data, and looks for possible explanations of this. Comment is made on impact of this research for government agencies.

6.1.1 The Settings

Japan is generally considered to be a stable and highly controlled society, with a homogeneous population of over 100 million. It is seen as politically conservative, emerging from centuries of isolation, and facing considerable change, especially if it wishes to maintain its global economic influence. It has a highly developed telecommunications infrastructure, an extensive broadband network, and high Internet usage rates (67.2% of the population in 2005) [INT07]. Regular scandals in the news media involving politicians and prominent businessmen and other aspects of Japanese culture lead to an overall lack of trust in government [TAN01] and concerns about Internet security, which may affect the confidence that citizens may have in the way that government agencies handle their personal information, especially in the online environment.

New Zealand is a very different country, a former colony of Great Britain, with a population made up of the indigenous Maori population (currently around 15% of the population), a large Caucasian population (mainly British in origin) which dates back to the early nineteenth century, large and rapidly growing migrant Polynesian groups from the many Pacific island states (Samoa, Tonga, Vanuatu, Tuvalu, the Cook Islands, etc.), and growing numbers of Asian and Middle Eastern migrants. The total population of 4.3 million people is spread out over a country roughly the same area as Japan, the largest city Auckland accounting for over one million of the population. New Zealand has a far less developed technology infrastructure and a significantly lower uptake of broadband Internet connectivity at the time the two studies were conducted, but a similar rate of Internet use. It is generally considered to be a more relaxed and informal society, strongly influenced by the indigenous Maori culture (reinforced by large Polynesian communities), and the population has been found to be relatively trusting both of government and the exchange of information on the Internet [BEL08, GO03, HER06].

6.1.2 Research Questions

The chapter focuses on citizen's concerns about the privacy of their personal information held by government in New Zealand and Japan, and investigates in both countries:

- The concerns that citizens express about their information privacy in relation to information held by government
- The extent to which citizens are aware of the existing protections of their right to privacy
- How trustworthy citizens believe government organizations are in relation to information privacy
- Whether, if an individual believes an organization has violated his or her privacy, this affects the individual's trust in that organization
- The extent to which a breach of privacy by one government organization affects the individual's perception of the trustworthiness of other government organizations
- Which channel citizens trust most when they are required to provide personal information to government organizations.

Finally, the chapter poses the question: what differences exist between the responses of Japanese and New Zealand participants in the studies? Knowledge of these differences can enhance understanding in Japan and New Zealand, as well as in other countries, of the different attitudes that may be held by citizens, and the need for government agencies to be aware of these.

6.2 Concepts of Information Privacy

Privacy is acknowledged and valued across many political systems, as is shown by Article 17 of the United Nations' *International Covenant on Civil and Political Rights*, which states: "No one shall be subjected to arbitrary or unlawful interference with his privacy, family, home or correspondence, nor to unlawful attacks on his honor and reputation" [UNI66]. Similar protections are also included in Article 12 of the *Universal Declaration of Human Rights* [UNI48]. However, although it is argued that privacy is a necessary requirement for citizens in modern democratic states [WES67, DEM03] and that it contributes to an individual's personal autonomy and dignity, at the same time there is general agreement that privacy is not an absolute right. For example, it is often argued that, in certain situations, an individual's right to privacy may be outweighed by the public interest in the disclosure of personal information (e.g., the location of convicted sexual offenders' residences, or the salaries of certain government employees). Thus, it is argued, tradeoffs must be made to promote a balance between these seemingly competing interests: "either too much or too little privacy can create imbalances which seriously jeopardize the individual's well-being" [WES67, p. 40].

6.2.1   Government and Citizens' Personal Information

The investigations reported here are concerned with information privacy, defined by Westin as "the claim of individuals, groups, or institutions to determine for themselves when, how and to what extent information about them is communicated to others" [WES67]. In many situations, the provision of personal information to government organizations is compulsory, in contrast to the nature of the exchanges that individuals engage in with private companies, where citizens may make their decision about which companies they choose to entrust with their personal information. This compulsion results in an unequal power relationship. As Dempsey et al. note: "Governments have special privacy obligations arising from the concept of democracy, which includes the establishment of rules mediating the power relationship between government and citizens" [DEM03, p. 1].

With the increasing use of electronic means of communication between citizens and government, citizens may perceive an even greater risk to the privacy of their personal information supplied to government. As Dempsey et al. also note:

> Governments are increasingly using the Internet as a means to deliver services and information. This development allows users to register for government services; obtain and file government forms; apply for employment; comment on public policy issues; and engage in a growing number of other functions – all on-line. The trend towards e-government and the electronic delivery of services has further expanded government collection of personally-identifiable data. [p. 1]

This information may be of a highly personal and sensitive nature, including financial or health-related information; it requires careful handling to ensure that information is kept confidential, used only for the purpose for which it is collected, and by those with authority to access it. The greater facility of exchanging information between agencies gives governments even greater power. With this power goes a greater responsibility.

This applies across all levels of society. As Raab and Bennett note, although those in lower socioeconomic groups may be more vulnerable to breaches of information privacy in relation to their personal living circumstances, due to the need to claim income support, "those higher up the socioeconomic ladder are more likely to be part of the credit-card economy" [RAA98, p. 264] exposing them to greater risk not only from the private sector, direct marketers, and online retailers, but also to government-related trading agencies, and the core agencies themselves. As governments seek to enhance their service delivery by meeting the expectations of citizens that they will meet or better the online service delivery of the private sector, they also "face the same challenges of balancing information privacy against potential service enhancement" [HER06].

6.2.2   Concepts of Information Privacy in New Zealand and Japanese Culture

Research in New Zealand to date has shown that New Zealanders have an above-average perception of "safety" in providing personal information to government over the Internet, and that this perception has increased considerably among groups of New Zealanders who make regular use of online government services [GOO3]. This is despite the fact that, like citizens in many other countries, New Zealanders' trust in government has been declining throughout the twentieth century, although there is no evidence that this decline is related to government performance, rather an overall lack of respect for authority throughout the western world [BAR02].

In most Asian cultures, privacy is seen as a "western" concept that coexists along with traditional values based on the communal nature of family or community life, close living quarters, hierarchical (feudal) social systems, and collectivist social values, and the Confucian, Buddhist, and in the case of Japan, Shinto religions [KIT05]. An additional cultural dimension that may have an impact on privacy concerns, and trust in government is encompassed by Hofstede's concept of power distance, which indexes the degree to which a society tolerates greater or lesser levels of inequality in power between individuals [HOF91]. Hofstede's studies of national and organizational culture identified initially four, then extended to five, *Dimensions of Culture* which are described as:

> *Low Versus High Power Distance* – Power distance refers to the "tendency of a society to be hierarchical" with "considerable social distance" between the higher and lower ends of society and an acceptance by less powerful members of society that power is distributed unequally. New Zealand is generally identified as a low power distance culture, with a strong egalitarian ethos, Japan (along with other "Confucian" cultures), as a high power distance culture.
> *Individualism Versus Collectivism* – Individualism refers to the extent to which people see themselves as autonomous, and independent of others; collectivist cultures have strong sense of group identity, which may be tribal, religious, or national (as in Japan).
> *Masculinity Versus Femininity* – Refers to the value placed on traditionally male or female values (as understood in most Western cultures). In high masculinity cultures men and women play very different roles.
> *Uncertainty Avoidance* – Reflects the extent to which members of a society attempt to cope with anxiety by minimizing uncertainty. Japan is usually ranked high on uncertainty avoidance, and more rigid and less innovative in social behavior.
> *Long Versus Short Term Orientation* – (initially described by Michael Bond as Confucian dynamism) Describes a society's "time horizon." Japan is usually identified as a culture focused on long-term orientation, with value placed on thrift, patience, and perseverance. Short-term cultures tend to value immediate results, and focus on recreation over a work ethic with long-term gains [LAW07, pp. 12–14.]

New Zealand is generally depicted as a low power distance, individualist culture, compared with Japan, which is characterized as being at the opposite end of the spectrum on these five dimensions. However, New Zealand also has a substantial minority population which is made up of indigenous Maori and immigrant Polynesian communities. These cultures are also strongly collectivist. This should not, however, be taken to imply that Polynesian culture has a similar profile to Japanese culture when measured on Hosftede's dimensions. Japan can be categorized as a fairly classic "hierarchical-collectivist" society as opposed to countries such as Israel, which has been described as "egalitarian-collectivist" [GOO99]. Although Polynesian cultures are strongly collectivist, they differ among themselves in the degree to which they are hierarchical, and their customs and mores change when they come into contact with and are embedded in the larger New Zealand society. Contemporary Maori society is less hierarchical than traditional Maori society, but these differences vary from group to group. In addition, whereas Maori and other Polynesian cultures share with Japanese culture a differentiation between male and female roles, they do not share the characteristics of uncertainty avoidance and long-term orientation that are attributed to the influence of Confucianism in Japanese society.

There are few studies as yet which relate citizens' concerns with information privacy in relation to government with this approach to cultural differences. Bellman et al. [BEL04] identified differences in information-related privacy concerns among respondents from 38 countries, based on differences in cultural values, and differences in Internet experience. They found that participants from cultures considered to be high on power distance indicators, and low on individualism indicators had concerns about inaccurate information held about them, and the secondary use of information. This is in contrast to the findings of the more widely recognized work of Milberg et al. which their study draws on, which suggests that high power distance cultures, which tolerate greater levels of inequality of power, have greater mistrust of powerful groups, such as companies, whereas groups with low individualism (collectivist societies) have a greater tolerance of intrusion on the private life of the individual [MIL00]. It is commonly assumed that Japanese culture fits within this definition, however, Polynesian cultures, both Maori and Pacific, with their emphasis on the extended family, and communal ownership of land and intellectual property, are also identifiable as high power distance and collectivist social groups. This is a factor which clearly needs to be taken into account in this study. A further element, however, may also come into play. Dinev et al. [DIN05] have identified a counter element to the influence of culture on citizens' trust in government, and that is the impact of an individual's "propensity to trust" which may interact with the individualistic or collectivist nature of his culture.

Focusing specifically on the concept of privacy in Japan, and the common perception, both within and outside Japan, that privacy is a foreign concept to the Japanese, Mizutani, Dorsey, and Moor discuss the introduction of the "loanword" *puraibashii*, meaning privacy, into the Japanese language [MIZ04]. They argue that the concept of privacy was not and is not foreign to the Japanese mindset, that there are related concepts of "secret," and "forbidden" matters in the Japanese language, but that the concept of privacy itself is different in the Japanese tradition. In particular they note the strong influence of Buddhism which advocates the effacement of the self, and the sublimation of the self to the group. In addition, they link the concept of privacy to the traditional Japanese lifestyle, where close proximity to family and neighbors has meant that things observed or overheard inadvertently are not to be repeated or acknowledged in any way. (This is sometimes identified with the iconic monkeys of the Japanese temples at Nikko, representing the precept "see no evil, hear no evil, speak no evil.") Thus privacy conventions in Japan, the authors argue, are based on the important role of the group within Japanese culture, and the need for self-imposed restraint in relation to the privacy of others. Although privacy may be a less individualistic concept in Japan than in western culture, privacy conventions are no less developed and firmly rooted in Japanese culture, the authors suggest. In fact, the traditions of group culture and privacy within it may, in fact, be so strong, they argue, that the need for regulations that would extend the concept of privacy to the world of ICTs and the Internet has not been seen as sufficiently urgent.

6.2.3   Privacy Legislation in Japan and New Zealand

In New Zealand, the Privacy Act (1993) protects how any individual's personal information can be collected, stored, used, and disclosed by government or any individual or organization.[1] The essence of the law is encapsulated in 12 *Privacy Principles* which place restrictions on how people and organizations can use and disclose information, and give individuals protections against unauthorized or improper disclosure of their personal information. It also gives individuals the right to access their personal information held by an agency and request correction of it. The Act gives the Privacy Commissioner the power to issue codes of practice across any specific industry or domain of activity (e.g., the health sector) that then become part of the law. It also limits

- The manner in which information can be made available from public registers
- Re-sorting or combining public register information for commercial gain
- Electronic transmission of public registers
- Charging for access to public register information

The Act sets out a complaints mechanism and contains rules regulating data matching between government agencies (e.g., to identify those in employment who may also be wrongfully claiming a welfare benefit), each case requiring to be reported to parliament. It also prohibits the government from issuing one single number for citizens to use in their dealings with agencies.

Privacy legislation in Japan is more recent. Despite a preference by the Japanese government for self-regulation in relation to information and data privacy, the government responded to heightened citizen concern amidst media reports of privacy violations by government and businesses, and passed the Personal Information Protection Act, amid considerable public discussion, on 30 May 2003. [FRE05] The Act came into effect on 1 April 2005. [JAP03] It establishes mandatory guidelines for central, local, and regional government agencies, and assigns individual ministries to develop equivalent guidelines for business and other institutions in their specific sector. The Act protects only living individuals, and is confined to information about an individual that distinguishes her from other individuals, such as name, date of birth, postal and email addresses, job title, photograph, employment information, and the like. The provisions of the Act are focused on the responsible management of information held in databases, rather than privacy protection covering more sensitive personal information, such as health or financial information, as in comparable legislation in other jurisdictions. The right to control one's personal data is also included as an important part of the right to privacy that is guaranteed under Article 13 of the Japanese Constitution.

6.3   The Two Parallel Studies

6.3.1   The New Zealand Study

The New Zealand data reported here are taken from a larger research project on breaches of privacy and their impact on trust in government, published on the New Zealand e-government website REI06. The data used for comparison in this chapter have been previously reported in more detail [CUL07, CUL08a, CUL08b], and are based on data derived from a series of focus group interviews with groups of citizens across a wide range of ages, ethnicities, occupations, and socioeconomic levels. Participants in the focus groups were given an initial questionnaire consisting of general questions regarding their concerns about their personal information and their trust in the government to handle it appropriately. Where appropriate, in an effort to avoid uncertainty inherent in phrases such as, "How concerned are you about your privacy in dealing with the government?" the questionnaire used more specific statements such as, "I feel confident that my personal information will be handled properly and be adequately protected by government agencies I deal with," and, "I think the rules governing the way in which government organizations collect and exchange information about me are adequate," with responses available on a five-point Likert scale (from Strongly Agree to Strongly Disagree). A group interview followed, which began with a discussion of five general questions, including how the participants defined information privacy, and their knowledge of the Privacy Act, and then centered on five scenarios for discussion. These were designed to present individuals with a situation involving improper use of information, or a breach of privacy of personal information to get as realistic a view as possible of the participants' responses to breaches of privacy, and its impact on their trust in government. A total of 58 participants were interviewed in this way.

Scenario 1 outlined circumstances in which a letter from an agency which contained personal financial information was sent to another person in error; however, the intended recipient was notified by phone and an apology offered. Scenario 2 outlined an incident in the offices of the local government where papers containing information about a neighbor's property taxes, and the neighbor's heated dispute about this matter, were left lying around and were seen by the participant. Scenario 3 involved a breach of privacy concerning personal health data in a hospital. Scenario 4 involved the prosecution of a government employee who had sold tax information to a debt recovery firm. Scenario 5 concerned the use of NZ Post's change of address system, which allows individuals to notify several government agencies at once of their address change. Unfortunately this was made available to other organizations as well, resulting in unwanted unsolicited mail.

6.3.2   The Japanese Study

In the reiteration of the study in Japan, most of the participants were interviewed individually in English, to enable the interviewer to ensure concepts were understood, and a small number interviewed in Japanese. Each individual was asked to complete the preliminary questionnaire, answer the five general questions, and then asked to comment and reflect on each of five scenarios. The scenarios used were the same as in New Zealand (apart from small changes of wording to reflect the Japanese context), except for Scenario 5, which was replaced with a reference to the introduction of a national resident registry network, known as Juki Net. Juki Net is a national identification system that links all municipalities and prefectures through the Local Government Wide Area Network, so that central and local governments can share four basic pieces of information about residents: name, address, sex, and date of birth, attached to their personal ID number (issued to all citizens). Citizens can obtain a photo ID card to be used to facilitate transactions such as registering a change of address or a vehicle, and also register an electronic signature to be used when tendering services to local government. The introduction of the system generated considerable controversy (some prefectures not adopting the system initially), and cases brought by citizens concerned about the privacy of their personal information were only resolved by a Japanese Supreme Court decision in March 2008.[2] A total of 34 participants were interviewed in Japan.

6.4   Findings

6.4.1   Questionnaire Data

Age range was relatively evenly spread across the participants in both New Zealand and Japan (see Table 6.1), and occupations were varied in both groups, although the occupations of the Japanese participants reflected their higher socioeconomic status overall, because of the bias introduced by interviewing the majority in English. The ratio of females to males in the NZ groups was 33:25; in the Japanese group this balance was reversed with 15 females:19 males. (More detailed analyses of responses in both of these studies can be found in the original report and in two successive conference presentations at HICSS 41 and 42 [CUL07, CUL08a].)

In the New Zealand groups 22 males and 25 female respondents (~81%) used the Internet, whereas 3 males and 8 females did not. All but one of the Japanese participants used the Internet (Table 6.2).

Table 6.1 Age of participants

Age	Number in NZ Study	Number in Japanese Study
Under 20	2	0
20–29	14	5
30–39	15	11
40–49	9	2
50–59	6	9
60–69	8	4
70+	4	3
Total	58	34

Table 6.2 Participants' use of online services

Online activity	NZ	NZ (%)	Japan	Japan (%)
Online banking	29	50	12	35.3
Online trading	21	36.2	27	79.4

The initial questionnaire which asked participants to respond to a series of statements about their privacy-related concerns, attitudes, and behaviors used a Likert scale of options, that is, 1 = strongly agree, 2 = agree, 3 = neutral (unsure), 4 = disagree, 5 = strongly disagree. Response data from these questions are shown in Table 6.3.

In Table 6.3, responses to statement S6 suggest that the majority of participants in both countries (73% in Japan, and 86% in New Zealand) are concerned about the privacy of their personal information when it is communicated via the Internet. Although only half the respondents in both countries (50% in Japan, and 52% in New Zealand) expressed concern about the amount of personal information collected by government (S10), Japanese respondents showed far more concern about the adequacy of the rules governing the way in which government organizations collect and share information (S13), with only 27% agreeing with the statement. Responses from New Zealand respondents to this question, at 48%, match more clearly the level of concern about the amount of information collected.

This difference is also apparent when we look at whether a more general concern about personal information on the Internet translates into an equivalent level of concern about government management of personal information in the online environment. Responses to S7 and S8 indicate that Japanese respondents are inclined to trust government agencies less than they trust businesses, whereas New Zealand responses are the opposite, showing only a slight gap between participants' levels of confidence in government organizations and private organizations (and overall levels of trust much higher).

Responses from the Japanese respondents show far lower levels of trust in government agencies, and in the ability of government servants to treat their personal information with respect than the trust shown by the New Zealand respondents; this is particularly evident in responses to statements S8, S9, and S13. This greater confidence of Japanese respondents in business is also shown in the higher rates of shopping online, and lower rates of concern about the exchange of information in the online environment. However, despite their overall extremely low levels of trust, Japanese respondents seem to be less proactive in assuring themselves, to the extent that they can, of privacy protection; that is, they are less likely to agree than NZ respondents that they will seek statements about security of information provided to government, or withhold personal information when it is requested (S11, S14).

Respondents were asked about their preferred medium for exchanging information with an agency. In the New Zealand study 42 out of the 56 people who answered this question (75%) preferred "in person," whereas a smaller percentage in Japan (22, or 65%) selected this as their first choice, followed by 19 (29%) who selected the postal system (whereas only 10 New Zealanders did so.) The telephone was nominated as a first choice by only four New Zealand respondents, and by no Japanese respondents, and only two respondents in each sample (4% and 6%, respectively) selected the Internet.

Table 6.3 Reported Attitudes in Japanese and New Zealand Respondents (strongly agree and agree responses, reported in (*rounded*) percentages)

Statement	Japan (n=34) Strongly agree	Japan Agree	Japan (n=34) Total agree	NZ Strongly agree	NZ Agree	NZ (n=58) Total agree
S6. I am concerned about the privacy of my personal information when it is exchanged online via the Internet.	10 (29%)	14 (41%)	24 (73%)	31 (53%)	19 (33%)	50 (86%)
S7. I feel confident that my personal information will be handled properly and be adequately protected by the *private businesses* (e.g., stores, banks, etc.) I deal with.	0 (0%)	12 (35%)	12 (35%)	11 (19%)	22 (38%)	33 (57%)
S8. I feel confident that my personal information will be handled properly and adequately protected by the *government organizations* I deal with.	0 (0%)	9 (27%)	9 (27%)	13 (22%)	22 (38%)	35 (60%)
S9. I trust government employees to treat my personal information with appropriate respect for my privacy.	0 (0%)	9 (27%)	9 (27%)	15 (26%)	19 (33%)	34 (59%)
S10. I am generally concerned about the amount of information that various *government organizations* hold about me.	7 (21%)	10 (29%)	17 (50%)	15 (30%)	15 (30%)	30 (52%)
S11. I usually seek or check statements about the way in which my personal information will be protected before I supply information to *government organizations*.	5 (15%)	7 (21%)	12 (36%)	18 (31%)	19 (33%)	37 (64%)
S12. I usually seek or check statements about the way in which my personal information will be protected before I supply information to a *business* that I deal with.	11 (32%)	9 (27%)	20 (59%)	20 (34%)	25 (43%)	45 (78%)
S13. I think the rules governing the way in which government organizations collect and exchange information about me are adequate.	2 (6%)	7 (21%)	9 (27%)	3 (5%)	25 (43%)	28 (48%)
S14. I sometimes refuse to provide information to a government organization if I feel they do not have an adequate reason to ask for such information.	4 (12%)	15 (44%)	19 (56%)	11 (19%)	30 (52%)	41 (71%)

The final questions in the questionnaire asked respondents if they made distinctions between government agencies in terms of the trust they accorded them. In both countries there were clear differences in how agencies are viewed. Even though in the New Zealand study 34 (59%) of respondents stated that they made no distinction, in subsequent discussion most people said they trusted some departments more than others. New Zealand agencies least trusted include the welfare agency Work and Income, and the taxation agency Inland Revenue. Contradictorily, participants also placed Inland Revenue at the top of the most trusted list, followed by the Ministry of Health (significantly absent from agencies trusted by Japanese respondents.) In Japan, 15 out of 34 (44%) respondents indicated that they made distinctions in the level of trust they accorded government agencies. Specific agencies which were mentioned as well trusted were limited to the Ministry of Justice, and the judiciary. Agencies mentioned as less trusted included the ministry in charge of pensions, the police, and the newly created Ministry of Defense (although this appeared to be more related to its recent change in status from a department to a ministry, a matter of public concern in view of Japan's traditional post-World War II nonmilitarist policy, than the activities of the agency itself). Concerns were expressed by some respondents about the trustworthiness of local government agencies, but local government and "City Hall" were specifically mentioned by five respondents as most trusted, in contrast to others who named "central government agencies" as more trusted than local agencies.

6.4.2   Concepts of Privacy and Privacy Protection

Although the study did not seek to develop a new definition of privacy, participants' views on what the term "privacy" meant to them were of interest. The interviews and discussion groups in both countries therefore gave participants an opportunity to define the term and what it meant to them. In New Zealand, many participants mentioned that they believe privacy is related to being able to control "who knows what" about things related to their private lives. Some individuals defined privacy in terms of types of information that they feel should be kept private and confidential (e.g., health, finances, etc.). Other individuals, notably in the groups of Maori and Pacific peoples, Polynesian cultures where the extended family is a very dominant concept, explained that their view of privacy is primarily concerned with keeping family information private and protecting the honor of their family's name and reputation. (See [CUL08b] where this is discussed in considerably more detail.)

The majority of Japanese respondents listed concerns and issues that they would like to keep private, or have control over the disclosure of, as some put it. These commonly included: personal details such as their name and address, age, date and place of birth; their income and the value of their assets and savings (and other business affairs); family matters (ages of their children, if any, and other family concerns); health data concerning themselves and their family; and details of their education and career. (Some of these concerns related to fears expressed about the rising crime rate, and recent abductions. Such people felt any information disclosure made them vulnerable.) However, some went further, and added personal habits, thoughts, religious ideas, and philosophies to this. Some respondents indicated that they had their employer in mind when defining what they wanted kept private, and some commented that practices within the workplace could be sharpened up in regard to privacy, explaining that as employees were moved in and out of the human resources departments at their workplaces, common practice in Japanese management culture, the pool of people who had access to their personal, income, and health data increased every year. The concept of "shutting out the world" to keep one's information secure was memorably expressed by one respondent who talked about keeping personal information safe within "my castle." He then explored that concept further, and commented on the difference in protections offered by Japanese law and privacy laws in other countries by describing his Japanese castle as being made of wood, not stone.

A number of Japanese respondents explained how, in their view, privacy was a "western" concept that had been introduced into Japan with modernization, and in particular with the postwar Constitution. The concept, they explained, was not well understood in Japan, and differed from the way it was perceived in other countries. This theme was picked up later, in discussions of the last scenario. For a small minority of participants, privacy was not a concern, both older and younger participants stated that they had "nothing to hide," and therefore no concerns.

6.4.3   Discussion of Scenarios

6.4.3.1   New Zealand Responses

Discussion of the scenarios varied slightly between the two parts of the study, because of the ways in which the two studies were conducted. In the focus groups conducted in New Zealand, discussion was more wide-ranging, prompted by, rather than responding specifically to, the five scenarios. A view commonly expressed by the New Zealand participants, was that although they had more confidence in government than private business because of the greater accountability of government, they were not surprised by the breaches, which they put down to incompetence, rather than deliberate harmfulness. "I think a private organization is more likely to *sell* my information, whereas government would be more likely to *lose* it." Their responses to the scenarios, and how these breaches of privacy would affect their trust in government tended to center around two themes: the way the organization disciplines the employee responsible for the breach, and the way the organization handles the situation with the individual whose privacy was breached; if both of these were satisfactorily addressed, it was less likely trust would be withdrawn. Breaches in one agency, would not, in this case, have an impact on trust in another agency.

Concern was greater among those with the least knowledge of technology, individuals reporting stories from the media which reinforced the stories recounted in the scenarios. Concerns focused on the security of computers and the Internet, increased potential for privacy breaches through the use of technology, and a lack of understanding about what happens to information submitted to organizations. Most had heard of the Privacy Act when reminded by others in the group, however, they knew little of its provisions.

In each group, participants explained how the various scenarios would affect the degree of trust they placed in different organizations. This included their reactions to previous personal experiences, as well as their responses to the hypothetical scenarios presented by the researchers. The overwhelming majority of individuals reported that breaches of information privacy have an impact on their trust in organizations (i.e., affect their assessment of the trustworthiness of the organization). Their responses suggest that a number of variables influence the magnitude of the impact on individuals' trust. These factors included:

1. *The perceived cause of the breach*: Respondents distinguished between an honest mistake, staff incompetence, deliberate wrongdoing, and/or a breach of privacy motivated by financial gain.
2. *How sensitive was the information involved*: The more sensitive the information, the greater the impact a breach would have. Individuals generally reported that health information and financial information were the most sensitive, and a few individuals claimed that their contact details were the most sensitive (these individuals explained that they did not want previous acquaintances to be able to find them).
3. *What happened to the information*: If the information was improperly disclosed, the magnitude of the impact was influenced by the entity to whom it was disclosed.
4. *How the organization handled the situation*: Individuals emphasized the importance of an organization's response to any privacy-related situations, for example, how they responded to a complaint, and what they were doing to ensure the breach would not occur again.
5. *Had this type of event happened before and is it consistent with, or contradictory to, the organization's reputation*? When explaining how much an event would affect their level of trust, individuals commonly said this would depend on whether the problem was perceived to be a "one-off" occurrence. Individuals were more likely to "give the organization the benefit of the doubt" in cases where an event appeared to be a unique aberration from an organization with an otherwise trustworthy reputation.

Although some people reported being relatively unconcerned about their privacy, many others became quite emotional as they recounted personal experiences. This type of response was most often shown by individuals who reported having a negative personal experience of a breach of privacy by a government department in the past.

A recurring theme, central to most of the group discussions of the scenarios, related to the unique context of the relationship between the state and its citizens. In contrast to their relationship with the private sector, people reported feeling they had little power in their relationship with the state and little control over what information the state collects about them and how it is used. A number expressed great concern about programs sharing data between agencies, some stating that they viewed this as a breach of privacy, others that data-sharing programs contributed to their feeling that they had little control over who had access to their information. This concern was heightened among Polynesian respondents, who expressed a strong view that not being able to control information about themselves, and in particular their families, exposed them to an unacceptable risk of harm. There was a considerable minority, however, who expressed qualified support for certain data-sharing arrangements, noting that there were situations where data sharing is necessary and acceptable, provided that this is done ethically, and that the individual perceives some benefit from the activity, such as not having to provide the same information to a number of different agencies.

6.4.3.2   Japanese Responses to the Scenarios

Japanese responses were much more specific to each of the scenarios, inasmuch as individuals were in private conversation with the researcher. However, responses were often very mixed. Scenario 1, for example, which outlined circumstances in which a letter from an agency that contained personal financial information was sent to another person in error,[3] raised concern in most participants. Nearly half the respondents stated that they would be angry and upset, and although most agreed to accept an apology from the agency, half of these again stated that they would seek an explanation, and changes in procedure. For at least one third of respondents such an incident would reduce their trust in government, although some noted that their trust was already so low that the incident would have little impact. A number of respondents confirmed that this sort of mistake was not uncommon; by and large it was put down to incompetence.

Scenario 2, which outlined an incident where papers containing information about a neighbor's dispute over tax were left lying around and were seen by the participant, caused considerable distress, many people stating that this was out of concern for their neighbor. A number stated that they would attempt to put the information "out of their mind," "draw down the veil," not wanting to know negative things about others. Over half indicated that this kind of breach would lower their trust in government, although some saw the incident as one of process not personal failure, or laxness. For a minority, this incident was less upsetting because their own privacy was not breached.

Breaches of health information, as in Scenario 3, were almost unanimously regarded as both serious and commonplace. Teaching hospitals, especially, were considered to be lax in regard to privacy. Both in this case, and in the case of the theft of data from Inland Revenue (Scenario 4), which had serious impacts on trust, many respondents thought systems should be better designed to protect the privacy of individuals. However, there was a strong view in all these cases, that the quality of staff employed by government agencies had deteriorated in recent years and that "morals" and attitudes were declining. Many people expressed the view that systems could and should be made more robust to prevent such incidents, and counter this lack of standards amongst government servants.

Scenario 5 was the only one that differed from the scenarios used in the New Zealand study, and referred to the introduction in 2002 of the online database for registering residents, Juki Net. Ten respondents stated that they had a Juki card (although five of these had either lost it, did not use it, or did not know how they could use it). Nineteen (55%) did not have a card and were mostly strongly opposed to having one; a further five respondents had mixed feelings about it, but did not state whether they had one. Of those without a card, some stated that although their initial concerns about the system had abated they still had not felt motivated to get one, even though they could see that for people without other forms of photo ID it could be useful and convenient. Others were adamant that the system was flawed, that their privacy was at risk, and that they were opposed to the system. More knowledgeable respondents were able to point to weaknesses in the network, and problems related to staff access. The active user group (numbering seven, one a more recent convert who had initially been opposed) were very positive about its convenience and did not have concerns about privacy in relation to the card, although they were aware that many people did.

How personal privacy is protected in Japan was certainly not well understood by most participants. Exactly half of the respondents indicated that they knew of some law or regulation that protected privacy, but few could name the recently implemented Personal Information Protection Act, although some were aware that this act worked in conjunction with the Constitution to ensure privacy in relation to government-held information, and that private and commercial companies needed to take responsibility for their own measures to ensure the protection of personal information. In the view of some, maintaining privacy was a personal responsibility, possibly leading to the high rates of withholding personal information requested by government.

When asked if they felt that attitudes to privacy had changed in Japan in recent years, most agreed there was greater concern, prompted by three factors, breaches of privacy by government agencies or individuals reported in the media, the public discussion that took place at the time the Personal Information Protection Act was passed, and concerns about the security of credit card information in the media. Although older respondents were inclined to the view that young people were less concerned about privacy, there were some very concerned respondents in the younger age groups, many of whom had personal experience of privacy violations. A number of older respondents (50 years of age and over) spoke of traditional Japanese society, in both rural and urban areas (including the suburbs of Tokyo prior to and immediately after World War II) that was more community minded, and in which neighbors knew of and took an interest in each other's business. Along with the developing concepts of individuality and privacy in Japan, they perceived a loss of the sense of community and mutual caring which characterized traditional Japanese society, while recognizing the intrusions on personal privacy of the communities of the past. In such an environment, people were expected to exercise personal restraint, ("hear no evil, see no evil, speak no evil"), a concept echoed by those who referred in some way to "drawing down the veil" if they heard something untoward about a neighbor. This may also relate to the need to take personal responsibility for one's own privacy.

6.5   Discussion

Reviewing the data derived from both the more formal questions, as well as the free-ranging discussion prompted by the scenarios, it is clear that among both New Zealand and Japanese participants there is a range of views. In both countries there are some people who are less concerned with privacy, and less upset by breaches of privacy. This may be a matter of personality, and a factor of an individual's "propensity to trust" that can cut across cultural dimensions. [DIN05]

However, although New Zealanders in general display a higher level of trust in government according to the data reported here, in both countries the majority of respondents express considerable concern about how government collects and handles their information. This concern is exacerbated among Maori and Pacific people because of the greater emotional, cultural, and spiritual significance given to personal information within Polynesian cultures, and the strongly collectivist nature of Polynesian society. This is in line with observations in earlier studies that people from Polynesian cultures express strong concerns about the secondary use of information, feeling they are losing control of an innate part of their family heritage [CUL08b]. At the same time, Japanese respondents express considerable mistrust in the way in which more powerful entities handle their information, while displaying a greater tolerance for intrusion on their personal privacy. The data reported here therefore appear to support Belman's claims, that people from cultures high in power distance and high in collectivism will have concerns about inaccurate information held about them and the secondary use of information [BEL04]. It also supports Milberg's claims that the same groups although having mistrust of powerful groups (whether corporate or government) will have a greater tolerance of intrusion on the private life of the individual [MIL00]. Thus, the origins of the concerns expressed in the responses reported in these studies seem to be derived from deeply felt cultural beliefs. In the case of some Japanese and Maori and Polynesian respondents these beliefs exacerbate the general concerns expressed by the majority of respondents about the way government agencies handle their personal information.

In addition, the concerns of Japanese respondents are reinforced by the strong belief among many that problems concerning information privacy in Japan lie more with individual government employees and their attitudes than with the system. This may be the reason why Japanese respondents were less inclined to actively protect themselves by checking privacy statements on government websites, or by refusing to provide information to the government. The noticeably low levels of trust in the government's ability to adequately protect their information, as shown in questionnaire responses of the majority of Japanese respondents, are reinforced by comments made in their reflective responses to the scenarios, which attributed many privacy breaches to poor attitudes of staff and declining moral standards. New Zealand respondents, by contrast, assume incompetence more at the systemic than the individual level; government servants as individuals are relatively well trusted. Both groups, although for slightly different reasons, believe systemic change is warranted to offer greater protections of personal data.

In the case of New Zealand citizens, there is, in fact, more than adequate legal protection for personal information held by government agencies, and it could be argued that in Japan there is at least a modest level of protection. Although in neither country was there much awareness of the specific details of these protections, the changes sought appeared to be more at the level of practice, than policy. This possibly influences several areas of response. The preference in both countries for exchange of information in person, and the overwhelming lack of enthusiasm for exchange of information through the Internet, the fact that a breach of privacy in one agency is likely to lead to lack of trust in that specific agency in future, but not necessarily across all agencies, suggest that participants are observing instances of poor practice, and want to see a change to better practice across government. The awareness shown by New Zealand respondents of the citizen's lack of power in relation to the state, reinforces the observation of Dempsey et al., that the state has special privacy obligations [DEM03, p. 1] for this reason, and a greater responsibility to observe good practice. In both countries, citizens show an awareness of the tradeoff necessary between personal privacy, and the needs of the state, however, individuals differ in where they perceive that tradeoff to lie, and where the state has overstepped the boundary. In an age where more and more information is being acquired and stored by governments these boundaries need to be clearly and publicly defined.

6.6 Conclusions

Trust in the state is a precious commodity, critical to effective government [COU05]. Breaches of privacy threaten that trust as much as other factors. This comparative study, despite the small numbers participating, reveals some genuine concerns of citizens regarding the privacy of their personal information, and some meaningful differences in attitudes towards information privacy and trust in government in two very different countries. Although some of the distrust expressed by Japanese participants in this study clearly originated as much in overall distrust of government as in breaches of privacy, the way in which personal information is managed by government agencies, and their responsiveness to citizen's concerns can play a very positive role in maintaining trust. The high levels of concern expressed by both New Zealand and Japanese participants in this study demonstrate a clear need for a change in the culture and privacy practices of government agencies in both countries, at the local and national level. In countries such as New Zealand where there are many cultures living side by side, immigrant populations alongside indigenous and long-established European settler populations, these differences become an important factor for government agencies to be aware of when they are considering privacy policies and dealing with citizens concerns.

In both countries, respondents blamed incompetence on the part of government, and in the case of Japan, declining standards, for breaches of privacy, however, in both countries participants were looking for remedies across government, focusing on the development of more robust systems for protecting privacy, and sensitivity to their concerns. These are issues that governments should be aware of and should be seeking to address: through the development of robust and culturally appropriate privacy legislation, through the education of citizens to ensure they are aware of and alert to their protections under such law, and, most important, that civil servants are also educated in their responsibilities, as agents of the state, in regard to information privacy when dealing with citizens' personal information.

Notes

[1] See the Privacy Commissioner's website at: http://www.privacy.org.nz/a-thumbnail-sketch-of-the-privacy-principles/.

[2] *Japan Times Online*, March 18, 2008. http://search.japantimes.co.jp/cgi-bin/ed20080318a2.html.

[3] This is one of the most common breaches of privacy in Japan. Much mail delivery from government agencies is outsourced. Source: Personal communication to the author by Japanese privacy researcher, Fumio Shimpo, University of Tsukuba, 21 February, 2007.

References

BAR02   Barnes C., Gill D. "Declining government performance? Why citizens don't trust government," Working paper, New Zealand State Services Commission. 2002. Retrieved 15 April 2009, from http://www.ssc.govt.nz/display/document.asp?docid=4549

BEL04   Bellman S., et al. "International differences in information privacy concerns: a global survey of consumers," The Information Society, 20, 2004, p. 313–324.

BEL08   Bell. A., et al. *World Internet project: New Zealand. International comparison 2008. Highlights from a New Zealand perspective.* Wellington, National Library of New Zealand, 2008.

COU05   Council for Excellence in Government. "A matter of trust: Americans and their government 1958–2004," Washington, 2005. Retrieved 15 April 2009, from http://www.excelgov.org/usermedia/images/uploads/PDFs/AMOT.pdf.

CUL07   Cullen R., Reilly P. "Information privacy and trust in government: a citizen-based perspective from New Zealand", Proceedings 40th Hawaii international conference on system sciences (HICSS 40), Waikaloa, Hawaii, January 2007.

CUL08a   Cullen R. "Citizens' concerns about the privacy of personal information held by government: a comparative study, Japan and New Zealand", Proceedings 41st Hawaii international conference on system sciences (HICSS 41), Waikaloa, Hawaii, January 2008.

CUL08b   Cullen R., Reilly P. "Information privacy and trust in government," Journal of IT and Politics, 4(3), 2008, p. 61–80.

DEM03   Dempsey, J.X., Anderson, P., and A. Schwartz. *"Privacy and E-Government: A report to the United Nations Department of Economic and Social Affairs as background for the World Public Sector Report: E-Government"*, Center for Democracy and Technology, Washington D.C., USA, 2003, from http://www.internetpolicy.net/privacy/20030523cdt.pdf, retrieved July 7th, 2009.

DIN05   Dinev T., et al. "Internet users' privacy concerns and attitudes towards government surveillance – an exploratory study of cross-cultural differences between Italy and the United States." 18th Bled eConference: eIntegration in Action. Bled, Slovenia, 2005.

FRE05   Freshfields, Bruckhaus, Derringer. Personal Information Protection Law, Japan. June
         2005. Retrieved 13 June 2007, from http://www.freshfields.com/places/ japan/publica-
         tions/pdfs/11704.pdf.
GO03   GO2003. Government Online, a national perspective 2003 – New Zealand, Taylor
         Nelson Sofres. Retrieved 19 May 2006, from http://www.e.govt.nz/plone/archive/
         about-egovt/programme/go-survey.html
GOO99   Goodwin R. "*Personal relationships across cultures*", New York, Routledge, 2009.
HER06   Hernon, P and R. Cullen. *Citizen's response to E-Government*, In Hernon, Peter
         Rowena Cullen, and Harold C. Relyea (eds). Comparative perspectives on E-Government:
         Serving Today and Building for Tomorrow. Lanham, MD; Scarecrow Press, 2006.
HOF91   Hofstede G. "*Cultures and organizations: software of the mind*," New York, McGraw-
         Hill, 1991.
INT07   Internet World Stats. Japan. Retrieved 12 June 2007, from http://www.internetworldstats.
         com/asia/jp.htm.
JAP03   Japan. Personal Information Protection Act 2003. Retrieved 12 June 2007, from http://
         www5.cao.go.jp/seikatsu/kojin/foreign/act.pdf.
KIT05   Kitiyadisai K. "Privacy rights and protection: foreign values in modern Thai context",
         Ethics and Information Technology, 7, 2005, p. 17–26.
LAW07   Lawlor J, Walumbwa F, Bai B, "National culture and cultural effects," In Harris M.
         (ed.), *Handbook of research in international human resource management*, Mahwah,
         NJ, Lawrence Erlbaum, 2007.
MIL00   Milberg S.J., Smith H.J., Burke S. "Information privacy: corporate management and
         national regulation," Organization Science, 11(1), 2000, p. 35–57.
MIZ04   Mizutani M., Dorsey J., Moor J. "The internet and Japanese conception of privacy,"
         Ethics and Information Technology, 6, 2004, p.121–128.
RAA98   Raab C., Bennett C. "The distribution of privacy risks: who needs protection?," The
         Information Society, 1998, 14, p. 263–274.
TAN01   Tanaka A. "Does social capital generate system support in Japan?" Paper presented at
         the annual meeting of the American Political Science Association, San Francisco,
         2001.
UNI48   United Nations. Universal Declaration of Human Rights. Geneva, Department of Public
         Information, 1948. Retrieved 14 April 2009, from http://www.un.org/Overview/rights.
         html
UNI66   United Nations. International Covenant on Civil and Political Rights. Geneva, Office of
         the High Commissioner for Human Rights, 1966. Retrieved 14 April 2009, from http://
         www.unhchr.ch/html/menu3/b/a_ccpr.htm
WES67   Westin A. *Privacy and freedom*, New York, Atheneum, 1967, p. 7.

Chapter 7
Strategic Issues Relating to Data Quality for E-Government: Learning from an Approach Adopted in Belgium

Isabelle Boydens

Abstract Data quality is a strategic matter in the context of e-government as the integration of services requires authentic, coherent, and reliable data. However, establishing databases that are devoid of duplication, redundancy, or ambiguity isn't simple either in theory or in practice. In the context of e-government, this problem has been neglected for too long, particularly because administrative databases have often been wrongly regarded as "simple." We demonstrate in this chapter that this is not the case at all, in particular because of the questions of interpretation that they raise. This chapter is based on case studies stemming from the Belgian federal administration (social security, business directories, federal authentic sources, etc.). Contrary to the assertions of common theories postulating a permanent bijective relationship between data and the corresponding reality, we argue that an empirical information system evolves over time along with the interpretation of the values that it allows one to determine. To address data quality, we propose a temporal framework that provides new operational strategies to improve administrative data quality (mainly, new ways to define quality indicators for continuous monitoring and re-engineering strategies). We finally demonstrate how our approach is generally applicable in the context of empirical information systems.

7.1 Introduction

The dematerialization of information and the placing online, via the Internet, of transverse services for citizens, based on electronic government, make the question of data quality more crucial than ever. We present firstly a general outline of the "data quality" concept and its practical challenges (Sect. 7.1.1) and, secondly, offer an introduction to the strategic data quality issues for e-government (Sect. 7.1.2).

I. Boydens (✉)
Département Sciences de l'Information et de la Communication – CP 123,
Université Libre de Bruxelles, Faculté de Philosophie et Lettres,
CP 123 Avenue F.D. Roosevelt, 50, B-1050, Bruxelles, Belgium
e-mail: iboydens@ulb.ac.be

S. Assar et al. (eds.), *Practical Studies in E-Government: Best Practices from Around the World*, DOI 10.1007/978-1-4419-7533-1_7,
© Springer Science+Business Media, LLC 2011

7.1.1 The Quality of Data

The quality of data is today considered as a strategic matter [BAT06]. The question is of significant importance when the information is used as a tool to assist with decision making, or even with real-world action. For example, in May 1999, during the war in Kosovo, NATO mistakenly bombed the Chinese embassy in Belgrade: the mapping databases then used to guide the missiles contained a plan of the city that was obsolete and therefore inadequate, hence, the untimely attack and the diplomatic incident which followed [BOY07].

The quality of a data element denotes its adequacy with respect to the objectives assigned to it. "Total quality" does not exist, because the concept is relative: on the basis of a cost–benefit type analysis, the most pertinent quality criteria (freshness of information, rapidity of data transmission, relevancy, etc.) must be adopted for a given context (*fitness for use*) [BOY11].

These questions are of increasing concern in the private sector [MAD09]. Several surveys carried out in the United States indicate that factors such as the multiplication of partially redundant heterogeneous sources and of incomplete or poorly documented data could entail a cost of up to 15% of businesses' revenue [RED01]. Added to this are the costs incurred for the implementation of new technologies [FRI07] as well as the consequences in terms of credibility in the eyes of clients or users.

7.1.2 Strategic Quality Issues for E-Government

Although the problem is just as significant in the context of electronic government, it has been neglected for too long, particularly because administrative databases have often been wrongly regarded as "simple" information systems. We show in this chapter that this is not the case at all. The management of such systems is complex, not only because of the questions of interpretation that they raise, but also because administrative information gives rise to rights and duties. The quality of the corresponding online services is therefore of considerable importance in social and financial terms. For example, every quarter, the Belgian social security databases store approximately four million records, with several hundred corresponding attributes. These databases allow the collection and redistribution of some 40 billion euros each year. Every quarter, hundreds of thousands of formal anomalies are detected (one finds similar proportions in other countries and other sectors, such as the banking sector: "Recent works about the quality of large databases have shown that about 10% of XML documents (or data records) contain at least one error. This level of quality is unacceptable for many applications" [VAN03]).

On the basis of our research work in the area of administrative database quality [BOY99, BOY11] and of our practical experience in consultancy [BOY07], we propose to examine these questions in greater depth. In Belgium, we are head of a "Data Quality Competency Center" for evaluating and improving the quality of databases deployed in electronic government, which has been created at Smals.[1]

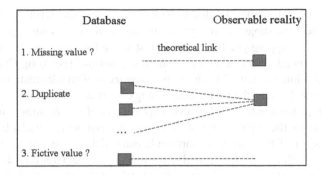

Fig. 7.1 Typology of formal data quality problems

This Data Quality Competency Center covers various domains (social security, business directories, federal authentic sources, etc.) and aims, by improving data quality, to strengthen the responsiveness of the administrations in the context of online services provided to citizens. We then demonstrate the generalisable character of this in the context of electronic government globally.

The integration of services requires that authentic, coherent, and reliable sources be put in place. For instance, in order to allow a company to fulfill its tax and social security obligations, or indeed to notify any events (e.g., change of address), via a set of integrated services on the Internet, there must be a back-office body of homogeneous databases relating to the target population (companies, in our example). These databases must be pertinent, accurate, up to date, and documented, because they are liable to be used transversely by various departments according to their respective needs. As we show, establishing files that are devoid of duplication, redundancy, or ambiguity is not a simple matter in practice. Two types of cases may arise: formal data quality problems and formal data interpretation problems.

Formal data quality problems (Fig. 7.1) may include the following situations.

1. *Missing values*: for instance, due to a lack of reactivity, a new company created in the "observable reality" is not yet registered in a database.
2. *Duplicate*: due to a lack of organization and harmonization, an international company created in the "observable reality" is registered twice because, for instance, two social security institutions in various countries use different metadata types and formal identifications to categorize a same item.
3. *Fictive value*: a company that stopped its activities (because it is bankrupt, for instance) did not inform the institution in charge of the database management.

Data quality interpretation problems are due to the fact that administrative databases are empirical information systems subject to human experience. Administrative databases, by their nature, raise particularly complex questions of interpretation that we tackle in this chapter. For example, the notion of "principal activity" of a company, which is fundamental information in businesses registers, is a mutable factor whose reliability is difficult to evaluate (for instance, in the woodwork sector, the difference between manufacture and installation, as "principal economic activity," may be very subtle and evolutive). These problems are also encountered on a daily basis by labor inspectors doing fieldwork: "In almost 30 years of doing this job [...], I have seen many points become subject to interpretation, and therefore to challenge. It's a little like a policeman stopping you for going too fast and telling you that you're driving at a "dangerous" speed. You could easily contest this notion" [BAR06]. Consequently, there is no "absolute reference" to check the correctness of an administrative database (nor, as we show later, of the correctness of any empirical database).

Moreover, in the context of a shared exploitation of information gathered in a single flow, as in the architecture of electronic government, a tradeoff may arise among the needs of the various departments using that single source. We see this phenomenon in the case of the multifunction online declarations developed in Belgium in the field of Social Security. For legal reasons associated with the payment of fixed-date welfare benefits, some user bodies need to have the information very quickly, in spite of any anomalies by which it may be tainted. Conversely, other social security institutions prefer all formal anomalies to be dealt with before the data are distributed. There is therefore a problematic tradeoff between the speed of distribution of administrative information and its relative reliability, with the quality criteria varying according to the respective uses.

However, if the deployment of electronic government raises new challenges regarding the quality of information, it also offers fresh prospects for improving the quality of data. Thus, it is now possible to provide citizens with online simulation environments in order to facilitate the declaration of social security contributions, for example, and to strengthen the partnerships between public and private sectors. Furthermore, it is essential to document the services offered and the corresponding digital resources. Meta-information systems for documenting administrative regulations through their successive versions, but also for generating the corresponding XML schemas (with regard to social security legislation, in particular), can now be made available to all.

The remainder of this chapter is structured as follows: after this introduction, we describe the characteristics of the data exploited in the field of electronic government (Sect. 7.2) on the basis of various operational definitions. It is then possible to specify the most appropriate quality indicators for the objectives pursued (Sect. 7.3). We then consider methodological recommendations for evaluating and improving the quality of the corresponding databases, including the new prospects now offered by electronic government (Sect. 7.4). By way of conclusion (Sect. 7.5), we present future work and widen the question to include other empirical information systems.

7.2   Characteristics of Administrative Data

Electronic government services rely essentially on data directories. For instance, the governmental business databases mentioned in the introduction may be exploited for a variety of purposes by different institutions. In Belgium, the directory of business companies can be used by various authorities, such as social security institutions or the agency responsible for monitoring the food chain. This agency needs the addresses of the production units of food sector companies in order to carry out its functions (food safety supervision). It is thus important for the various data (relating to the businesses and their production units) to be interpreted in the same way by each institution and handled in a homogeneous and reliable manner. For this reason, we consider in greater depth the characteristics and the nature of administrative data.

Administrative databases exhibit a number of distinctive characteristics: frequency and nature of legislative changes, compliance with probative force, volume of data and of formal anomalies to be handled, and finally, the social and financial stakes.

The structure of administrative databases evolves according to changes in the corresponding legal directives. In the domain of Belgian social security, for example, legislative changes, entailing an equivalent number of schema versions, must be implemented every 3 months. The question becomes more complex when these changes are retroactive: even if contested, retroactive changes occur frequently in administrative life in various European countries. Furthermore, the successive versions must be jointly maintained at least for the period of prescription, which specifies the time for which the administrative files must legally be taken into account. In the case of Belgian social security, this period varies from 5 to 30 years depending on the sector concerned.

Moreover, most of the original administrative information entered into the databases has a probative force status: in other words, it serves as court evidence in the event of any dispute. This is true, for example, of the quarterly declarations submitted by employers to prove payment of their employees' social security contributions. Consequently, the original information, even if tainted by formal anomalies, must be conserved. Similarly, the history of its processing must also be retained for several schema versions (these anomalies may be corrected or validated following inspections on the ground or after the interpretation of legislation). Ultimately, no error tolerance is theoretically permitted within databases. Citizens legitimately expect their administrative affairs to be handled equitably, whether with regard to taxes to be paid or welfare benefits to be received.[2]

Finally, administrative databases are generally extremely voluminous. Potentially, they may house the files of an entire state's population. Considerable social and financial stakes are involved in their management, as already mentioned in the introduction of this chapter.

7.3 Quality Indicators

Any process aimed at improving the quality of information involves the prior specification of indicators. These will then make it possible to evaluate the progress made with respect to the objectives pursued. In order to identify the most appropriate indicators, it is first necessary to examine the nature of the handled concepts.

To this end, we consider in succession the following three questions (in the light of the administrative information characteristics, as cited in the previous point): what is a data element (Sect. 7.3.1), what is a "correct" data element (Sect. 7.3.2), and how is the information progressively constructed (Sect. 7.3.3).

7.3.1   What Is a Data Element?

A data element is a set of three components (i, d, v): an identifier (i), referring to a concept (e.g., a category of activity); a domain of definition (d), comprising a set of formal assertions specifying all the values admissible in the database for this concept (e.g., a controlled list of alphabetical values), and finally, a value (v) at a time t (e.g., the chemicals sector). In addition, there are also interactions among the different components of the database schema, which we do not consider here.

It is important to distinguish *deterministic data* from *empirical data*. The first are characterized by the fact that there is, at any moment, a theory which makes it possible to decide whether a value (v) is correct. This is the case with algebraic data: inasmuch as the rules of algebra do not change over time, we can know at any time whether the result of a sum is correct. But for empirical data, which are subject to human experience, theory changes over time along with the interpretation of the values that it has made possible to determine. This is true, for example, in the medical domain, where theory evolves with the accumulation of experience, as witnessed, for instance, in the current research into influenza A(H1N1)) and the economic domain (e.g., with regard to the calculation of national wealth), but also in the legal and administrative realms, where the interpretation of legal concepts changes with the constant evolution of real-world circumstances and jurisprudence. For example, when "copy centers" first began to appear, (i.e., shops offering photocopying services to their customers), the nomenclature for European business activities (used in administrative databases to categorize companies) was quickly found to be inadequate for their classification: the best it could offer were the categories of "printing," "book retailing," or "secretarial services." To take the category "copy centers" into account, it was first necessary to amend the regulatory texts, and then to adapt the structure of the administrative databases accordingly. Problems related to empirical data quality remain crucial in the context of electronic.

7.3.2   What Is a "Correct" Data Element?

For obvious operational reasons, the functioning of a database is predicated on the *closed world assumption*, according to which any value not included in the domain of definition (d) is regarded as false. However, in the case of empirical data, if we step outside this formal framework, it may happen that between the moment at which the structure of the database was formalized and the moment at which the information was entered, new characteristics have appeared within the domain in question (contrary to the assertions of some theories postulating a permanent bijective relationship between data and the corresponding empirical reality [WAN96]). In this case, it is impossible to verify the correction of the database values automatically. Consequently, when an inconsistency appears between a value entered in the database and the reference tables which allow the validity of that value to be tested, it may become essential, depending on what is at stake, to carry out a manual verification, for example, by contacting the citizen or company concerned.

There is therefore no "absolute" formal reference for testing the correction of a huge empirical database. Let us take an example. We know that social legislation differs according to whether it is applied to manual or clerical staff, with these two groups being distinguished in the law according to the preponderant nature of their manual or intellectual activities. In practice, this distinction is not easy to apply, but no fuzziness is tolerated in a database: everything must be clear-cut. In order to arrive at a clear-cut answer, it will often be necessary to be doing fieldwork to interpret de facto situations and examine supporting documentation. As new interpretations are made and jurisprudence evolves, the meaning of the notions of "clerical" or "manual" staff will evolve over time.

We can conclude from this discussion that data are not a given: they are progressively constructed. It is all the more essential for these conclusions to be taken into account when several institutions are involved. Thus, as mentioned in the introduction, in Belgium, electronic government projects have given rise to the adoption of a multifunction declaration (one information flow can be used for multiple administrative institutions) in the social security sector, so that the citizen now has to enter his or her information online only once, this information then being exploited by the various social security sectors. Consequently, the question of conceptual interpretation also takes on a multifunctional dimension. As we saw in the introduction, this question may give rise to tradeoffs according to the needs of the institutions, particularly between the relative quality of the information and the speed of its distribution.

7.3.3 How Are Data Progressively Constructed?

Braudel's temporal framework (*"temporalités étagées"* [BRA76]) can be applied in the database field. Three levels of transformation are interacting within the information system: the evolution of jurisprudence, the changes made within databases, and the categories observable in the field. These three levels of reality are interlinked, interlinked, but asynchronous [BOY04]. They operate, according to their nature, on different timescales. Thus we have the long-term for legal rules, renewed from one quarter or one year to the next, the medium-term for the management of databases, and the short-term for the observable reality, that is, that of the citizens or companies subject to administration, which is continuously evolving. Companies regularly merge, split, or disappear altogether, and new professions or categories of activity not covered in the official nomenclature are constantly being born, as with the diversification of IT jobs, for example. From a dynamic point of view, an ideal database should therefore match the rhythm of its updates to the (unforeseeable) division into "layered timescales" of the changes in the reality that it seeks to grasp. To what looks like a gamble we must add the necessity, always revealed a posteriori, to integrate unforeseen observations, prohibited a priori by the closed world assumption.

Let us take an example in the domain of employment creation initiatives (Fig. 7.2). Following the directives issued by the European Council in Brussels in December 1993, on the basis of Jacques Delors' white paper on growth,

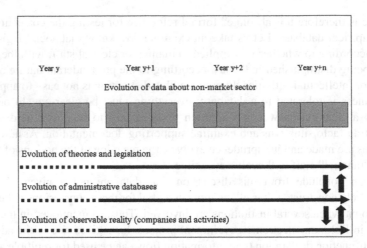

Fig. 7.2 Transformation mechanisms to interpret administrative data

competitiveness and employment, multiple job creation initiatives have been taken in most European countries with the aim to fight unemployment. Among this legislation, reductions in social charges have resulted in lowering the social security contributions payable by employers, in order to enable them to take on additional employees. In many countries of the European Union, these initiatives have produced a flood of legislative directives and adjustments which complicate not only their implementation but also the evaluation of their effectiveness.[3] The problem is ever-present: owing to the proliferation of legal texts in France, in March 2006 the Council of State proposed drafting a law to reduce their number: "[...] to the 9000 laws and 120,000 decrees on the books in 2000, an average of 70 laws, 50 orders and 15,000 decrees have been added every year [...]" [DEM06].

In the case of Belgium, during the implementation of a governmental directive aimed at the "nonmarket" sector, the question arose with regard to the reality that is progressively reflected in the database, of whether this "nonmarket" sector should include private nursing homes, which were a priori excluded because they operate for profit. Initially regarded as "erroneous" cases with respect to the domain of definition for the "nonmarket sector," these businesses were eventually included after legal interpretation. This led to a restructuring of the database schema. This restructuring was the result of a human decision aimed at bringing the model temporarily into line with the new observations. This phenomenon of transformation corresponds to the so-called "strange loop" mechanism defined by Hofstadter [HOF80]. In the absence of such an intervention, the gap between the database and the reality widens. We show later (Sect. 7.4) the operational extensions of these mechanisms when it comes to evaluating and improving the quality of administrative data.

What are the consequences of this analysis with regard to specifying appropriate quality indicators for administrative information? Because administrative data are empirical in nature, there is no direct frame of reference for testing their correction. Their appropriateness to the needs can be determined only indirectly, via a series of lateral indicators. Firstly, it is necessary to consider the relative relevance of the information with respect to the objectives pursued: relevance is a nonquantifiable indicator whose operational scope is examined in Sect. 7.4.1. ("Master Data Management"). Next, a series of quantifiable indicators relating to the detected anomalies and their handling may be produced with a view to deploying management strategies for the database (Sect. 7.4.2). Finally, in all cases, there must be a tool for the critical interpretation of the data: we present a meta-information system implemented to document the online services of the Belgian social security authorities (Sect. 7.4.3).

7.4   Methods for Improving the Quality of Administrative Databases

The methods presented below for improving the quality of information should ideally be applied during the design of a database, because questions of quality arise at the very outset. They should also be accompanied by continuous monitoring, carried out by a committee designed for this purpose, with a prohibition of hasty ad hoc actions [BLO05].

1. *Master Data Management* is a general methodology to analyze and improve the quality of the concepts and flows judged to be the most fundamental within the information system.
2. *Anomalies and Management Strategies* are an original operational approach that we applied in the scope of our research about interpretation of the Belgian social security database.
3. *Documentation of Application and Services* aims to present an electronic data dictionary (*glossaires de la sécurité sociale*) that was implemented in Belgium to improve interpretation of e-government databases by the Belgian Data Quality Competency Center presented in the introduction.

We do not consider the data cleansing technique here, which involves automatically smoothing the content of a database a posteriori by eliminating (using a set of formal correction algorithms) the values considered to be aberrant, for example. This technique has its place in the statistical domain, where an error tolerance is permissible. It is, however, not valid in the administrative domain, where each individual case must be considered [OLS03]. We must also mention that data cleansing does not act on the causes of the "no-quality." As suggested by Thomas Redman [RED01], an information system can be compared to a river: the algorithms of data cleansing clean up the river bed in an ad hoc manner, but they do not act on the procedures situated upstream. However, it should be noticed that these types of algorithms are useful operational techniques that facilitate the implementation of the three methods of data interpretation

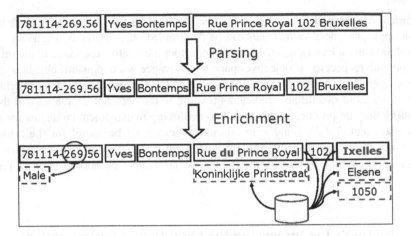

Fig. 7.3 Data standardization: illustration of data parsing and enrichment

improvement presented in the rest of this chapter (for instance, as illustrated in Fig. 7.3, to parse and automatically enrich multilingual data).

7.4.1 Master Data Management

On the basis of the core business and main needs of the application domain concerned, "Master Data Management" [LOS09] aims to analyze and improve the quality of the concepts and flows judged to be the most fundamental within the information system.

For instance, in the intersectorial relationships involved in electronic government, the question of the identification of citizens is crucial for reasons of security and confidentiality, but also for operational reasons. It is essential that a given citizen or a given company is correctly identified by the various services accessible online.

In the first instance, it will be necessary to check whether the unique identifier used corresponds to the intended target of the application domain [VOL06]. Service to the citizen must take precedence over internal organization: the identifier must therefore not include any "content" information. In the case of a bank, for example, a customer must be identified by a randomly generated number and not by his or her account number, inasmuch as this may change and generate double entries if it is used as the primary key.

This question has special implications in the administrative domain. Even if the above rule of Master management has been observed, problems may arise in relation to the unique identifier, because the flows that allow the creation of a company in a directory, for example, have been imperfectly defined. This may entail double entries or a phenomenon of "undercoverage" (absence of pertinent elements). Thus we sometimes see, in the architecture of an information system, the phenomenon of the "phantom factory" or the "factory within the factory," meaning the time and energy an organization devotes (unknowingly) to producing and correcting errors. In company directories, "overcoverage" is also sometimes observed (presence of "false actives" in the database) owing to realities in the field: for example, companies which have ceased trading but omitted to inform the administration that they are no longer active.

Finally, we must note that the handling of double entries requires complex procedures: firstly, it is necessary to define what constitutes a double entry and to implement procedures for identifying the corresponding cases. There are algorithms for this purpose which make it possible to take account of a certain imprecision where certain strings of characters (relating to a name or an address, for instance) may have been entered on several separate occasions, giving rise to double entries in the database. So-called "matching" techniques [BAT06] are used to compare the records of a database with those of an authoritative competing source (or "frame of reference"), and these also make it possible to detect any inconsistencies in the identifier. Once the double entries have been detected, homogeneous rules must be defined in order to use a priority number and resolve any discrepancies between the values associated with the fields of the various records constituting cases of double entries.

Finally – and this is specific to the administrative domain – procedures must be defined for carrying the correction made over into legislation. Thus, when errors of identification concerning companies with "legal person" status have been dealt with in the database, those companies' deeds of incorporation must also be amended. In Belgium, a procedure has been enacted into legislation for handling these cases in the directory of natural persons.[4] In Germany, the problem is complicated by the need to manage heterogeneous numbering systems relating to different sectors of the administration.

7.4.2 Anomalies and Management Strategies

Quantitative monitoring of anomalies and their handling allows the deployment of original strategies for database interpretation and management, with measurable cost–benefit results. The strategies we present here are based on analysis presented in Sect. 7.3 ("Quality Indicators") and have been implemented in Belgium by the "Data Quality Competency Center" of Smals.

There are several essential prerequisites for supporting this approach. A system for detecting anomalies at the time of entry, but also ex post, must be put in place (owing to the potential interactions between data elements, formal anomalies may arise subsequently after the correction of other anomalies). Clear procedures for their handling must be established, particularly when the database forms part of a federalized environment and several institutions are each responsible for a subset of the information. It must be clearly defined which authority handles which part of the database and what the authorized handling procedures are. This is often a tricky matter in practice, because it falls under the political responsibility of each institution concerned. The database must be structured in such a manner that traceability is guaranteed (i.e., the history of data handling operations is stored and can be queried). Finally, a clear procedure for the production of indicators at a given frequency must be defined.

On the basis of the analysis proposed in Sect. 7.3, we present an example of the operational exploitation of the presented quality indicators. Statistical monitoring of integrity constraint violations ("formal anomalies") makes it possible to detect not only "abnormal" increases in anomalies (with respect to a given threshold), but also increases in "validations" of anomalies during the handling phase. A validation operation means that, after examination, an operator has judged that the anomaly, which is a presumption of error, corresponds to a relevant value. The operator can "force" the system to accept the value. If the rate of these anomaly validations is high and recurring, there is a high probability that the structure of the database itself is no longer relevant. An algorithm then issues a "signal" to the database manager so that she can examine whether a structural modification of its schema is required. When there are large numbers of validations, it is worthwhile to examine the phenomenon closely: as we have seen (Sect. 7.3), a new circumstance (e.g., the emergence of a new category of activity or a change in the interpretation of a concept, such as the nonmarket sector as cited above) may have arisen, which requires a modification of the database structure. If the schema is not modified accordingly, the anomalies corresponding to these cases will continue to appear in large numbers, demanding a potentially large-scale manual examination and considerably slowing down the administrative file handling.

For the Belgian social security system, the implementation of this method has made it possible to improve the precision and speed of social security contribution handling, reducing by up to 50% the volume of formal anomalies, which had previously accounted for 100,000 to 300,000 occurrences to be managed manually every quarter [BOY99]. Other types of indicators for identifying, quantifying, and categorizing anomalies and the nature of their handling are essential for the implementation of efficient electronic government services. For example, it is possible to evaluate the speed of anomaly handling in order to determine the timeliest moment for the database exploitation. This type of method is all the more useful when data are collected at a single point and then exploited in a federalized manner by different departments, as with the procedures offered by electronic government [BOY11].

7.4.3 Documentation of Applications and Services

Because the legislation is complex and constantly evolving, an "electronic data dictionary" is regarded as highly necessary in order to facilitate the administrative information interpretation. To this end, in the framework of the services involved in electronic government, a collaborative multilingual meta-information system was designed within the Belgian social security department. This was deployed in a Web environment in order to document the XML messages exchanged between the citizens and the administration. This meta-information system was put into operation in 2001, and has been enhanced since then.[5] This Web-based application is aimed both at the IT personnel responsible for the management of the databases and at the authorities responsible for sending electronic messages, the goal being for all parties to work on a common basis.

We would note that meta-information systems are potentially prone to three pitfalls:

- The first is associated with the fact that these systems are infinitely expandable, particularly when the fields to be completed are "free," because the natural language is its own metalanguage. This involves significant management costs when there are numerous manual updates to be made.
- The second snag is that the metadata may themselves be erroneous or uncertain. When the data are contextual in nature, their validation cannot be made subject to rigorous integrity constraints.
- The third snag concerns the time lag between the updating of a data element and that of the corresponding metadata, because the latter, especially when it takes a textual form, is generally created only after the completion of an analysis phase.

These characteristics may appear in every empirical application domain [VAN06]. On the basis of these observations, a system aimed at preserving the coherence of the information and facilitating its management has been implemented by the Belgian Data Quality Competency Center. The system (*"glossaires de la sécurité sociale"*) includes the following functions.

- Semi-automatic management of multilingualism (via precontrolled tables).
- Reuse of common definitions via an inheritance procedure (see Figs. 7.4 and 7.5); generic definitions such as the codification of locations, addresses, and so on are updated only once and then propagated in all the specific documentary applications where they are used.
- Version management (when technical definitions evolve over time, as shown in Fig. 7.6, the system makes it possible to monitor the various versions and specifies, for each new version, the list of changes made with respect to the immediately preceding version).
- Implementation of the concept of WOPM ("Write Once Publish Many"): the application includes structured lists (postcodes, categories of activity, etc.) which, in practice, must be distributed not only for documentary purposes but also to test the data entered into the databases. In order to accommodate these two functions, the application was designed to automatically generate a single structured table (e.g., list of postcodes) in different formats: ASCII, XML, Word, Excel, and PDF. The same source can thus be used in interdependent applications.
- Navigation system and search engine.
- Validation procedures (Fig. 7.6): owing to the legal, social, and financial stakes associated with the management of databases and their documentation, each

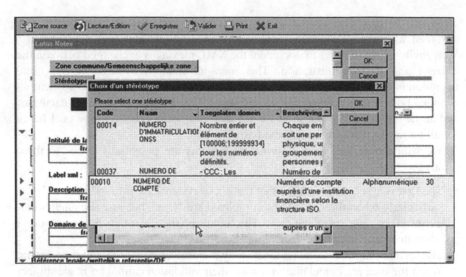

Fig. 7.4 Heritage of common definitions

Fig. 7.5 Heritage and reuse (multilingual framework)

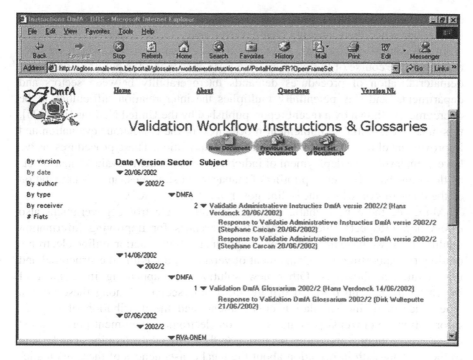

Fig. 7.6 "Glossaires de la sécurité sociale": validation procedures and version management

new version must be validated by the information manager in both technical and legal terms. In order to structure this validation process, a workflow system guides the deployment of the electronic dictionary. This system is enshrined in a procedure (a schedule rigorously specifies the timing of each update, validation, acceptance, and putting into production). The workflow is "piloted" in a centralized manner by a team dedicated to this task, and deployed in a decentralized manner in a Web environment. At the time of the creation of each new version, the history of exchanges between the various managers is conserved, so that the interpretation process can continue to be monitored.

The implementation of this kind of system facilitates management of the data that feed the online administrative services and helps to ensure their quality.

7.5   Conclusions, Future Work, and Generalization of the Approach

Examination of the quality of a database is a multidisciplinary process. It requires joint intervention both by technicians and by specialists in the concerned application domain. In this regard, the administrative concepts have certain specific characteristics, including their empirical nature: they are subject to human interpretation and their meaning changes over time.

In the context of electronic government, these characteristics, which we have detailed in the course of this chapter, pose fresh challenges: the pooling of data and dematerialization of procedures demands interoperability between sectors and departments, and this potentially multiplies the interpretation difficulties to be overcome. As shown by a recent report published by the United Nations [UNG05], this makes it essential to implement procedures for the continuous evaluation and improvement of the quality of administrative information. These procedures, as we have seen, involve the deployment of indicators for data quality evaluation, analysis of flows and basic concepts, piloting of management strategies, and documentation of the databases on which the online government services rely.

Alongside these new challenges, the takeoff of electronic government also offers new prospects, such as operational avenues for improving information quality. Thus, we have described the adoption of a multifunction online electronic dictionary, supporting the management of versions and feeding the structured and unstructured applications. Other new solutions are appearing in a spirit of increased partnership between private and public sectors. Among these are the emergence of online simulation environments and the distribution of targeted information via citizens' personal spaces on electronic government portals: a list of the most common anomalies occurring in their official declarations can be sent to them, along with information about the legal consequences of these anomalies and various courses of action for putting them right. On this basis, "process re-engineering" projects can be put in place: errors are frequently committed by certain declaring parties because of an inadequate or heterogeneous interpretation of the procedures or concepts to be handled. In collaboration with the administration, a procedure of "data tracking" allows us to examine the internal processes of the 50 Belgian companies with the highest numbers of anomalies in their social security declarations: the objective is to determine the reason (problem of data interpretation, of interface usability, of formal error, of internal or external organization, etc.) for this and remedy it at the source.

In conclusion, we would note that phenomena similar to those observed in the administrative sector are found in various empirical domains. This is true, for example, in the world of stratospheric databases: before the discovery of falling ozone levels by British researchers in the 1980s, the corresponding low values were, as a matter of course, treated as anomalies in NASA's database for more than a decade [BOY99]. The prevailing theory of the time, which was modeled in the NASA database, did not allow any entertainment of the possibility that such values might be correct. After the British discovery, NASA adapted the structure of its database, integrating the values previously regarded as "anomalies" into the set of permissible values. The management strategy described in this chapter therefore applies to all information systems whose structure evolves according to the interpretation of the realities which they aim to grasp [BOY11]. The body of propositions put forward elsewhere ("Master Data Management," Sect. 7.4.1, documentation of databases, etc.) are all the more essential when the information system is dynamic in nature. This is particularly true of administrative databases, in which the homogeneity of the formal codifications clashes with the heterogeneity of the empirical categories.

Notes

[1]ICT company supplying services to the Belgian federal administration (http://www.smals.be).
[2]Conversely, the statistical exploitation of a database may be predicated on error tolerance. Let us take a simple example: the total of all wages paid to salaried employees is used to evaluate the national wage bill, which in turn allows the calculation of statistical aggregates. If all the records used incorporate wage inversions, with the pay of an individual A incorrectly attributed to an individual B, the overall evaluation of the national wage bill will be unaffected. Such inversions are, however, extremely damaging at the level of individual administrative processings (B being paid the salary of A).
[3]As in France, where the 'stratification of measures, the short lifespan of mechanisms, the multiplication of the effects of policy announcements and the growing complexity of the field of these policies, which are still recent in terms of the history of social policy' complicate their long-term evaluation [DAN 98].
[4]Royal Decree of 8/02/91 on the composition and procedures for allocation of the identification number of natural persons not entered in the National Register of natural persons, *Belgian Official Gazette*, 19 February 1991.
[5]https://www.socialsecurity.be/lambda/portail/glossaires/dmfa.nsf/web/glossary_home_fr https://www.socialsecurity.be/lambda/portail/glossaires/dmfa.nsf/web/glossary_home_nl.

References

BAR06   Baroux R., "En première ligne sur le front du travail". *Le Monde*, 2006, p. 3.
BAT06   Batini C. and Scannapieco M., *Data quality: concepts, methodologies and techniques*, Heidelberg, Springer, 2006.
BLO05   Bloch L., *Systèmes d'information, obstacles et succès*, Paris, Vuibert, 2005.
BOY99   Boydens I., *Informatique, normes et temps*, Bruxelles, Bruylant, 1999.
BOY04   Boydens I., *La conservation numérique des données de gestion (Numéro spécial "Archivage et perennisation")*, vol°8, no. 2, Paris, Hermès Sciences, 2004, pp. 13–22.
BOY07   Boydens I., "Qualité de l'information et e-administration: enjeux et perspectives". In Assar S. and Boughazala I., (eds.), "Administration électronique: constats et perspectives," Paris, Lavoisier – Hermès Sciences, 2007, pp. 103–120 (chapter 5).
BOY11   Boydens I., Van Hooland S., "Hermeneutics applied to the quality of empirical databases". Journal of Documentation Emerald, volume 67, issue 2, 2011.
BRA76   Braudel F., *"La Méditerranée et le monde méditerranéen à l'époque de Philippe II,"* Paris, Armand Colin, 1976.
DEM06   De Montvallon J.-B. "Une Loi pour enrayer la prolifération des textes". *Le Monde*, 2006, p. 10.
FRI07   Friedman T., *Key Issues for Data Quality, 2007*. Gartner Research Note, 2007, no. G00147383.
HOF80   Hofstadter R. D., *Gödel, Escher, Bach: an eternal Golden Braid. A metaphorical fugue on minds and machines in the spirit of Lewis Carroll*, New York, Penguin Books, 1980.
LOS09   Loshin D., *Master Data Management*, Burlington, Elsevier, 2009.

MAD09 Madnick S. E., Wang R. Y., Lee Y. W., Zhu H., "Overview and Framework for Data and Information Quality Research," *ACM Journal of Data and Information Quality*, 2009, vol. 1, n 1, pp. 2–22.

OLS03 Olson J., *Data quality: the accuracy dimension*, San Francisco, Elsevier, The Morgan-Kaufmann Series in Database Management, 2003.

RED01 Redman T. C., *Data quality: the field guide*, Boston, Digital Press, 2001.

UNG05 *UN Global E-governement Readiness Report 2005. From E-governement to E-inclusion.* New York, United Nations, 2005.

VAN03 Van Der Vlist E., *Relax NG*, Cambridge, O'Reilly Media, 2003.

VAN06 Van Hooland S., "Spectator becomes annotator: possibilities offered by user-generated metadata for image databases," *Immaculate Catalogues: Taxonomy, Metadata and Resource Discovery in the 21st Century, Proceedings of CILIP Conference*, University of East Anglia, UK, 13–15 September 2006.

VOL06 Volle M., *De l'informatique (Savoir vivre avec l'automate)*, Paris, Economica, 2006.

WAN95 Wand Y., Wang R. Y., "Anchoring Data Quality Dimensions in Ontological Foundations," *Communications of the ACM*, 1996, vol. 39, n 11, pp. 86–95.

Chapter 8
Long-Term Verifiability of Remote Electronic Elections

Lucie Langer

Abstract Retention of election documents is essential for verifying the proper conduct of an election ex post. The documents retained provide for later review in case an election contest is filed. Moreover, the principle of public elections laid down in German basic law implies the need for public verifiability. This applies to remote electronic voting in particular as physical observation is not achievable in this case.

Although the retention obligations on paper-based elections are governed by electoral law, specifications for e-voting are still an open issue. We therefore address the following questions. With which existing legal obligations on retention of election data is it necessary to comply? How can they be transferred to the scenario of remote electronic elections?

We approach the issue as follows. Based on an analysis of the retention obligations specified in German electoral law, we identify the conditions that must be documented and are thus subject to long-term verifiability. Then we investigate how they can be adapted to the scenario of remote electronic elections. We also recommend how to conclusively document that these conditions have been met.

Our work contributes to establishing the basis for legally binding e-voting in Germany. As electoral law in Europe is rather consistent, this contribution might be useful to other countries as well.

8.1 Introduction

With regard to e-government, secure long-term retention of relevant documents is an important issue. The correct implementation of administrative processes must be verifiable and provable for years or even decades. Strict regulations are imposed here, and this applies in particular to elections as they embody democratic decision-making.

Remote electronic voting is an important part of the e-government strategy. It has been introduced in several European countries such as Estonia, the United Kingdom,

L. Langer (✉)
Technische Universität Darmstadt, Department of Computer Science, Cryptography
and Computer Algebra Group, Hochschulstraße 10, 64289, Darmstadt, Germany
e-mail: langer@cdc.informatik.tu-darmstadt.de

S. Assar et al. (eds.), *Practical Studies in E-Government: Best Practices*
from Around the World, DOI 10.1007/978-1-4419-7533-1_8,
© Springer Science+Business Media, LLC 2011

the Netherlands, France, Germany, Switzerland, and Austria. However, the elections were on different levels: In Estonia, legally binding political elections were carried out over the Internet in 2005 local elections and in the 2007 parliamentary elections. This was possible due to the high e-readiness of the Estonian population as well as a modern infrastructure and political sponsorship of e-government programs: with regard to online availability of public services, Estonia was the second highest ranked of the Member States of the European Union in 2006 [EUR06].

In Germany there have been several pilot applications of remote electronic voting in nationwide societies. The German Informatics Society (Gesellschaft für Informatik, GI) has been electing its executive committee over the Internet since 2004, while still retaining the option for postal voting. The German Research Foundation (Deutsche Forschungsgemeinschaft, DFG) adopted online elections of the review boards in 2007. As stated in the according electoral regulations, the evaluation records of the remote electronic election have to be retained for the term of office of the elected body, that is, 2 and 4 years, respectively [GI04, DFG06]. The provisions concerning retention are given in the section which regulates scrutiny procedures. This indicates that election documents must primarily be retained in order to prepare for scrutiny proceedings in case an election contest is filed. However, we show that providing and retaining election documentation is fundamentally related to the public nature of democratic elections.

The importance of appropriate recordkeeping for secure electronic elections has also been recognized on a European level [COU05, OSCE08]. In its recommendation on legal, operational, and technical standards for e-voting, the Council of Europe states that "any data retained after the election or referendum period shall be stored securely" [COU05]. However, it is not clear which data should be retained at all. A one-to-one mapping from the documentation of a paper-based election at the polling station to keeping records of a remote electronic election is not possible due to its differing implementation. Thus, different ways of identifying the according documents in an online election must be found.

We approach the issue by analyzing the retention obligations laid down in German electoral law on paper-based elections. We identify the conditions that have to be conclusively documented and transfer them to the scenario of remote electronic voting. Then we determine the documents which have to be retained in order to prove that these conditions have been met.

The chapter is structured as follows. In Sect. 8.2 we identify the objectives of retention for parliamentary elections. Section 8.3 provides an analysis of the retention obligations laid down in current German law on conventional paper-based elections. Section 8.4 identifies the conditions that are supposed to be documented by the records retained. According implications for online elections are derived in Sect. 8.5. Section 8.6 summarizes the results and concludes the chapter.

8.2   Retention Objectives

The primary objective of retaining election data is to prepare for scrutiny proceedings. The proper conduct of the election must be provable and thus conclusively documented. But what does the proper conduct of an election comprise?

First of all, the election has been conducted properly if the basic principles of electoral law have been followed. These principles are of prime importance and are thus laid down in German Basic Law (Grundgesetz, GG[1]) and also stated at the beginning of the German Federal Electoral Law (Bundeswahlgesetz, BWG[2]). According to §38 GG and §1 (1) BWG, the members of the German Federal Parliament (Bundestag) are elected in "universal, direct, free, equal and secret elections" by the Germans who have the right to vote. It is commonly accepted that parliamentary elections have to be free, equal, and secret, and the principles of universal and direct elections belong to the European electoral heritage [MIT03]. The principles of freedom and secrecy are also enshrined in the Additional Protocol to the European Convention on Human Rights [COU03] and are thus supposed to be reflected by national electoral law of the European countries. In the following we explain briefly what the five basic principles of electoral law mean. Similar interpretations have been provided by Grimm et al. [GRI07].

An election is *universal* if it is guaranteed that any eligible voter can participate and cast his or her vote. According to Schreiber [SCHR90], the right to vote may not be denied because of political, economic, or social reasons. The principle of *direct* elections postulates that the voters alone determine the composition of the parliament [SCHR90]. After polling is terminated, nobody may influence the results of the election anymore. Furthermore, a voter cannot transfer his right to vote to someone else who then votes on his behalf (§14 (4) BWG). However, auxiliary persons may be used to help disabled voters (§33 (2) BWG). *Free* elections exclude the possibility that voters are influenced unlawfully by others or even coerced to vote in a particular way. This applies also to the period after the votes have been cast: any control of the content of the particular vote must be excluded. Furthermore, voters must not be influenced by intermediate results of the election [SCHR90]. The principle of *equality* states that all votes cast by eligible voters have equal influence on the election results. This principle applies also to the eligible candidates in the sense that equal opportunities for all candidates should be ensured [SCHR90]. Finally, the principle of *secret* elections postulates that the voter's decision must be kept secret. It must not be possible to associate a vote with the voter who cast it. According to Schreiber, unrestricted freedom of the vote is only given provided that secrecy of the vote is ensured [SCHR90].

With regard to the proper conduct of an election, not only compliance with the five basic principles of electoral law must be provable: according to §31 BWG, an election of the German parliament must be conducted in public. The principle of public elections can also be derived from German Basic Law. According to §20 (2) GG, "All state authority is derived from the people. It shall be exercised by the people through elections and other votes and through specific legislative, executive, and judicial bodies." As the voter confers the state authority to the elected representatives, the voter shall maintain confidence in her successful participation. Thus, all essential steps of an election are subject to the possibility of public scrutiny unless other constitutional interests justify an exception [FED09].

In conventional paper-based elections taking place at polling stations the principle of public elections is implemented by allowing the interested public to be present during polling and tallying. This kind of physical observation is not achievable for remote electronic elections as the voting system is based on information technology and the underlying procedures are implemented by computers. Thus, compliance with the principle of public elections is a particular challenge for remote e-voting. According to the Organization for Security and Co-operation in Europe (OSCE), the infeasibility of physical observation implies that there must be a thorough examination of the relevant documentation [OSCE08], which in turn emphasizes the importance of a secure and conclusive retention of election documents. Missing documentation may be an indication of problems [OSCE08].

However, election observation by competent authorities alone is not sufficient to satisfy the principle of public elections. As noted by Mitrou et al., "the loss of visibility, seen as a loss of (direct) controllability, may undermine the confidence in election procedures and may result in the loss of legitimacy of the outcome" [MIT03]. Thus, the correct functionality of the electronic voting system should be verifiable by the voters and the public as well. This is reflected by the security requirements of individual and universal verifiability that are, among others, usually imposed upon electronic voting systems [LGT03]. However, both requirements must be considered not only between starting the poll and publishing the election results, but also beyond the election day.

8.3 Retention Obligations in German Electoral Law

In this section we analyze current German electoral law, focusing on obligations regarding the retention of election documents. We consider one example for parliamentary and one for nonparliamentary elections. For each we at first ascertain which documents have to be retained for which period of time. In the next step we analyze the concrete purpose of these legal retention obligations.

8.3.1 Federal Elections

Federal elections of the German Bundestag are held every 4 years. They are subject to the German Federal Electoral Law (Bundeswahlgesetz, BWG) and specified by the according Federal Electoral Regulations (Bundeswahlordnung, BWO).

8.3.1.1 Retention Obligations

The federal territory is subdivided into 299 constituencies, each of which comprises several polling districts. In each polling district an Electoral Board including an Electoral Officer is appointed (§6 BWO). Furthermore, each constituency appoints a Constituency Returning Officer (§3 BWO).

The voters' register must be closed the day before the election at the latest. Closure of the register is certified by completing Annex 8 of the BWO. Polling cards may be issued to voters registered in the voters' register upon application if they declare themselves outside their polling district on election day or unable to go to the polling station due to physical or other reasons. A notice is placed in the voters' register next to the name of each voter who applied for a polling card. The polling card issued may thereafter be used for postal voting or for voting in a different polling district of the same constituency. If the polling card is used for postal voting, the voter must sign an affidavit on the polling card certifying that she has voted personally.

After the poll has been closed, the Electoral Board shall establish the election result in the polling district (§67 BWO). Hereafter the ballots are collected and the pile of ballots as well as the pile of received polling cards is sealed by the Electoral Officer and handed over to the local authority of the commune. Each authority in charge must protect these documents against unauthorized access (§73 (1), (2) BWO).

According to §89 (1) BWO, the following documents must be retained and protected against unauthorized access:

- Voters' register
- Polling card register
- Register of polling cards which have been declared invalid according to §28 (8) BWO (affecting voters whose names have been canceled from the voters' register)
- Register of voters who shall vote before a moving Electoral Board according to §29 (1) BWO
- Forms with supporting signatures for nominated candidates
- Voter's notices which have been collected

Although the voter's notices have to be discarded immediately to ensure data protection and voter privacy (§90 (1) BWO), all other documents listed have to be retained for at least 6 months after the election (§90 (2) BWO). If electoral scrutiny proceedings are pending, further retention may be ordered by the Federal Returning Officer (§90 (2) BWO). According to §89 (2), (3) BWO, information on these documents may only be given to official authorities and may only be used for election statistics, scrutiny procedures, or in case an election fraud is suspected.

All other election documents may be discarded 60 days before a new German Bundestag is elected (§90 (3) BWO). These documents comprise the ballots and the postal vote documents (polling cards and ballots), as well as the election records, which are explained in the following.

According to §72 BWO, the clerk in each polling district shall compile an election record pursuant to the model provided in Annex 29 of the BWO. The election record documents the polling procedure and the determination of the election results. Furthermore, the election record contains decisions on the following.

- Admission or exclusion of voters whose voting right was questionable (§56 (7) BWO)
- Validity and content of questionable ballots (§69 (6) BWO)
- Validity or legal ownership of questionable polling cards (§59 BWO)

The ballots and the polling cards which correspond to the latter two items are enclosed in the election record. The completed election record must be approved and signed by each member of the Electoral Board. It is handed over to the local authority of the commune immediately, whence it is forwarded to the Constituency Returning Officer (§72 (3), (4) BWO). All authorities in charge have to ensure that the election records including the annexes are protected against access by unauthorized persons (§72 (4) BWO).

8.3.1.2 Analysis of the Retention Obligations

In the following we refer to the documents which have to be retained and consider at what their retention aims. We start with the election documents which according to §90 (3) BWO have to be retained for almost the whole election period and therefore are of special importance.

The *election record* is a public deed setting out that the election has been duly performed. The record documents that the members of the Electoral Board have been informed about their duties and responsibilities, in particular, discretion and impartiality. Any special incidents such as turning away voters in accordance with §56 (6) BWO (e.g., because they are not registered in the voters' register and do not possess a polling card) must be thoroughly documented in the election record. The record also accounts for the fact that proper surroundings for vote casting have been established: tables equipped with shields to protect voter privacy (§50 BWO) and a duly installed ballot box which has been checked to be empty before the election starts. The ballot box must be locked or sealed before the poll begins and it must not be opened again until the poll has been closed (§53 (3) BWO). If any changes to the voters' register are required (e.g., due to belatedly issued polling cards which require an according mark to be set beside the name of the affected voters), these must be documented, and the voters' register has to be closed before the election starts.

The election record also accounts for proper polling: the Electoral Board must take care and also confirm in writing that the voters have been unobserved while voting and that they folded the ballot paper after having completed it. The poll must be closed at 6:00 p.m., and only voters who are in line at that time are entitled to cast their ballots. Furthermore, the correct evaluation of the election documents and determination of the election results can be verified on the basis of the election record: polling and tallying must be conducted in public (see also §54 BWO). The ballots have to be counted by two members of the Electoral Board independently. In case there are doubts about the values written down in the election record, the ballots allow for retallying and hence verifying the correctness of the announced election results. The collected polling cards are considered below.

The *voters' register* allows for verifying the voting rights. It is retained to make this verification possible even after the election, for example, in case the election is contested because of alleged participation of persons who were not eligible to vote. According to §14 (1) BWO, the voters' register contains the first and last name of the voter as well as his day of birth and address. Furthermore, when a voter casts his ballot, this is acknowledged by placing a mark beside his name in the voters' register (§56 (4) BWO). Hence, the total of voters who have cast a ballot can be determined by these marks after the election has ended. Thus, the voters' register can be used to check that this value matches the one written down in the election record and, if required for verification, also the number of ballots cast.

The *polling card register* contains the names of voters who have been issued a polling card for postal vote or for voting in a different electoral district. This register should match the voters' register in the sense that each voter who is in the polling card register should have a corresponding mark beside her name in the voters' register. This way it can be checked that a voter who has obtained a polling card could not have voted twice. Because polling cards are first and foremost used for postal voting, this review may contribute to excluding the possibility that someone has cast a ballot in person and by postal vote as well. Furthermore, by comparing the *polling cards* received during the election with the *register of polling cards which have been declared invalid* it can be verified that only valid polling cards have been used for voting.

The *forms with supporting signatures for nominated candidates* testify to sufficient support for the candidates by the general public. These may be used as a justification for nomination of the candidates if challenged.

8.3.2   Works Council Elections

Works councils in Germany are elected every 4 years in secret and direct elections. The elections are subject to §7 to §20 of the Works Constitution Act (Betriebsverfassungsgesetz, BetrVG) and the according election regulations determined by the First Ordinance on the implementation of the Works Constitution Act (Erste Verordnung zur Durchführung des Betriebsverfassungsgesetzes – Wahlordnung, WO).

8.3.2.1   Retention Obligations

The Electoral Board is supposed to compile an election record (§16 WO) containing the following details.

- Total number of votes cast
- Number of valid and invalid votes cast
- Calculated maxima according to §5 BetrVG and §5 WO (explained below)
- Distribution of the calculated maxima to the lists
- Names of the elected candidates
- Any special incidents which occurred during the election

The maxima which have to be calculated according to §5 BetrVG and §5 WO are supposed to ensure that the staff gender ratio is duly represented by the works council.

§19 WO states that the election documents must be retained by the works council at least until the end of its term of office. These election documents comprise the election record described above as well as the ballots and the postal vote envelopes which have been received too late and hence cannot be counted. These envelopes remain sealed and are to be discarded 1 month after the announcement of the election results, as long as the election has not been contested (§26 (2) WO).

8.3.2.2 Analysis of the Retention Obligations

The ballots allow for retallying and hence for verification of the election results which have been announced. The values set down in the election record which correspond to the total number of votes cast, valid votes, and invalid votes, may be verified as well.

The calculated maxima and their distribution to the lists may be used to prove that the gender which represents the minority of staff is not discriminated with regard to the seats on the works council.

The postal vote envelopes which have been received too late may become relevant if an election contest is filed. The same applies to the special incidents if given.

8.4 Conditions to Be Documented

Hitherto we have analyzed the retention obligations laid down in the laws and regulations on federal elections and works council elections in Germany. As the retention obligations on parliamentary elections are most comprehensive, we henceforth restrict to retention obligations for federal elections.

In the following we consider the background of the retention obligations compiled in Sect. 8.3.1. We identify the conditions that must be demonstrably satisfied and thus conclusively documented. As observed in Sect. 8.2, the overarching retention objective for parliamentary elections is to document compliance with the basic principles of electoral law and to satisfy the principle of public elections. The proper conduct of the election must be documented for all three phases of an election: preparation, polling, and evaluation. We thus structure the conditions according to the election phase they refer to and relate each condition to the basic principle(s) of electoral law which it supports.

8.4.1 Preparation Phase

As shown in Sect. 8.3.1, documenting the correct preparation of the election aims at proving that the following conditions have been satisfied.

- Prep1: Instruction of election staff.
- Prep2: Proper installation and surroundings.
- The ballot box must be empty before the voting phase starts.
- The contents of the ballot box must not be disclosed before the polling phase terminates.
- The voter must have the chance to complete the ballot unobserved.
- Prep3: Closure of the voters' register.

- Prep4: Justified nomination of candidates.
- Prep1: First of all, the election staff must be instructed on the proper conduct of the election and advised of their obligation to maintain confidentiality and impartiality. If the Electoral Board could unduly influence the election results this would violate the principle of direct elections. Moreover, discretion of the election staff supports freedom and secrecy of the vote.
- Prep2: It must be verifiable that the polling station has been equipped properly. The Electoral Board must check that the ballot box is empty before the election starts. This aims at fulfilling the principle of universal elections in terms of excluding illegal ballots. Furthermore, the ballot box must be sealed or locked afterward in order to prevent untimely opening of the ballot box. This relates to the objective of free elections as voters must not be influenced by intermediate results of the election. The tables which are used for vote casting are supposed to be equipped with shields to protect voter privacy and hence support secrecy and freedom of the vote.
- Prep3: Although authorized corrections to the voters' register during the preparation phase are still possible, the voters' register must be closed before the election starts. This prevents illegal changes to the voters' register and hence may be viewed as supporting universal elections in the sense that no eligible voters are denied the right to vote and no persons not eligible are permitted to vote.
- Prep4: Nomination of candidates is justified by the forms with supporting signatures, which at the same time guarantees equal opportunities for all candidates and hence supports the principle of equal elections.

8.4.2 Polling Phase

As shown in Sect. 8.3.1, documentation of proper polling aims at proving that the following conditions have been met.

- Poll1: Special incidents.
- Poll2: Proper authentication of voters.
- Poll3: Secrecy of the ballot.
- The content of the ballot must be protected against unauthorized inspection from the time the ballot is completed until the end of the polling phase.
- If the vote is cast in an uncontrolled environment, the voter must affirm having voted personally.
- Poll4: Mutual exclusion of different voting channels.
- Poll5: Proper termination of the poll.
- Poll6: Public conduct of the poll.
- Poll1: Documenting any special incidents during polling, especially recording the names of voters who have been turned away, aims at accounting for the fact that no eligible voter has been excluded from the election and thus supports the principle of universal elections.
- Poll2: Correct voter authentication, for example, by verifying validity and legal ownership of polling cards, contributes to universal elections in terms of

ensuring that only persons who have the legal right to vote are permitted to participate in the election.

- Poll3: It must be verifiable that the ballots were cast properly, which means that voters cast their vote unobserved and folded their ballot papers before they were put into the ballot box. These measures clearly aim at secret and free elections. Opening the ballots only after the polling phase has terminated supports free elections as it prevents voters from being influenced by intermediate results. In case of postal voting, the affidavit which has to be signed by the voter to certify that the vote was cast personally aims at ensuring free and direct elections.
- Poll4: If multiple voting channels are provided, it must be ensured that only one vote per voter is counted. Mutual exclusion of voting in person and postal voting as well as checking the acknowledgements of voting provides for equality in terms of giving each voter equal influence on the election result.
- Poll5: Closing the poll in due time while allowing the present voters to cast their ballots aims at ensuring that voters who were present on time are not excluded from the poll and thus supports universal elections.
- Poll6: The obligation to conduct the poll in public does not directly relate to any of the basic principles of electoral law, but rather is important with respect to the principle of public elections. For conventional paper-based elections this condition is met by allowing the interested public to be present during polling as long as polling is not disturbed (§31 BWG).

8.4.3   Evaluation Phase

As shown in Sect. 8.3.1, documenting the correct evaluation of the election outcome aims at proving that the following conditions have been satisfied.

- Eval1: Repeated independent tallying.
- Eval2: Public conduct of the tally.
- Eval1: Verifying the tallying process by recounting the ballots supports universality and equality because repeated counting ensures that all ballots have been counted correctly. The same applies to having the ballots counted by two members of the Electoral Board independently.
- Eval2: As for polling in public (Poll6), the requirement of public tallying does not directly relate to any of the basic principles of electoral law, but rather is important with respect to the principle of public elections.

8.5   Transferring the Conditions to Remote Electronic Voting

In the previous section we compiled the conditions which must be documented in order to prove the proper conduct of an election. They were derived from the legal regulations on conventional paper-based elections. Nevertheless, these conditions apply to (parliamentary) elections in general, irrespective of whether the election is carried out electronically or in a conventional, paper-based way. What makes the difference between the two scenarios is how these conditions are met and which data must be retained in order to prove that they have been met.

In the following we review the different conditions identified in Sect. 8.4. Each condition is transferred to the scenario of remote electronic elections. We provide an according interpretation and recommend which data should be retained in order to demonstrate that the condition was met. As in the previous section we restrict to federal elections. Inasmuch as federal elections comprise all of the retention obligations which apply for works council elections (except for protection of minorities with respect to gender), guidelines for works council elections may easily be derived. However, for other, especially nonparliamentary types of elections, some of our recommendations for implementing the conditions apply only in a weaker form or not at all. We refer to this where necessary; otherwise, the particular recommendation applies to any type of election.

8.5.1 Preparation Phase

Let us first recall the conditions to be documented in order to prove the correct preparation of the election.

- Prep1: Instruction of election staff.
- Prep2: Proper installation and surroundings.
- The ballot box must be empty before the voting phase starts.
- The contents of the ballot box must not be disclosed before the voting phase terminates.
- The voter must have the chance to complete the ballot unobserved.
- Prep3: Closure of the voters' register.
- Prep4: Justified nomination of candidates.
- Prep1: When we turn to remote electronic elections, ascertaining the integrity and trustworthiness of the election staff concerns not only the Electoral Board. Several people are involved in setting up and maintaining the voting system, for example, software engineers and system administrators. Depending on the level of the election (parliamentary versus nonparliamentary), appropriate measures such as background and reference checking should be applied here and compliance with due diligence procedures should be verified and documented.
- Prep2: In the scenario of remote electronic elections, the ballot box is electronic. As for the physical ballot box, its electronic equivalent must be empty before the election starts. A time stamp issued at the very beginning of the voting phase can prove that the ballot box was in a correct state at that time: Time stamps are an effective means to certify that an electronic document existed in a certain form at a specific time (more details can be found in [KUN07]). The content of votes which are in the electronic ballot box must not be revealed as long as the voting procedure has not terminated. This can be established by several means, for

example, by encrypting the votes using a threshold encryption scheme and providing multiple talliers who jointly decrypt the votes after the voting phase is over. As to the use of shielded tables, remote electronic voting of course works differently here. The Electoral Board has no influence on the surroundings in which voters cast their vote, thus this condition cannot be transferred directly to remote electronic elections. We take up this matter in Sect. 8.5.2 (Poll3).

- Prep3: Closing the voters' register in a remote electronic election can be realized by providing a time stamp. This gives a conclusive document on the state of the voters' register to which it was referred for checking eligibility during the polling phase. It also allows for setting marks to indicate that a voter has already cast his vote or that he has used a specific voting channel. As time stamps can only prove that a document existed in a certain form at a specific point in time, a write-protected version of the voters' register should additionally be retained, for example, on a nonrewritable compact disc. This way data from the voters' register cannot be deleted, altered, or overwritten.
- Prep4: The collection of supporting signatures for candidate nominations should be retained for remote electronic elections as well. It may still be accomplished using pen and paper. An electronic variant may be applicable in the case that digital signatures are available to the public, for example, if electronic Citizen Cards have been issued to support e-government. However, this may be approriate for parliamentary elections only.

8.5.2   Polling Phase

We recall the conditions to be documented for proving the proper conduct of the polling phase.

- Poll1: Special incidents.
- Poll2: Proper authentication of voters.
- Poll3: Secrecy of the ballot.

    - The content of the ballot must be protected against unauthorized inspection from the time the ballot is completed until the end of the polling phase.
    - If the vote is cast in an uncontrolled environment, the voter must affirm having voted personally.

- Poll4: Mutual exclusion of different voting channels.
- Poll5: Proper termination of the poll.
- Poll6: Public conduct of the poll.
- Poll1: To document any special incidents that occurred during polling, system monitoring should be carried out and log files for the voting system should be created and retained. System monitoring is actually important not only with respect to special incidents, but also in order to document the correct execution of the voting software during the whole election process.

- Poll2: Proper authentication of voters should be documented by keeping a record of all voters who have cast a vote. This can be realized, for example, by placing a mark beside the names of affected voters in the voters' register and having this extended register signed by the Electoral Board after the end of the polling phase. This record must, however, not allow for establishing a link between a voter and her vote.
- Poll3: For paper-based elections which take place at the polling station the Electoral Board has to take care that polling happens unobserved. The scenario of remote electronic voting does not allow unobserved polling to be enforced by any supervising authority as voters complete their ballots by means of their computers at home or in the workplace. In the scenario of online works council elections, the employer should be obliged to ensure that each workplace offers sufficient privacy to the voter in order to avoid shoulder surfing. If this is not possible (as, for example, in open-plan offices), a separate computer for polling shall be set up in an environment which offers a sufficient level of privacy.

  Folding the paper ballot can be mapped to encrypting the electronic ballot in order to keep its content secret. However, the voting platform used by the voter might be compromised by malicious software in order to record the vote before it is encrypted. It is obviously beyond the power of the Electoral Board to check the voter's private computer for malware. There are, however, several measures to mitigate this threat: Before casting his vote, the voter should be informed of the duty to take appropriate measures in order to keep his voting client free from malware. The voter could even be required to sign an according declaration, although this might dissuade the voter from voting via Internet. Another possibility is to distribute the voting system on bootable discs which the voters use on their private computers. There could as well be supervised public terminals for voters who are not sufficiently confident in securing their home computers.

  As the scenario of voting at home in a remote electronic election is similar to postal voting due to the uncontrolled environment, the voter shall as well be required to digitally sign an affidavit certifying that the vote was cast personally.
- Poll4: Any voting system must provide secure procedures to exclude the possibility of having more than one vote per voter counted. If multiple voting via one or more voting channels[2] is permitted, policies are required to determine which vote is to be counted. This may be determined by a predefined priority mode of voting (e.g., voting in person with a paper ballot) or by the time the ballot was cast (i.e., the latest vote counts). This policy is to be published at least several days before the election in order to inform the voters. For each voting channel a list of the voters who used this channel shall be compiled. Alternatively, the voting system can place a corresponding mark beside the names of affected voters in the voters' register. The original voters' register amended by these marks or the channel-specific registers, respectively, should be digitally signed by the Election Board and retained.
- Poll5: Proper termination of the poll is a challenge for remote electronic elections. Although it must not be possible for the voter to start filling out the

ballot after the polls have closed, it must still be ensured that votes which are pending can enter the ballot box. This is in general referred to as the *last call problem* and has been discussed, for example, in [MEI04]. Secure procedures for intermediate storage must be provided to solve this problem. Deadlines regarding the period between closing the polls and closing the ballot box must be determined and published. If a voter has started to fill out the ballot and the polling phase is about to end, the voter shall be informed about the time remaining until the ballot box is closed. This notification is logged and thus part of the election documentation.

- Poll6: As mentioned before, in an election carried out electronically it is not possible simply to be present during polling. Therefore the log files of the voting system should be published after the election in order to allow for transparency and traceability. As source code is copyrighted according to §2 and §69 (a) of the German Copyright Act (Urheberrechtsgesetz – UrhG) it may not generally be possible to publish the programs and procedures on which the voting system is based. The source code shall, however, be open at least to election observers.

8.5.3 Evaluation Phase

As shown before, the following conditions must be documented in order to prove the correct evaluation of the election outcome:

- Eval1: Repeated independent tallying
- Eval2: Public conduct of the tally
- Eval1: If the ballots are electronic, tallying the election results is especially fast and efficient. For remote electronic elections it is often postulated that recounting the results should be open to all voters and moreover to the general public. This property, which is commonly referred to as *universal verifiability*, is considered to be one of the main features of e-voting systems [BUR03]. Requiring two members of the Electoral Board to count the electronic ballots independently does not add any significant value if the same tallying routine is used by both of them.[3] It is, however, reasonable to have third parties (e.g., election observers and official scrutiny authorities) perform a recount using the original tallying routine. Moreover, another certified tallying routine should be applied and it should be checked whether the same result as for the original routine is obtained. Thus, independent tallying comprises having the ballots counted by independent parties using different tallying routines. The different counting processes shall be logged and the results shall be documented and digitally signed by the Electoral Board or the third parties involved. If universal verifiability is a goal then retallying should also be open to the public. Note that remote electronic elections usually do not provide the possibility of a manual recount.
- Eval2: The tallying process should be made transparent by providing to the public an according routine for recounting the votes as described above. Voters

could even be invited to implement their own routines for a recount, provided that the according specification is published and followed. However, small-scale elections such as in societies require only small-scale scrutiny. In contrast, electing a parliament should offer a high level of transparency to the voters and should also allow for comprehensive assessment by election observers. The higher the level of the election, the more important public scrutiny is.

8.6 Conclusion

For remote electronic elections to become legally binding, the proper conduct of the election must be verifiable in the long term. This requires appropriate recordkeeping. The retention obligations on paper-based elections are governed by electoral law, however, according specifications for e-voting are still an open issue.

Based on a compilation of the retention obligations on paper-based elections laid down in German electoral law, we have identified the conditions that must be conclusively documented in order to provide evidence on the proper conduct of the election. These conditions were thereupon transferred to the scenario of remote electronic voting. We have recommended which data should be retained in order to conclusively document that these conditions were met. As a next step, the technical demands which apply to the records kept must be determined. This is important because meeting these demands is essential for preserving the probative value of the data retained (e.g., digital signatures must be renewed after a certain period of time). We regard this as future work.

The last section has shown that it is especially challenging to transfer the obligations which are related to the secrecy and freedom of the vote to online elections. This is due to the fact that the scenario of remote electronic voting does not allow unobserved polling in person to be enforced by any supervising authority. However, the same holds for the case of postal voting. In Germany, this voting channel was originally introduced in order to enhance the universality of elections at the expense of their secrecy. In the 2005 election of the German parliament almost 20% of the voters exercised the option to cast a postal vote. This shows that remote electronic voting is an important step towards meeting voters' needs in a mobile society. Further research is required on how to enforce secrecy and freedom of the vote in remote electronic elections.

We believe that our work may help legislative organs in terms of providing one piece of the background which is necessary to issue a legal framework on e-voting in Germany. As electoral law in other countries is similar, this profit might not be restricted to German legislation. Furthermore, our work may also be valuable to practitioners and developers of electronic voting systems in particular, as they should consider the issues of recordkeeping when designing and implementing a remote electronic voting system. In summary, we hope that our work will help to establish remote electronic voting as a true alternative to paper-based elections and hence contribute to advancing online elections, not only in Germany.

Notes

[1] Any laws and regulations are henceforth referred to by their official abbreviations.

[2] For example, in the 2007 Estonian parliamentary elections, voters could change their electronic vote either by voting again electronically or by voting with a ballot paper (Riigikogu Election Act §44 (6)). English version available at http://www.iuscomp.org/gla/statutes/BWG.htm.

[3] However, the approach of using two or more separate individuals or entities operating together (commonly referred to as *dual control*) is an important method to enhance the security of an online voting system. It should be adhered to where appropriate, for example, when starting or closing the poll is initiated by the Electoral Board.

References

BUR03   Burmester, M. and Magkos, E., "Towards secure and practical e-elections in the new era", Secure Electronic Voting, Advances in Information Security, Vol. 7, pp. 63–76, Kluwer Academic Publishers, 2003.

COU03   Council of Europe, Convention for the Protection of Human Rights and Fundamental Freedoms as amended by Protocol No. 11, September 2003, http://www.echr.coe.int/NR/rdonlyres/D5CC24A7-DC13-4318-B457-5C9014916D7A/0/EnglishAnglais.pdf [7 April 2009].

COU05   COU05 Council of Europe. Recommendation on legal, operational and technical standards for e-voting, Rec(2004)11. Council of Europe Publishing, Strasbourg Cedex, France, 2005.

DFG06   Deutsche Forschungsgemeinschaft, Wahlordnung für die Wahl der Mitglieder der Fachkollegien der Deutschen Forschungsgemeinschaft (DFG), 2006, available in German only: http://www.dfg.de/forschungsfoerderung/formulare/download/70_01.pdf [7 April 2009].

EUR06   European Commission. Online Availability of Public Services: How Is Europe Progressing? Web Based Survey on Electronic Public Services Report of the 6th Measurement, June 2006, http://ec.europa.eu/information_society/eeurope/i2010/docs/benchmarking/online_availability_2006.pdf [8 April 2009].

FED09   Federal Constitutional Court. Press release no. 19/2009 of 3 March 2009, http://www.bundesverfassungsgericht.de/pressemitteilungen/bvg09-019en.html [9 April 2009].

GRI07   Grimm, R., Krimmer, R., Meißner, N., Reinhard, K., Volkamer, M. and Weinand, M., Security Requirements for Non-political Internet Voting, [online], Arbeitsberichte des Fachbereichs Informatik, Nr. 06/2007, Universität Koblenz-Landau, Koblenz, Germany, 2007, http://www.uni-koblenz.de/~aggrimm/arbeitsberichte/arbeitsberichte_6_2007.pdf [10 April 2009].

KUN07   Kunz, T., Okunick, S. and Viebeg, U., "Long-term security for signed documents: services, protocols, and data structures", in Schmidt, A. U., Kreutzer, M. and Accorsi, R., (Eds.), Long-term and dynamical aspects of information security: emerging trends in information and communication security, pp. 125–139, Nova Publishers, New York, 2007.

LGT03   Lambrinoudakis, C., Gritzalis, D., Tsoumas, V., Karyda, M. and Ikonomopoulos, S., "Secure electronic voting: the current landscape", Secure Electronic Voting, Advances in Information Security, Vol. 7, pp. 101–124, Kluwer Academic Publishers, 2003.

MEI04   Meißner, N., Hartmann, V. and Richter, D., "Verifiability and Other Technical Requirements for Online Voting Systems", Electronic Voting in Europe, Lecture Notes in Informatics, Vol. 47, pp. 101–109, GI, 2004, http://www.e-voting.cc/static/evoting/files/meissner_hartmann_richter_p101-109.pdf [10 April 2009].

MIT03   Mitrou, L., Gritzalis, D., Katsikas, S. and Quirchmayr, G., "Electronic voting: Constitutional and legal requirements, and their technical implications", Secure Electronic Voting, Advances in Information Security, Vol. 7, pp. 43–60, Kluwer Academic Publishers, 2003.

OSCE08   Office for Democratic Institutions and Human Rights. OSCE/ODIHR Discussion Paper in Preparation of Guidelines for the Observation of Electronic Voting, Warsaw, 24 October 2008, http://www.osce.org/documents/odihr/2008/10/34647_en.pdf [7 April 2009].

SCHR90   Schreiber, W., Handbuch des Wahlrechts zum Deutschen Bundestag: Kommentar zum Bundeswahlgesetz, Heymann, Köln, Germany, 1990.

Chapter 9
Law-Based Ontology for E-Government Services Construction – Case Study: The Specification of Services in Relationship with the Venture Creation in Switzerland

Abdelaziz Khadraoui, Wanda Opprecht, Michel Léonard, and Christine Aïdonidis

Abstract The compliance of e-government services with legal aspects is a crucial issue for administrations. This issue becomes more difficult with the fast-evolving dynamics of laws. This chapter presents our approach to describe and establish the link between e-government services and legal sources. This link is established by an ontology called "law-based ontology." We use this ontology as means to define and to construct e-government services. The proposed approach is illustrated with one case study: the specification of services in relationship with the venture creation in Switzerland and in the State of Geneva. We have selected the Commercial Register area which mainly encompasses the registration of a new company and the modification of its registration.

9.1 Introduction

The institutional activities are governed by legal sources represented by a set of laws which regulates their execution. The contents of laws are mandatory for the institutional domain and represent a reference for the professionals (managers) as well as for the e-government designers. The compliance of e-government services with legal sources is a very important issue in e-government engineering.

At present, compliance issues with a legal aspect typically rely on experiences and the reference of the laws is manually done by business stakeholders and e-government designers. In other words, the legal sources are not properly

---

A. Khadraoui (✉)
Department of Information Systems, University of Geneva, Battelle, CUI,
7 Route de Drize, CH-1227 Carouge, Geneva, Switzerland
e-mail: abdelaziz.khadraoui@unige.ch

S. Assar et al. (eds.), *Practical Studies in E-Government: Best Practices from Around the World*, DOI 10.1007/978-1-4419-7533-1_9,
© Springer Science+Business Media, LLC 2011

considered in most existing approaches for e-government architectures [TAM01, AP005a, CHU02, PER06, LEN02]. These approaches lack a systematic framework for the compliance of e-government services with legal sources. This issue becomes more difficult with the fast-evolving dynamics of laws (i.e., the amendment of a law, the abrogation of a law, and the introduction of a new law).

Our goal in this chapter is to present our approach to describe and establish the link between e-government services and legal sources. This link is established by a law-based ontology. In other words, this ontology is used to define and construct the e-government services.

The chapter is structured as follows. Section 9.2 introduces our proposed framework for the construction of e-government services. Section 9.2.1 describes the method for extracting ontology from legal sources. Section 9.2.2 presents the conceptual basis for discovering and constructing e-government services. Section 9.3 discusses difficulties related to the deployment of the proposed approach in public administration. Finally, Section 9.4 summarizes the chapter.

9.2 Framework for the Construction of E-Government Services

Our goal in this work is to use the ontological level extracted from legal sources as means to define and to construct e-government services. We present a method to describe the ontological level for e-government services construction. This is composed of two steps: Step 1 is ontology construction from legal sources and Step 2 is e-government services identification (Fig. 9.1).

9.2.1 Ontology Construction from Legal Sources

In the context of Information Systems (IS) engineering, we define an ontology as a conceptual information model that describes some specific domain in terms of concepts, facts, and business rules. An ontology is a reference model which supports information interoperability and shares information: (1) it supports human understanding of the domain under consideration and communication, and (2) it facilitates the interoperability across different parts of IS.

The meaning of ontology considerably evolved from its origins in philosophy to its current usage in IS for e-government. Although ontology in the philosophical sense roughly means a categorization of all the entities that exist in the world and the relationships among them, ontology in the IS sense is only considered as a limited universe of discourse [ZUN01]. In our research work, laws are considered as a universe of discourse for IS engineering. The concepts and business rules

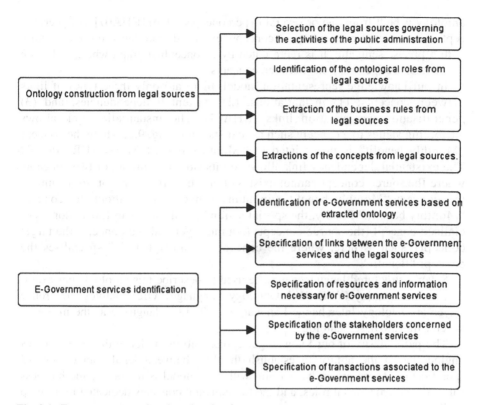

Fig. 9.1 E-government services based on legal sources

extracted from the appropriate laws are used to build the ontological aspects of the corresponding domain.

Legal texts describe concepts, business rules, and roles governing the given institutional domain. The usage of these sources of knowledge permits us to enhance IS adequacy and compatibility with institution activities and to find stable common information for IS engineering for e-government in the perspective of sustainable development.

Law-based ontology is a new approach for IS engineering that allows establishing and clarifying the links between laws and IS, in particular the alignment between the amendment of laws and the evolution of IS. This link is established by the law-based ontology. In other words, we use laws as a source of knowledge to analyze and construct the ontological level of an institutional domain. The exploitation of these sources of knowledge permits us to find stable concepts. For us, an ontology contains the stable common information of the IS domain.

As we said previously, the aim of our work is to establish the link between e-government services and a legal framework. In our approach, the law-based

ontology is built from one or several hyperconcepts (Hcp) [KHA07]. A hyperconcept is constructed on a subset of concepts extracted from laws, forming a unity
with a precise semantic. It is represented by a conceptual graph where nodes are
concepts and edges are links between concepts.

In our knowledge representation model, there are only three types of links
between concepts: (1) instantiations, (2) existential dependencies, and (3)
generalisation–specialisation links [KHA07]. The instantiation link allows
attributing values to a concept such as that shown in Fig. 9.2, where the concept
"Monthly benefit" is instantiated by "Monthly benefit value=EUR 1000.-".
The existential dependency link allows, on its side, the linking of two concepts
where the source concept cannot exist without the target concept: for example,
the concept "Monthly benefit minimum" cannot exist without the concept
"Monthly benefit." Finally, the specialisation link allows us to link a more specialised concept (the source concept) to a more generalised concept (the target
concept), such as here, where the concept "Monthly benefit" specialises the
concept "Benefit."

Several structured languages may be used to describe this ontology. For example, we can employ OWL (Web Ontology Language), OIL (Ontology Inference
Layer or Ontology Interchange Language), or TELOS language as the means to
specify the law-based ontology.

The particularity of our knowledge representation model in the context of IS
engineering is the ability to establish the link between legal sources and IS
specification. More precisely, our aim with this model is to specify the business
rules, the organizational roles, and the fundamental concepts dedicated to develop
an IS and to specify e-government services.

The hyperconcept schema must satisfy a set of conformity rules including
connectivity and concept completeness. The connectivity guarantees that each

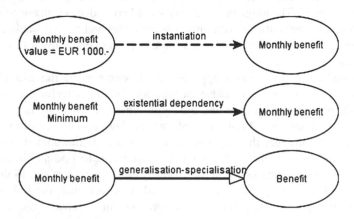

Fig. 9.2 The three ontological relationship types

concept of a hyperconcept is related to at least one other concept from the same hyperconcept. In this case, the hyperconcept represents a homogeneous zone and not a discontinuous unit. If the concept C1 belongs to the hyperconcept Hcp and is linked to the concept C2, then C2 also belongs to Hcp.

The process model of the construction of an ontology from laws is expressed as a map (i.e., strategic guideline) [RPB99] where the nodes represent the intentions and the links between the nodes represent the strategies. An intention indicates the desired goal and a strategy specifies the manner with which the intention can be carried out. In order to extract an ontology from law texts, we have identified five intentions, which are as follows.

1. Select the laws governing the IS domain and e-government services. This intention is reached by a strategy using expertise.
2. Define the ontological roles. This intention is reached by a strategy of organisation study.
3. Define a hyperconcept. This intention is reached either by a strategy of law analysis or by a strategy of information study relating to the ontological roles.
4. Build a hyperconcept. This intention is reached by a strategy of extraction of concepts and business rules from laws (or by re-evaluation of the hyperconcept).
5. Validate a hyperconcept. This intention is reached by a strategy of validation regarding its form and completeness.

In [KHA07], we proposed guidelines and method components for the extraction of the law-based ontology. Each guideline can be composed of a set of more detailed subguidelines or, on the contrary, be a part of some more complex guideline.

9.2.1.1 Guideline for the Selection of the Laws Governing the IS Domain

The first proposed guideline permits the selection of the legal framework that governs the IS under consideration. For a given domain, we propose firstly to identify the set of legal texts such as laws or application regulations which formalize the IS domain. The study of each of these texts should be made only in the perspective of IS engineering.

The laws contain information and knowledge of a purely legal nature, which cannot be considered in the IS. Only the key concepts of the domain and business rules are identified and retained. The analysis and interpretation of certain laws is a complex process. An important effort is required to carry out this process. Collaboration with an expert in legislation is necessary.

9.2.1.2 Guideline for the Definition of the Ontological Roles

An ontological role is a specialised organisational role which is described in law texts. The guideline to define an ontological role can be achieved through analysing the domain of the corresponding IS or through analysing laws which formalise the IS domain.

9.2.1.3 Guideline for the Definition of a Hyperconcept

There are two strategies to define a hyperconcept: the first strategy is based on the analysis of the texts of laws and the second is based on the study of the information related to ontological roles.

9.2.1.4 Guideline for the Construction of a Hyperconcept

The construction of a hyperconcept is carried out by the extraction of concepts and business rules from laws.

9.2.1.5 Guideline for the Validation of a Hyperconcept

The validation of a hyperconcept is carried out by the application of validation criteria. A hyperconcept can be rejected, which causes its re-evaluation. This reevaluation is expressed by the addition of new elements to the hyperconcept or by the removal of existing elements belonging to the hyperconcept.

The proposed method is illustrated with one case study: the specification of services in the relationship with venture creation in Switzerland and in the State of Geneva. We have selected the Commercial Register area which mainly encompasses the registration of a new company and the modification of its registration. This case study includes services about company registration, raising finances, tax payments, employee hiring, social insurance, and business premises.

With this case, our main goal is to exemplify our methodology, that is, to define and to build e-government services by the extraction of key concepts from laws. We consider legal sources as prominent, as an absolute referential.

In order to select the most appropriate legal sources at the federal level regarding the Commercial Register and the related services which may be offered, we have used a Swiss doctrinal source[1] which is considered as a reference by legal experts. The main law regarding the Commercial Register is the "Ordonnance sur le Registre du Commerce."[2] We have thus begun to analyse this legal source. We have then extracted the most significant concepts from the select laws. Here is an example of a hyperconcept, *examination of the registration of an association,* based on the articles 97-98-111a regarding the registration of an association to the Commercial Register. An association is one out of the 15 legal forms of organisation handled by the Swiss Commercial Register (Table 9.1).

The following ontological business rules can be extracted from these law fragments.

• The registration of an association in the Commercial Register must indicate the statute date, the association name, the head office, the objective, the resources, the organisation, the representation, and the signature mode.

- The registration query must be signed by the association's manager.
- The registration query must appear together with a legal abstract of the General Assembly minutes, an indication of the authorized people to sign, the signature mode, and a copy of the statutes. Figure 9.3 illustrates the hyperconcept schema.

Table 9.1 Example extracted from the Swiss federal law ("Ordonnance sur le Registre du Commerce")

4. Associations

Art. 97

The registration of an association indicates:

    a. The statutes date

    b. The name

    c. The head office

    d. The objective

    e. The resources

    f. The organisation, the representation, and the signature mode

Art. 98

The registration query is signed by the association's manager. It comes together with:

    a. A legal abstract of the General Assembly minutes which adopted the statutes and designed the bodies, as well as the indication of the authorised people to sign and the signature mode (if necessary)

    b. A copy of the statutes (art. 28, al 4[110])

10. Examination by the commercial register office

Art 111a

    a. The associations registered at the commercial register receive an identification number

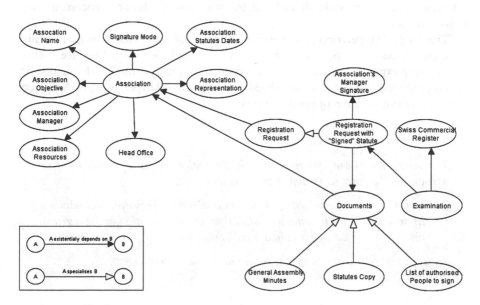

Fig. 9.3 Hyperconcept examination of the registration of an association

The following ontological roles can be extracted from these law fragments.

- Association
- Association's manager
- Commercial Register Office (Cantonal Administration/Swiss Commercial Register)

9.2.2 Public Administration Services Identification

The model presented below could serve as the conceptual basis for identifying public administration services. The overall model is presented in Appendix 9.1. The textual description follows.

9.2.2.1 Hyperconcepts and E-Government Services

E-government services are subject to government regulation. As we said previously, we used the legal framework to define public administration services. More precisely, the constructed hyperconcepts are used as a means to define and build e-government services. The key element of the proposed model is the entity "Service."

A service is defined by a name, a description, a type, and a goal. A subset of services can be defined and proposed based on the established ontology. This task is carried out by analysing the semantics of the constructed hyperconcepts. This analysis requires the validation of the business actors who are concerned with e-government.

The entity "Hyperconcept – Service" in Fig. 9.4 expresses a many-to-many relationship between the entity "Hyperconcept" and the entity "Service." This relationship expresses the fact that one hyperconcept can be used to define one or several services. A service can be defined on one or several hyperconcepts. A service may need the invocation of other services.

The semantics of the hyperconcept "Examination of the registration of an association" allows us to define two services:

- *The first service allows getting information about the registration conditions.*
- *The second service permits the validation and examination of the registration request by the Swiss commercial register.*

These two services are clearly identifiable in the hyperconcept.

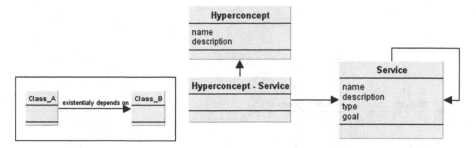

Fig. 9.4 Links among hyperconcepts and services

A hyperconcept is defined on the basis of one or several law fragments (see Fig. 9.5). A law fragment (LF) can contribute to the definition and the construction of one or more hyperconcepts. We express this semantic relationship by the introduction of the entity "Hyperconcept – LF." An Ontological Business Rule (OBR) is extracted from one or several law fragments and a law fragment can contain several ontological business rules. We express this relationship by the introduction of the entity "OBR – LF" in the model. We express the link between services and law fragments by the entity "Service – LF."

A stakeholder can be concerned with one or more services. A service for its execution can involve one or more stakeholders. There are three categories of stakeholders: enterprise, public administration, and person (citizen). The public administration is the entity that provides the service to the enterprise, the citizen, or to itself internally. In other words, the enterprise or the citizen interacts with the administration to get all relevant information about services. The entity "Public administration" in the proposed model specifies the departments, divisions, and branches in which public administration services are performed (Fig. 9.6).

The relationship between the "Stakeholder" entity and the "Ontological role" entity expresses the facts that a part of defined stakeholders can be found in an ontological role described in laws. An ontological role represents a set of necessary responsibilities, authorities, and capabilities, expressed in laws, to perform the execution of the activities of the development process or to watch the execution of activities performed by the other roles.

> In our example, the following ontological roles are considered as stakeholders.
>
> • Association
> • Association's manager
> • Commercial Register Office (cantonal administration)

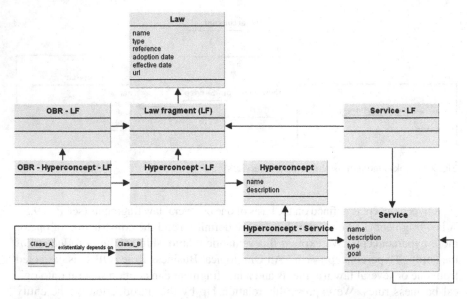

Fig. 9.5 Links among services, hyperconcepts, law fragments, and ontological business rules

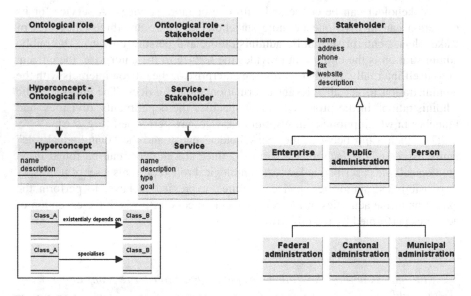

Fig. 9.6 Links among services, stakeholder, and ontological roles

E-Government services are governed by preconditions which are expressed in our model (Fig. 9.7) by the entity "Resource and Information" (usually specified as an ontological business rule which is extracted from laws).

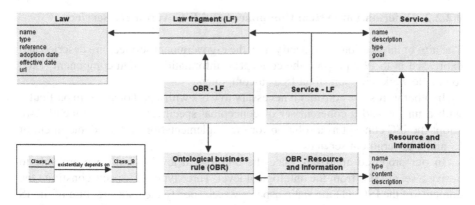

Fig. 9.7 Links among service, resource, and information and ontological business rule

An ontological business rule can specify one or several resource/information. A resource/information is concerned by one or several ontological business rules. This relationship is expressed by the "OBR – Resource and Information" entity.

The business rules are used to help the administration to better achieve goals, communicate between principals and agents, between the organization and interested third parties, demonstrate the fulfillment of legal obligations, operate more efficiently, and perform analysis on current practices. Consequently, business rules are very significant because they guarantee the conformity of services with the legal framework.

Resource/information which governs the "Validation and examination of the registration request" service are:

- *The registration of an association with the Commercial Register must indicate the statute date, the association name, the head office, the objective, the resources, the organisation, the representation, and the signature mode.*
- *The registration query must be signed by the association's manager.*
- *The registration query must appear together with a legal abstract of the General Assembly minutes, the indication of the authorised people to sign, the signature mode, and a copy of the statutes.*

Resource/information is clearly expressed, at the ontological level, in terms of ontological business rule associated with the hyperconcept "Examination of the registration of an association".

9.2.2.2   Information System Component and E-Government Services

The aim of this section is to specify how the e-government services are descried and expressed in IS. We propose the concept of information system component (ISC) to enable work with part of an IS as a component.

In other words, we consider it necessary to work with a part of an IS, in particular with a unique and a coherent set of conceptual specifications. Consequently, we adopt the ISC concept as a solution for the implementation and the deployment of IS and e-government services.

In our proposed approach, once the ontological level is built, we are able to derive a set of ISCs from the ontological level. Three types of aspects constitute the contents of the ISC: (1) the static aspects which specify the data structure of the IS by using the concept of hyperclass with its set of classes and hypermethods [TUR05], (2) the dynamic aspects which express the behaviour of different elements of the IS, and (3) the integrity constraints aspects which specify the rules governing the behaviour of the IS elements. The integrity constraints of an IS generally represent the business rules of an organisation. An integrity constraint is a logical condition defined over classes and verified by transactions or methods.

We do not detail in this chapter the process of ISC derivation from the ontological level. Below, we propose a model to establish links among services, hyperconcepts, ISC, and transactions. As we see in Fig. 9.8, one hyperconcept then corresponds to one or more services, and a service corresponds to one or more ISC. The entity "Service – Transaction – ISC" expresses the direct link among Service, Transaction, and ISC.

9.2.2.3   Implementation of the Proposed Model

We have implemented our proposed model to define and construct e-government services based on legal sources with the ontology editor called Protégé (Protégé-Frames).[3] This editor provides us with an interface to construct and store frame-based domain ontologies, to customize data entry forms, and to enter instance

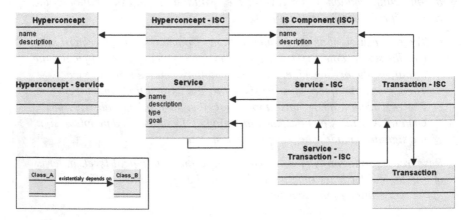

Fig. 9.8 Links among service, hyperconcept, ISC, and transaction

data. The knowledge model implemented by Protégé-Frames is compatible with the Open Knowledge Base Connectivity protocol (OKBC). In this model, an ontology consists of a set of classes organized in a subsumption hierarchy, a set of slots associated with classes to describe their properties and relationships, and a set of instances of those classes.

Firstly, we have deployed our conceptual model for identifying public administration services as a class ontology: each concept in our model corresponding to a class in the Protégé ontology, and each class attribute in our model to a class attribute in the Protégé ontology. The relations of type "existential dependency" have been realized through an attribute of value type "instance" in the source class, whereas the relations of type "specialisation" have been realized through the class hierarchy in Protégé. Secondly, we have developed one form in Protégé for each class of our ontology. Thence, we have been able to populate the ontology (to instantiate the class ontology) by (1) laws and law fragments, and (2) related hyperconcepts, ontological business rules, stakeholders, and the like.

9.2.2.4 Usage of the Ontology Editor Protégé

In order to support our work regarding the identification of e-services for the venture creation in Switzerland from laws, we have decomposed each law into fragments (i.e., law articles) and we have stored them in the Protégé editor as an instance of the class "Law Fragment (LF)." Then, we have decomposed each law fragment into hyperconcepts and stored them in the class "Hyperconcepts." We have done the same for each concept of our conceptual model.

An example of usage for the service "Information about the registration conditions" is shown in Fig. 9.9. In the left-hand frame, the list of classes belonging to the proposed model is displayed, and in the right-hand frame, a detailed instance of

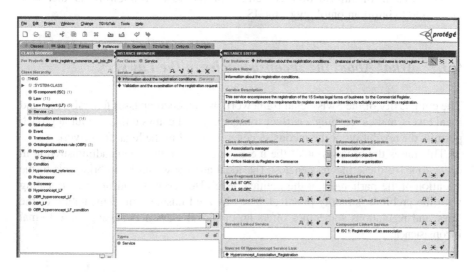

Fig. 9.9 Example of navigation among concepts in Protégé

"Service." In this example, the service "Information about the registration conditions" originates from two law fragments: art. 97 and art. 98 ORC. It is bound to several stakeholders ("association," "Office Fédéral du Registre du Commerce," etc.) and to several information and resources ("association name," "association objective," "association organisation," etc.).

9.3 Discussion About Difficulties Related to the Deployment of the Proposed Approach

Implementing this approach in the public administration certainly creates strong reactions and raises several issues. In this context, we suggest basing the creation of institutional IS engineering and online services on the existing laws, because these legal texts are the unquestionable source of information for the public administration.

One of the main advantages of such an approach is to explicitly match the legal framework, which provides the basis of the activities of a public administration, to the provided services, especially online services. Although not written to build IS, laws nonetheless contain relevant and potentially very valuable information to build an IS.

The laws studied in our research – Swiss federal laws, but also cantonal laws and their application regulations – supply information and business rules. Moreover, this analysis also reveals the roles and functions that the public administration (in our case the State of Geneva) has to perform. These elements in the laws have to be transposed in the institutional IS of the State of Geneva, either through software applications and databases, or through other specific organisational functions.

The wealth of information contained in the legal framework is therefore processed to build an ontology of the IS.

9.3.1 What About the Inconsistencies in the Laws?

The complexity of the Swiss legal framework, which encompasses federal, state, and local levels, makes reaching a perfect consistency of the laws unlikely. Our approach permits the revelation of the inconsistencies included in the legal framework.

This raises the broad issue of the means allocated in the public administration in order to solve these inconsistencies. The ideal answer would be to bring this to the attention of the parliament at the political level. However, this ideal way of dealing with the problem is hardly practical. The observed business implementation of the laws and regulations sometimes offers an empirical way of bypassing these formal inconsistencies.

9.3.2 What Skills Are Required to Implement This Approach?

The hierarchical structure of the laws and the specific legal terms are certainly essential elements to be taken into account when modelling the IS from the laws. This brings us to the following questions.

Should this analysis be performed by the legal experts who write the laws? In this case, should these experts be able to model IS? This analysis could broaden perspectives as far as conceiving and writing the laws, while verifying their consistency. This would raise awareness about consistency issues and offer a means of dealing with the problem.

- Should this analysis only be performed by IS designers? In this case, should they take into account the laws as their source for modelling? In order to clarify the legal texts and resolve ambiguities, collaboration with a legal expert is essential.

9.3.3 The Law Doesn't Correspond to Business Practice

One of the difficulties we have encountered with this approach is in the assessment of the correspondence between legal fragments and the existing practice. Indeed, there are three possible cases where a legal fragment does not correspond to the practice. To begin with, there is the case where the law does not completely cover a business practice. Then, there is the case where the law is inconsistent with the practice. Finally, there is the case where there is a legal vacuum. These three cases require handling by a legal expert.

9.4 Conclusion

This chapter illustrated two specific problems:

- How to take into account the legal sources in e-government architecture
- How to build e-government services based on legal sources

In this chapter, we presented our approach in the field of e-government services construction. The ontological level extracted from legal sources is used as means to define and construct e-government services. As we said previously, one of the main advantages of such an approach is to explicitly match the legal framework, which provides the basis of the activities of a public administration, to the provided services, especially online services. This approach allows the identification of a first set of services. It may not be exhaustive, but it is nonetheless based upon an unquestionable source of information, the laws themselves. This constitutes a strong basis in order to help develop a sound e-government project.

9.5   Appendix 1: The Conceptual Basis for Identifying Public Administration Services

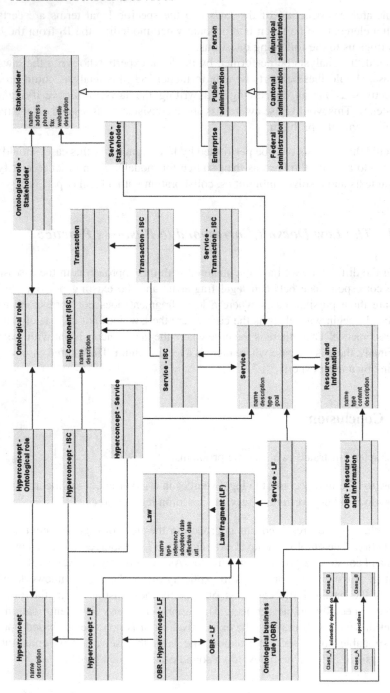

Notes

[1] Fiches juridiques suisses. http://www.fjs.ch.
[2] Ordonnance du 7 juin 1937 sur le registre du commerce (ORC), RS 221.411. http://www.admin.
ch/ch/f/rs/c221_411.html.
[3] http://protege.stanford.edu.

References

AKK04   Akkermans, H., "Value webs: using ontologies to bundle real-world services". IN:IEEE
        Intelligent Systems, July–Aug. 2004, pp. 57–66.
APO05a Apostolou D., Stojanovic L., Pariente Lobo T., Thoenssen B., "Towards a Semantically-
        Driven Software Engineering Environment for e-Government", {TCGov2005, IFIP}
        International Federation for Information Processing, 2005.
APO05b Apostolou, D., "The ontogov (FP6 – IST) project experience". Technical report, IST
        Call 4 Infoday, 2005.
BEN 97 Bench-Capon, T. J. M., and Visser, P. R. S. "Ontologies in legal information systems;
        the need for explicit specifications of domain conceptualisations". In International
        Conference on Artificial Intelligence and Law, 0-89791-924-6, pages 132–141,
        Melbourne, Australia, 1997. ACM Press New York, NY, USA.
CHU02   Chutimaskul, W., "E-government analysis and modeling. In Knowledge Management
        in e-Government", KMGov2002, 3rd International Workshop on Knowledge Manage-
        ment in e-Government. University of Linz and University of Roskilde, Copenhagen,
        Denmark., 23–24 May 2002.
DIN04   Le Dinh, T., "Information System Upon Information Systems: A Conceptual
        Framework", Phd Thesis, University of Geneva, November, 2004.
FRA03   Fraser, J., "Knowledge management applied to e-government services: the use of an
        ontology". In Springer, editor, Knowledge Management in Electronic Government
        (KMGov2003), Island of Rhodes, 2003.
GRO00   Grönroos, C., "Service Management and Marketing: A Customer Relationship
        Management Approach", 2nd edition. John Wiley & Sons, 2000.
KHA07   Khadraoui, A., "Method Components for Institutional Information System Engineering",
        Phd Thesis, University of Geneva, 2007.
KHA05   Khadraoui, A., Arni-Block, N., Léonard, M., Ralyté, J., "Laws-based Ontology for
        e-Government Information Systems", The Second International Conference on
        Innovations in Information Technology IIT'05, Dubaï, September, 2005.
KOT88   Kotler, P., "Marketing Management: Analysis, Planning, Implementation and Control",
        6th edition. Prentice Hall, Englewood Cliffs, NJ, 1988.
LEN02   Lenk, K., Traunm"uller, R., and Wimmer, M., "Electronic Government – Design,
        Applications and Management. The Significance of Law and Knowledge for Electronic
        Government". Hershey, Idea Group Publishing, 2002.
LOV01   Lovelock, C., "Services Marketing: People, Technology, Strategy", 4th edition. Prentice
        Hall, 2001.
RPB99   Rolland, C., Prakash, N., Benjamin, A., "A multi-model view of process modelling",
        Requirement Engineering J4(4):169–187.
PHA05   Pham, T., "Integration of Static, Dynamic, Organizational Aspect of Information
        System", Phd Thesis, University of Geneva, October, 2005.
PER06   Persisteras, V., Tarabanis, K., "Reengineering Public Administration through semantic
        technologies and the GEA domain ontology. IN: Proceedings of the 2006 AAAI Spring
        Symposium on The Semantic Web meets eGovernment (SWEG), Mar. 27–29, 2006,
        California, USA.

TAM01   Tambouris, E. "An integrated platform for realising online one-stop government : The egov project". In In proceedings of the DEXA International Workshop "On the way to Electronic Government", Los Alamitos, 2001. IEEE Computer Society Press.

TUR04   Turki, S., Aïdonidis, C., Khadraoui, A., Léonard, M., "Ontologies for Institutional IS Engineering", Open INTEROP Workshop On "Enterprise Modelling and Ontologies for Interoperability"; EMOI – INTEROP 2004; Co-located with CaiSE'04 Conference, Riga (Latvia), June, 2004.

TUR05   Turki, S., "From hyperclasses to components in information systems engineering", Phd Thesis, University of Geneva, 2005.

ZEI96   Zeithaml, V., Bitner, M. J., "Services Marketing", McGraw-Hill, New York, NY, 1996.

ZUN01   Zúñiga, G. L., "Ontology: Its transformation from philosophy to information systems". In Christopher Welty and Barry Smith, editors, Proceedings of the International Conference on Formal Ontology in Information Systems (FOIS'01), ACM Press, Ogunquit, Maine, USA, October 2001, pp. 187–197.

Chapter 10
Architectural Principles for Orchestration of Cross-Organizational Service Delivery: Case Studies from the Netherlands

Anne Fleur van Veenstra and Marijn Janssen

Abstract One of the main challenges for e-government is to create coherent services for citizens and businesses. Realizing Integrated Service Delivery (ISD) requires government agencies to collaborate across their organizational boundaries. The coordination of processes across multiple organizations to realize ISD is called orchestration. One way of achieving orchestration is to formalize processes using architecture. In this chapter we identify architectural principles for orchestration by looking at three case studies of cross-organizational service delivery chain formation in the Netherlands. In total, six generic principles were formulated and subsequently validated in two workshops with experts. These principles are: (i) build an intelligent front office, (ii) give processes a clear starting point and end, (iii) build a central workflow application keeping track of the process, (iv) differentiate between simple and complex processes, (v) ensure that the decision-making responsibility and the overview of the process are not performed by the same process role, and (vi) create a central point where risk profiles are maintained. Further research should focus on how organizations can adapt these principles to their own situation.

10.1 Introduction

The focus of the research presented in this chapter is on the delivery of services that require multiple public agencies to collaborate across the boundaries of their own organization. An example of such a service is the creation of a new enterprise. Setting up a new enterprise usually requires requesting a VAT number from the Inland Revenue Service, registering at the Chamber of Commerce, and registering for permits at the local government level. To create better service delivery for citizens and businesses, governments increasingly aim to realize *Integrated Service Delivery* (ISD). ISD is achieved when multiple organizations, each

A.F. van Veenstra (✉)
Delft University of Technology, Jaffalaan 5, 2628 BX, Delft, The Netherlands
e-mail: a.f.e.vanveenstra@tudelft.nl

S. Assar et al. (eds.), *Practical Studies in E-Government: Best Practices from Around the World*, DOI 10.1007/978-1-4419-7533-1_10,
© Springer Science+Business Media, LLC 2011

performing a specific part of the service delivery process, act in a coherent manner, which is perceived as integrated service delivery by customers [VEE09]. In this chapter, we adopt the customer metaphor for businesses and citizens to emphasize their benefits, instead of political or societal motives. From the perspective of a client, traditional – nonintegrated – service delivery consists of taking multiple steps and dealing with more than one organization. ISD has the advantage that citizens or businesses no longer need to contact multiple organizations, provide the same information to multiple government agencies, and integrate the separate responses into one. Instead, when ISD is realized, customers and businesses will be able to make one request to one organization, provide information only once, and receive one coherent response to which more than one organization have contributed. In the example of setting up an enterprise, this would mean that a single request to set up an enterprise would lead to all three government agencies performing their part of the service. By minimizing the number of interactions, transaction costs for citizens and businesses are reduced and accordingly lower their administrative burden.

Integrated service delivery has to deal with the problem of fragmentation of governments within constitutional, legal, and jurisdictional limits [SCH07]. One way to perform a service in an integrated manner is by forming service delivery chains that run through a network of government organizations. In such a service delivery chain, every organization performs one or more steps of the process and these steps are invoked in a coordinated manner. However, the formation of cross-organizational chains proves to be a great challenge due to the inherent fragmented nature of public administration. Different organizations need to manage and coordinate their activities and dependencies to create a single service as if it were created by one organization. Coordination of the processes of various organizations or departments to realize ISD can be called *orchestration* [JAN06]. Within this context orchestration can be defined as "the management of the interdependencies among agencies by one of those agencies, with the aim of ensuring that individual organizations collaborate in a coherent and consistent way to provide an integrated response to citizens" [JAN09]. Orchestration can, thus, be seen as a specific kind of coordination to manage the activities necessary for realizing ISD. Without orchestration customers interact with multiple government organizations and each organization deals with each customer; in a situation with orchestration, the interactions with customers as well as between the parties involved in the service delivery chain are performed in accordance (see Fig. 10.1.).

Realizing orchestration and cross-organizational chains requires interoperability on the level of organizations, management, semantics, syntaxes, and technology. As individual organizations often serve different purposes from the service delivery chain, it is necessary to make these dependencies explicit. One way of formalizing interoperability is to make use of IT, information, or enterprise architecture. IT architecture serves as a guide, roadmap, and communication tool for the development of information technology within an organization [ZAC87]. An important element of architecture is a set of generic principles

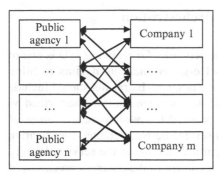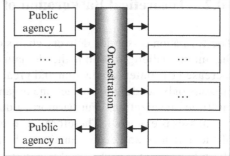

Fig. 10.1 Interactions with and without orchestration

that guides the design of these information systems. The goal of these architectural principles is to direct the development of the information technology in an organization and they are a reflection of a commonly agreed-upon strategy and way of thinking, in such a way that it is unrelated to the specific technology used [PER02]. Architectural principles are formulated as general rules or guidelines that are intended to endure and to be seldom amended that inform and support the way in which an organization sets about fulfilling its mission [PER02, RIC90].

The research presented in this chapter aims at identifying architectural principles for orchestrating the processes of multiple government organizations to create ISD. However, not much is known about the design issues that need to be addressed when orchestration is realized. By examining three case studies of cross-organizational service delivery chain formation in the Netherlands, this chapter explores this topic. All three case studies are in the government-to-business (G2B) domain. In total, six generic architecture principles have been induced from the case studies and were subsequently validated in two workshops with experts. For generalizability purposes these principles remain at an abstract level, but their practical use is explained in the case studies. This research, thus, not only addresses a gap in literature on the collaboration of public agencies aiming for ISD, but it is also of interest to practitioners. In the Netherlands, as in other countries, government organizations experience difficulties when aiming to create cross-organizational chains. The principles that are derived in this chapter are, therefore, discussed in detail and examples from case studies given to show how they can be applied to creating and improving service delivery chains.

This chapter is structured as follows. In the next section the theoretical background of orchestration is presented. Then, three in-depth case studies from the Netherlands are described and the characteristics of orchestration observed in these cases analyzed. In the following section, architectural principles for orchestration, which were found on the basis of literature and the case studies, are discussed by giving examples from practice. Finally, conclusions are drawn and recommendations are made for further research as well as for practitioners.

10.2 Theoretical Background of Orchestration

The formation of service delivery chains or networks for realizing ISD is one of the main challenges within the domain of e-government as it aims to bring increased customer satisfaction and greater efficiency. Its results should include citizens only needing to contact one organization to have a service performed by multiple organizations. Furthermore, a decrease of the administrative burden of businesses is expected. Therefore, to form service delivery chains, coordination of the activities and dependencies of the parties making up the service delivery chain is necessary. However, this requires a change in the business processes of the autonomous organizations that take part in the service delivery chain, as these organizations need to collaborate and adapt their processes to those of the service delivery chain. Achieving this degree of cooperation presents a major challenge to the chain formation as the goals of the individual organizations might differ from the objectives of the service delivery network. Orchestration, thus, needs to deal with the fragmented nature of the public sector.

10.2.1 Technical Dimension of Orchestration

Various views on orchestration can be found in the literature. Hagel-III et al. focus on value creation by managing a network of specialized organizations and see network orchestration as the coordinated mobilization of resources supplied by many enterprises at many levels of the value chain [HAG02]. From another perspective orchestration can be seen as "coordinating the processes of various organizations or departments to realize ISD" [JAN06], where coordination more generally deals with managing the dependencies between different parts [MAL90]. The theoretical underpinning of this necessity for coordination follows from the constraints that influence the outcome of a certain task, such as the maximum lead-time, the information availability and quality, and the dependencies between tasks [MAL90].

In the case of orchestration, these constraints are influenced by the requirement of realizing ISD. In essence, ISD means that customers only seem to interact with one organization, whereas, in reality, the service is being performed by multiple organizations. This leads to the following requirements for orchestration: in addition to ensuring that customers do not need to provide information more than once, all information and services that are provided to the customer should be in accordance with each other, even when they have been performed by different organizations, and the *orchestration role* (the role of integrating the different activities and pieces of information into one service) should be performed by the service delivery organizations instead of by the customer. Thus, the first challenge for orchestration is to create an overview of all the different activities, dependencies, and resources to design coordinated processes for ISD.

Ways to realize orchestration include many different coordination mechanisms [MAL94] that vary from centralized to decentralized or distributed architectures for orchestration and from hierarchical to network-oriented approaches. For example, Janssen et al. propose an architecture for Web service orchestration based on the Business Process Execution Language (BPEL) for Web services [JAN06]. Web service orchestration using BPEL invokes the time-dependent sequence of Web services by creating a process flow from the point of a single stakeholder [FRE02]. The orchestrating entity is the orchestrator, which is often a person, department, or organization. This results in a centralized coordination entity that has an overview of all necessary activities. Sheng et al. take an opposite approach and propose a distributed architecture based on events [SHE08]. The orchestration layer consists of a set of agents that collaborate with each other by events. Both centralized and decentralized approaches have their merits and disadvantages.

In a hierarchy the activities in the chain are coordinated through adjacent steps, controlled and directed at a higher level in the managerial hierarchy [MAL87], which could be called the orchestrator. As a response to the hierarchical approach, networks have emerged aimed at overcoming the problems associated with hierarchies and to create greater structural effectiveness and responsiveness [CLE93, POW90]. Whereas in a hierarchy processes are directed by the highest in the hierarchy stressing straightforward and well-defined processes, in networks many processes and relationships are possible. And whereas in a hierarchy the orchestration role is solely allocated to one single entity (the highest in the hierarchy), in networks various organizations might have the orchestration role. The choice between a hierarchical or a network approach for orchestration will depend on the relationships among stakeholders.

10.2.2   Organizational Dimension of Orchestration

The move towards ISD requires extensive process changes across organizational boundaries. This challenge is similar to Business Process Re-engineering (BPR) or the radical redesign of business processes, to achieve dramatic improvements [O'NE99]. Re-engineering service delivery processes is a complex endeavor as it involves stakeholders having different interests in mind. Stakeholder theory originates from management studies and advocates addressing the concerns of all stakeholders in a firm [FRE84]. Mitchell et al. propose to analyze stakeholders based on their power, legitimacy, and urgency attributes [MIT97]. It is commonly agreed that stakeholders influence the design process, (see for example [BRU02, PFE81]), and therefore it is likely that stakeholders influence the outcomes of the design of orchestration.

Another major challenge is for different organizations to collaborate. The success of the service delivery chain is dependent on the ability of individual organizations to collaborate, although they often have different objectives for a certain activity than that of the chain as a whole. This influences the transaction costs of collaboration between different parties involved and the dynamics of principal–agent relations. Transaction cost theory, which is concerned with the collaboration or transaction costs between two companies and the influence of these costs on the decision to cooperate or source activities, holds that the costs of cooperation are usually higher in a network situation than in a hierarchical situation, as a result of costs that have to be made, for example, for negotiation between different parties [MAL87]. Therefore, unless one organization holds strong power over the other organizations in a service chain and it can enforce its will in a hierarchical manner, the costs of setting up a service delivery chain are expected to be high, even though the use of information technology generally decreases transaction costs [MAL87]. Principal–agent theory holds that agents (in this case the individual organizations) do not always perform their tasks in the best possible manner for the principal (the chain), thereby making it impossible to ensure that the agent behaves in the optimal way for the principal without incurring any extra costs [JEN76]. This, in turn, is also likely to affect the degree to which organizations are willing to collaborate. Therefore, in addition to designing mechanisms for keeping track of the process, mechanisms coordinating the dependencies also need to be put in place when designing orchestration.

10.3   Case Studies of Orchestration

In the previous section, requirements for orchestration and two main challenges have been derived from the literature. In order to derive architectural principles for orchestration, three cases of orchestration of service delivery chains were examined and analyzed in this research. All cases were set up in the context of a government-sponsored program to diminish the administrative burden for businesses. In all cases, therefore, the (main) customers are businesses. The cases are used by this program to create lessons-learned for other organizational networks aiming to orchestrate their service delivery processes. The cases are situated in different industries, in different networks of public (and sometimes private) organizations and also lead-times vary greatly. However, as in all cases orchestration was the main focus for diminishing the administrative burden of their customers, from these very different cases some generalizations could be made.

The case study analyses were carried out by first examining relevant documents mapping the *as-is* situation and designs of the *to-be* situation, mainly on the level of business processes, responsibilities, and information flows. Furthermore, for each case multiple interviews were held with different project leaders involved in the process of redesigning the orchestration process and building a prototype. To examine and analyze all cases using the same systematic approach, first an overview was made of the key characteristics, such as number of actors involved in the chain, lead-time, process steps, and information flows. Then, all cases were analyzed to identify whether the main project and design objectives were likely to be met. However, as the case studies examined were not yet operational, only the designed *to-be* situation could be analyzed. Therefore, an analysis was also carried out to test whether this design was likely to meet the requirements of orchestration when implemented. This systematic analysis was necessary to be able to identify architectural principles afterwards.

We looked at three case studies in this research. The first case is concerned with the integration of separate permit requests to diminish the administrative burden by supporting the process of filling out the integrated request. In the second case the process of inspecting veterinary products that are imported through the Rotterdam harbor is orchestrated leading to reduced administrative burden for the importers. The third case is concerned with the orchestration of the process of asbestos removal including the required inspections to decrease illegal removals. Although the second and third cases turned out to be good examples of orchestration as they implemented a central coordination system for the processes of different organizations, the first case was identified to not yet realize full-fledged orchestration.

10.3.1   Case Study 1: Preparation Module for Joint Permit Requests

The first case study concerns the integration of previously separate permit requests at the local level into one. Until recently, businesses and citizens had to request a separate permit for all (building) activities related to the direct environment of homes and company sites. Recently, a law was introduced specifying that the permit request for all permits related to the direct environment have to be filed through a specific information system handling these requests. The aim of this project is to decrease lead-times and diminish the administrative burden of citizens and businesses as they no longer have to provide the same information for all the requests, but they can fill these requests only once. However, filling out this integrated form can become complicated when a request does not concern a single permit, for instance, for building an extension to a house, but for building a whole shopping center instead. Therefore, a preparation module was designed as an extension to this information system to prepare for the process of the actual filing of the request. The process supported by the module is shown in Fig. 10.2. The rationale behind this module is that by preparing the request thoroughly, the number of requests that is sent back for reasons of being incomplete or faulty (which often sets back the building process by a few months) is likely to decrease.

This preparation module presents the possibility of consulting experts on permit issuing, ensuring that the number of faulty forms will decrease. However, consulting representatives of the local government beforehand, who will decide about the permit request later on, is likely to make the process of filling out the permit request less transparent. Instead of designing a clear business process in

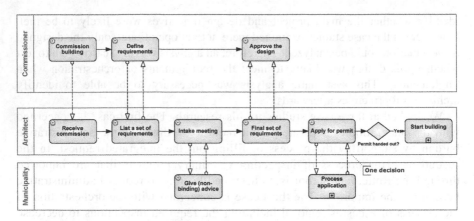

Fig. 10.2 Process of joint permit request in the preparation module

which the individual activities can be held accountable for their output, the system was designed around informal contact, in which not all decision-making information is likely to be stored, even though the information exchange via this preparation module enables capturing all the information exchanged between the different parties involved. Furthermore, although this case is expected to successfully diminish the administrative burden and decrease lead-times, it is unclear whether all requirements for orchestration will be met. Because of the lack of clear process steps and responsibilities not being clearly allocated to these steps, the requirements of information and services having to be in accordance with each other and the orchestration role being taken over from the client are only partially met. Although the designed situation without clear processes and information decoupling is expected to increase the quality level of the permit request being filled out leading to diminished administrative burden, the risk of incomplete or missing information or lack of transparency or losing track of the process is large, and, therefore, the chance that in either of these cases the client needs to take on the orchestration role is still large.

10.3.2   Case Study 2: Information System for Import of Veterinary Products

The second case concerns the process of importing veterinary products (predominantly meat) via the Rotterdam harbor. Rotterdam is the third largest port in the world and a smooth import process is important for keeping a competitive advantage over other ports or airports. Before veterinary products can enter the Netherlands or before they can be exported to other countries in Europe or beyond, these products need to be inspected to ensure they meet certain quality standards. These inspections are carried out by the Food and Consumer Product Safety Authority (in Dutch: VWA). The import process, however, is the responsibility of Customs, which is a subdivision of the Inland Revenue Service. As Customs has the responsibility over a lot of different products that are being imported, they already have a number of information systems implemented to support the import and inspection processes. However, the VWA uses different information systems. Therefore, much time is being lost by communicating the arrival of imports and the allocation of products to a specific inspector by fax. Furthermore, in the current situation all containers containing veterinary products need to be checked by a veterinarian, even those that are not opened. It should be possible, however, to allow Customs to check the information on these products as the specific skills of a veterinarian are not required.

To make the process more efficient and to decrease the lead-time of the inspection process, Customs is developing an information system that will link the existing systems of Customs, the VWA, the importing company, and the system that ships use to declare the goods they carry. This system supports the whole process from the moment (around 24 h before arrival) a ship declares its load to Customs, to the moment both the VWA and Customs approve the veterinary products for entrance into the country. All interactions with the system (called Supd@x, represented by activities within the dotted line) are shown in Fig. 10.3.

During this process all organizations can trace the incoming products, supply the information necessary for inspection, and perform administrative checks by using the new information system, even though it is owned and maintained by Customs. A second objective of the system is to decrease the administrative burden of the customer, who should only have to provide information on the import products once. After information has been entered into the system, all organizations have access to it by logging into the system and they can reuse it by linking the system to their own systems. Thus, in this case, orchestration was realized successfully, as all three requirements were met.

During the design phase of the project, however, it became clear that only some of the process inefficiency was caused by suboptimal information exchange between the different parties. Another major problem was that the office of the VWA was only open at specific times, resulting in a situation where products needed to be stored for quite some time before inspection. Widening opening times of inspections could contribute even more to decreasing the lead-time of the import process. This, however, cannot be solved by orchestrating the process alone, but requires additional agreements between the organizations involved. Furthermore, the design phase allows for interventions in the business process and the reallocation of responsibilities, for instance, by enabling Customs to take over some tasks from the vets of VWA. However, this redistribution of responsibilities needs new legislation. Although orchestration is likely to be realized in this case, additional agreements or changes in the law are likely to achieve more improvements.

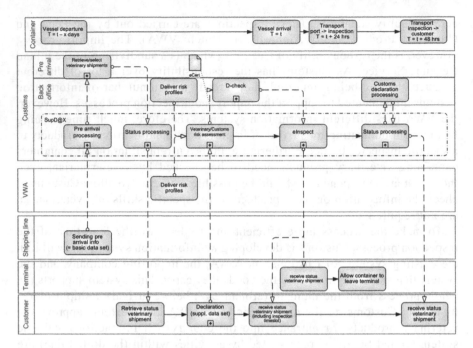

Fig. 10.3 Redesigned import process of veterinary products (Source: [AUD08])

10.3.3 Case Study 3: Information System Supporting the Asbestos Removal Process

The information system under development to improve the process of asbestos removal is the third case looked at in this research. Asbestos is a mineral that has been used in the building sector since the end of the nineteenth century because of its resilience and resistance to heat. However, the use of this material was banned in the mid-1980s after it became known that inhaling its fibers is toxic. Currently, many buildings still contain asbestos, and when the material is discovered, for example, during reconstructions, it needs to be removed in a safe manner. The removal process includes reporting the discovery of asbestos, requesting a removal license, taking a sample of the finding, and finally removing it. Currently, this process takes 6 weeks on average after the discovery of the asbestos is reported. Installing the information system is thought to decrease this lead-time radically to approximately 1 week.

Orchestrating the asbestos removal chain, however, has an even more important reason than decreasing lead-times. It is estimated that many asbestos removals are currently carried out in an illegal manner. Organizations without a certificate issued by the national certifying agency carry out the removal in an illegal manner because these organizations cannot be tracked by inspections. This means that there is no agency inspecting the manner in which these assessments and removals take place, for instance, by checking whether safety and health regulations are followed. Therefore, the main reason for undertaking this orchestration project is to get a firmer grip on the asbestos removals taking place in the Netherlands and reducing the number of illegal removals. The system designed has a similar function to that of the support system for the import of veterinary products, as it supports the information flow through the whole process (see Fig. 10.4).

As soon as asbestos is found at a specific location, this finding is reported to the Asbestos Following System (AFS). The parties with access to this system are the local government that has to issue a license for the removal and the agencies inspecting the removal process. Currently, an asbestos discovery has to be filed into the system at least 2 weeks before an assessment or removal company visits the site where the asbestos has been found. The reason for this is that the assessments and removals have to be carried out according to specific regulations and inspections have to be scheduled. As the asbestos removal process is already a step-by-step process where parties have clear responsibilities of the different steps that need to be taken, this process will not be redesigned, but merely supported by information technology capturing all the relevant information on the asbestos discovery. This means that at all times, all the parties involved can follow the status of the removal. The rationale behind this system is that by getting a firmer grip on the asbestos removal process by requiring all information to be stored and kept up to date in the system by all organizations involved, the process can be sped up. This will lead to a more efficient removal process as well as diminishing the administrative burden as information can be provided once. All requirements for orchestration are thus met.

However, the main objective for orchestrating the process was to decrease the number of illegal removals by increasing compliance to the certifying and

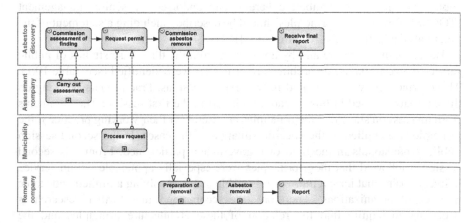

Fig. 10.4 Asbestos removal process supported by orchestrator

inspection agencies. To achieve this goal, additional improvements need to be made in addition to installing an orchestrator. Therefore, the organizations involved in the process have taken the first steps to force organizations by law to register at the certifying agency and to use the orchestrating information system that will subsequently be owned and maintained by this agency. In this instance the implementation of an orchestrator has changed the legal status of one organization, which will, in turn, lead to further process improvements and efficiency gains.

10.4 Architectural Principles for Orchestration

Supporting the formation of service delivery chains and realizing ISD requires the development of comprehensive integrated architectures [JAN05]. The goal of architecture is "to define and interrelate data; make hardware, software, and communication resources available; and have the staff to efficiently and effectively process transactions, produce information, and support a variety of domains of human activity" [RIC90]. Architecture should, thus, support business processes and be closely linked to the goal and strategies of the enterprise [JAN05]. Furthermore, architecture can be used as a roadmap for future decisions on information technology. As such, it can be used for communication purposes as well.

Architectural principles form the most important element of an architecture [RIC90]. Their goal is to formalize the underlying rules for the role of information technology (IT) within the organization. To be able to do this properly, it is important that they are clearly related to the goal of the organization and that they provide a guideline for future IT development [TOG08]. Therefore, principles should be written in a language that is understood and used by the business, they should be limited in number, coherent, and endorsed by senior management [TOG08]. Furthermore, principles should be described including a statement of the practical implications that result from it [RIC90].

Based on the literature and by abstracting from the three case studies of public service delivery chains, six architecture principles were identified (see Table 10.1). These principles were evaluated in two expert sessions. Practitioners working on the case studies used in this research took part in the first session. The comments from this session show that the principles are useful for their working practice if the principles are applied to the specific situation of the cases. In the second session public professionals in the field of e-government participated. From this second session it followed that these principles were especially applicable within service delivery chains that have a more or less stable nature involving a limited and stable number of organizations. Therefore, we recommend that further research is necessary to inquire into the relation of these architecture principles and the structure of the service delivery chain or network. Each of these six principles is discussed by giving examples from the case studies.

Table 10.1 Architectural principles for orchestration

Issue	Challenge	Principle	Implications	Theoretical background
1. Information and service aggregation	Create integrated service delivery and a single point of access	Move intelligence to the front office	Specify the information needs of the organizations involved	Coordination theory; principal–agent theory
2. Process coordination	Coordinate the dependencies in between the organizations; realize accountability	Process steps have a clear starting and end point, clear responsibility, and unambiguous links with adjacent steps	Specify simple "points of decoupling of activities"; appoint responsibilities for specific tasks	Coordination theory
3. Process overview	Create "tracking and tracing"	Build a central work flow application for creating an up-to-date and real-time process overview	Process information needs to be stored centrally	Coordination theory
4. Process optimization	Optimize the business process for greater efficiency	Differentiate between simple and complex processes that interfere, resulting in increased lead-time	Prioritize service requests by installing a selection mechanism at the start of the process	Transaction costs theory
5. Differentiate workflow and decision making	Ensure the transparency of process outcomes	Divide process control and decision authority responsibilities over different roles	Keep track of process centrally; appoint responsibility for decision making to the proper authority	Principal–agent theory; Coordination theory
6. Maintain risk profiles	Create adaptive processes that can be adjusted easily in case of law amendments	Maintain risk profiles used as selection mechanisms centrally	Other process chains can re-use maintenance functionality; creation of shared service	Principal–agent theory; coordination theory

10.4.1 Architectural Principle 1: Information and Service Aggregation

The first architectural principle follows from the requirements for orchestration. Orchestration requires that single coherent services can be delivered and that customers only need to provide information once to the service delivery chain. In short, the orchestration role needs to be taken over from the client. This means that services provided to the client that have been performed by separate organizations need to be integrated, ensuring that the client receives information that is complete and not contradictory. Furthermore, the client information that is provided at the start of the service request also needs to be disaggregated and distributed to the parties that need this information to perform the service.

In the cases examined, this information and service (dis-)aggregation took place by implementing information systems that allowed for entering and storing information from the client, which could consequently be reused by all the parties allowed to log on to the system. To ensure that this (dis-)aggregation is performed in the right way, moving intelligence to the front office will be necessary. This first architectural principle can be implemented by installing a knowledgeable employee in the front office using the orchestration system interpreting all the incoming and outgoing information or by setting up a software system in which all possible scripts have been programmed beforehand. An important implication of this principle is that all the information required by the service-providing organizations needs to be made explicit beforehand in order for the information system to store and request all this information from the client.

10.4.2 Architectural Principle 2: Process Coordination

Orchestration was defined as the coordination of processes and services to allow for ISD to be realized. Often, organizations performing a specific service are dependent on the information provided by the client or by other organizations. Therefore, these dependencies need to be mapped and the process needs to be redesigned according to the objectives of the service delivery chain. From the case studies it becomes clear that defining the starting point and end of process steps, the responsibility for the activity, and the links with the adjacent steps are important for being able to identify the separate activities and coordinating them. Furthermore, being able to hold individual steps of the process accountable for their actions and decisions appeared to be an important prerequisite for implementing orchestration. The cases in which clear steps of activities and information flows were designed were considered better practices of orchestration than the case in which a risk of opaque decision making was identified.

Furthermore, process coordination could lead to further process optimization, as it becomes possible to identify bottlenecks in the process. Implications are that "points of decoupling" need to be identified clearly to ensure that process steps have a clear starting and ending point and also responsibilities need to be allocated. Orchestration can only work if the process is accountable. If the client is dissatisfied with the service delivery, it needs to be clear where in the process a decision has been made for a certain part of the service, otherwise it is impossible to make arrangements between the organizations involved in the service delivery chain.

10.4.3   Architectural Principle 3: Process Overview

From the case studies the importance of lead-time becomes clear. Clients would like to be served as quickly as possible; for businesses the adage is: "Time is money." Furthermore, in some cases, such as the case of the joint permit request, legislation has defined the maximum lead-time for the process. Organizations involved in the service delivery chain need to rely on each other to ensure that they do not exceed this maximum lead-time, as in case of the permit request this requires the permit to be allowed automatically, for example. Therefore, it is important that not only the different organizations know of each other where a request or service is within the service delivery chain at any given time, but also the client likes to know how long the service might still take before it will be delivered. Therefore, not only coordinating the service delivery process is important for orchestration, but also giving an overview is necessary to improve service delivery: a "tracking and tracing" functionality should be added.

For this to be realized, however, process information on where a service request is being processed at any time has to be exchanged within the service delivery chain. Therefore, the third architectural principle is that a central work flow application for creating an up-to-date and real-time process overview needs to be installed. The implication of this principle is that to provide tracking and tracing information to customers at any given time, process information needs to be stored centrally. This allows organizations involved in the service delivery chain to update process information constantly that is stored in a database connected to the orchestration system.

10.4.4   Architectural Principle 4: Process Optimization

For service processing there is no single size that fits all. When process coordination is realized properly, this could lead to a next step for designing orchestration: process optimization. In order truly to improve service delivery by, for example, decreasing lead-times, removing bottlenecks from the process is important. When the different process steps have been identified and their dependencies are clear, it is possible to shift activities to different actors, as long as such reallocation of responsibilities is permitted. In case of the import of veterinary products, this can be observed, as the redesign of the process foresees a redistribution of tasks between the VWA and Customs.

Furthermore, in all cases it has been observed that one of the first process steps is a risk assessment of either the necessity of controlling the goods or of the complexity of the specific request. In these cases, simple and complex requests are separated and a different pathway through the service chain is followed. This allows for process differentiation and optimization as simple requests can be dealt with easily without having to wait for the more complex cases to be processed, and complex cases can be given more attention without this process being interrupted by simple requests. In the case of the joint permit request this, for instance, means that only complex requests make use of this preparation module. The relatively simple cases are directly referred to the information system used for the actual request of the permits.

This architectural principle is related to the first principle that enough intelligence should be installed in the service-delivering front end in order to recognize the difference between simple and complex requests. Criteria should be provided to the front office for it to be able to distinguish between simple and complex requests.

10.4.5 Architectural Principle 5: Differentiation of Workflow and Decision Making

The fifth architectural principle follows from the risks identified in the case of the joint permit request. In this case, the risk of nontransparency was identified and although the situation is set up to help clients, there is a danger of the process becoming compromised if not all steps are performed or if not all clients are treated in the same manner. Therefore, it is important to distinguish between the decision-making functionality of the service delivery chain and the workflow functionality guiding the service through the chain. To ensure the transparency of the process and its outcomes, these functionalities should not overlap in the same process role. Thus, although process information should be stored centrally, the decision-making functionality should be appointed to the proper authority being entitled to make these decisions.

10.4.6 Architectural Principle 6: Maintain Risk Profiles

In all cases a risk assessment step is designed in the orchestrated process. This risk assessment step will have one of two functions with the same overarching goal: to differentiate between simple and complex processes. In the case of the joint permit requests, an informal assessment is made when a citizen or business contacts the local government as to whether the request concerns a single permit request or a multiple permit request. Furthermore, the complexity of the request will be assessed. Principle four stated that complex processes should be treated differently, as they are expected to be more difficult to process and chances are higher that the request will be incomplete. Therefore, more attention is given to these complex requests. In the case of asbestos removal, the function of the risk assessment is to assess the complexity of the discovery. For instance, is the discovery small or large, are there multiple finds in a building, or is the asbestos located only at one spot. The complexity of the asbestos discovery is likely to have implications for the removal process as well as the inspections to be carried out.

The risk assessment process step in the case of the import of veterinary products has a slightly different functionality. Here, risk profiles are set up beforehand on the basis of pattern recognition of previous imports by the same company and the origins of the products. In the case where an importer has built up a strong name and imports are usually of impeccable quality, the frequency of inspections is decreased. In time, this is likely to lead to a more advanced system of inspections in which mainly the suspicious imports will be inspected and trusted products will be released often without inspection, accelerating the import process.

However, in both cases, risk profiles are partly dependent on legislation. In the case of importing veterinary products, legislation could decide that certain countries need to be checked more thoroughly, for instance, because of a recent breakout of a disease. And in the other two cases, risk assessment criteria may change as a result of changing legislation, for example, if European criteria for asbestos removal require a change in Dutch legislation. In order for these changes of law to be noticed clearly, it could be useful to maintain risk profiles centrally. In that way, business processes are not affected by any changes in legislation and maintaining these profiles centrally, specialized lawyers could be given responsibility over the risk assessment of service delivery chains, resulting in shared services.

10.5   Conclusion

The case studies show that although various approaches to orchestration can be taken, some similarities could be identified that are translated into generic principles. Architectural principles form an important part of any IT architecture as a way to formalize the underlying rules for the role and design of systems within the organization. In this chapter we derived six architecture principles for orchestration of cross-organizational service delivery based on theory and practice. These principles are: (i) build an intelligent front office, (ii) give processes a clear starting point and end, (iii) build a central workflow application keeping track of the processes, (iv) differentiate between simple and complex processes, (v) ensure that the decision-making responsibility and the overview of the process are not performed by the same process role, and (vi) create a central point where risk profiles are maintained. The case studies show how these principles can be used in practice for creating ISD by developing cross-organizational service delivery chains. They can guide the process of re-engineering supply chains in which many stakeholders take part.

The use of the architectural principles will avoid problems at a later stage by creating adaptive processes and increasing transparency. In the case studies these principles were used to lower the administrative burden, to improve the effectiveness and efficiency of the service delivery process, and to increase customer satisfaction. Evaluation of these principles showed that they can be used to design orchestration arrangements in public service networks and in this way the advantages of orchestration for improving cross-agency service delivery processes can be exploited fully. However, these principles were formulated based on case studies in stable service delivery chains in the Netherlands in which a fixed number of parties are involved. Furthermore, for purposes of generalization, these principles were formulated in an abstract manner. Therefore, we recommend organizations to adapt and customize these principles to their situation. This is likely to result in more specific principles that are easily understood and directly applicable to their specific situations.

Further research should be carried out to learn more about the effectiveness of architectural principles in other cross-organizational processes. The case studies in our example employ SOA and Web service orchestration (BPEL) technology, whereas there are also other approaches and standards for realizing ISD. Currently a shift is occurring towards the use of Event-Driven Service-Oriented Architecture (EDSOA) in which events are communicated instead of messages and receivers must determine whether and how to react to an event [OVE09]. Although there are no examples found in practice yet, this development should be monitored and used to determine whether the principles remain valid and if new principles can be derived. Moreover, further research should focus on other ways of evaluating cross-organizational chains. The case studies in this chapter were analyzed from a BPR perspective analyzing the main process steps and information flows. Other methods include using a Delphi method or by carrying out action research. A Delphi method relies on a panel of experts that can be used to evaluate and extend the principles. Other ways of evaluating the principles are determining the actual use in practice of either the principles alone or of architectures developed based on the principles.

References

AUD08   Audenaerdt, R., de Wit, J., "Toekomstvisie veterinaire importproces Zeehavens, versie 1.0." Ministerie van Economische Zaken, Programma SGGV (voorheen Ketenherinrichting), 2008.
BRU02   de Bruijn, H., ten Heuvelhof, E., in 't Veld, R., Process management. Why project management fails in complex decision making processes. Dordrecht, Kluwer, Academic Publishers, 2002.
CLE93   Clemons, E.K., Row, M.C., "Limits to interfirm co-ordination through information technology: Results of a field study in consumer packaged goods distribution." Journal of Management Information Systems, vol. 10, no. 1, 1993, pp. 73–95.
FRE84   Freeman, R.E., Strategic management: A stakeholder approach. Boston, Pitman Publishing, 1984.

FRE02   Fremantle, P., Weerawarana, S., Khalaf, R., "Enterprise services. Examine the emerging files of web services and how it is integrated into existing enterprise infrastructures." Communications of the ACM, vol. 45, no. 20, 2002, pp. 77–82.

HAG02   Hagel-III, J., Durchslag, S., Brown, J.S., "Orchestrating loosely coupled business processes: The secret to successful business collaboration." Unpublished manuscript, 2002. Available online at http://www.johnhagel.com/paper_orchestratingcollaboration. pdf, accessed Oct. 4, 2010.

JAN05   Janssen, M., Cresswell, A.M., "An enterprise application integration methodology for e-government." The Journal of Enterprise Information Management, vol. 18, no. 5, 2005, pp. 531–547.

JAN06   Janssen, M., Gortmaker, J., Wagenaar, R.W., "Web service orchestration in public administration: Challenges, roles, and growth stages." Information Systems Management, vol. 23, no. 2, 2006, pp. 44–55.

JAN09   Janssen, M. "Orchestrating networks for Integrated Service Delivery." Paper presented at Advances in E-government and E-governance, 2009.

JEN76   Jensen, M.C., Meckling, W.H., "Theory of the firm: Managerial behavior, agency costs, and ownership structure." Journal of Financial Economics, vol. 3, no. 4, 1976, pp. 305–360.

MAL90   Malone, T.W., Crowston, K., "What is coordination theory and how can it help design cooperative work systems?" Proceedings of the Conference on Computer-Supported Cooperative Work CSCW'90, 7–10 October, Los Angelos, California, 1990.

MAL94   Malone, T.W., Crowston, K., "The interdisciplinary study of coordination." ACM Computing Surveys, vol. 26, no. 2, 1994, pp. 87–119.

MAL87   Malone, T.W., Yates, J., Benjamin, R.I., "Electronic markets and electronic hierarchies." Communications of the ACM, vol. 30, no. 6, 1987, pp. 484–497.

MIT97   Mitchell, R.K., Agle, B.R., Wood, D.J., "Toward a theory of stakeholder identification and salience: Defining the principle of who and what really counts." Academy of Management Review, vol. 22, no. 4, 1997, pp. 853–886.

O'NE99   O'Neill, P., Sohal, A.S., "Business process reengineering. A review of recent literature." Technovation, vol. 19, no. 9, 1999, pp. 571–581.

OVE09   Overbeek, S.J., Klievink, B., Janssen. M., "A flexible event-driven service-oriented architecture for orchestrating service delivery." IEEE Intelligent Systems, vol. 24, no. 5, 2009, pp. 31–41.

PER02   Perks, C., Beveridge, T., Guide to enterprise IT architecture. New York, Springer, 2002.

PFE81   Pfeffer, J., Power in Organizations. Boston, Pitman Publishing, 1981.

POW90   Powell, W., "Neither market nor hierarchy: Network forms of organization." In: Staw, B.M., Cummings, L.L. (eds.), Research in organization behavior. Greenwich CT, JAI Press, 1990.

RIC90   Richardson, G.L., Jackson, B.M., Dickson, G.W. "A principles-based enterprise architecture: Lessons from texaco and star enterprise." MIS Quarterly, vol. 14, no. 4, 1990, pp. 385–403.

SHE08   Sheng, Q.Z., Benatallah, B., Maamar, Z., "User-centric services provisioning in wireless environments." Communications of the ACM, vol. 51, no. 11, 2008, pp. 130–135.

SCH07   Scholl, H.J., Klischewski R., "E-Government Integration and Interoperability: Framing the Research Agenda." International Journal of Public Administration, vol. 30, 2007, pp. 1–32.

TOG08   The Open Group, TOGAF 8.1.1 Online, part IV: Resource Base, Chapter 29: Architecture Principles. http://www.opengroup.org/architecture/togaf8-doc/arch/ chap29.html, accessed Nov. 24, 2008.

VEE09   van Veenstra, A.F., Janssen, M., "Orchestratie van Ketens: Techniek, bestuur en organisatie. Een onderzoek voor de Alliantie Vitaal Bestuur (AVB)." Delft University of Technology, 2009. http://www.overheid20.nl/widgets/edit_entry/filesharing/134, accessed Nov. 4, 2009.

ZAC87   Zachman, J.A., "A framework for information systems architecture." IBM Systems Journal, vol. 26, no. 3, 1987, pp. 276–292.

Chapter 11
Achieving Interoperability Through Base Registries for Governmental Services and Document Management

Yannis Charalabidis, Fenareti Lampathaki, and Dimitris Askounis

Abstract As digital infrastructures increase their presence worldwide, following the efforts of governments to provide citizens and businesses with high-quality one-stop services, there is a growing need for the systematic management of those newly defined and constantly transforming processes and electronic documents. E-government Interoperability Frameworks usually cater to the technical standards of e-government systems interconnection, but do not address service composition and use by citizens, businesses, or other administrations.

An Interoperability Registry is a system devoted to the formal description, composition, and publishing of traditional or electronic services, together with the relevant document and process descriptions in an integrated schema. Through such a repository, the discovery of services by users or systems can be automated, resulting in an important tool for managing e-government transformation towards achieving interoperability.

The chapter goes beyond the methodology and tools used for developing such a system for the Greek government, to population with services and documents, application, and extraction of useful conclusions for electronic government transformation at the global level.

11.1 Introduction

As the development and deployment of electronic government solutions continues, the system complexity, multiplicity, and diversity in the public sector is posing extreme challenges to common interoperability standards. In this quest for collaborative operation, e-Government Interoperability Frameworks (eGIFs) are a cornerstone for the provision of one-stop, fully electronic services to businesses and

Y. Charalabidis (✉)
Department of Information and Communication Systems Engineering, University of the Aegean, School of Sciences, Karlovassi, Samos, 83200, Greece
e-mail: yannisx@aegean.gr

S. Assar et al. (eds.), *Practical Studies in E-Government: Best Practices from Around the World*, DOI 10.1007/978-1-4419-7533-1_11,
© Springer Science+Business Media, LLC 2011

citizens [IDA07]. Such interoperability frameworks aim at outlining the essential prerequisites for joined-up and Web-enabled Pan-European E-Government Services (PEGS), covering their definition and deployment over thousands of front-office and back-office systems in an ever-extending set of public administration organizations.

Embracing central, local, and municipal government, e-government interoperability assists public sector modernization at business, semantic, and technology levels. As more and more complex information systems are put into operation every day, the lack of interoperability appears as the most long-lasting and challenging problem for governmental organizations that emerged from proprietary development of applications, unavailability of standards, or heterogeneous hardware and software platforms.

11.2 Background and Scope

In order to effectively tackle the transformation of public administration, the European Union has set key relevant priorities in its "i2010 eGovernment Action Plan" [EUR07]. At the national level, most European Union member states have produced their own national digital strategies (e.g., the Greek Digital Strategy 2006–2013 [GRE07], or the Estonian Digital Strategy [EST06]) which include measures and strategic priorities aimed at developing e-government.

Within this context, most countries have tried to face the interoperability challenge with the adoption of national e-GIFs covering areas such as data integration, metadata, security, confidentiality, and delivery channels, which fall into the technical interoperability layer. Such frameworks have issued "sets of documents" guiding system design but to date have not developed appropriate infrastructures, such as repositories of XML schemas for the exchange of specific-context information throughout the public sector, observed only partially in the United Kingdom's e-GIF Registry [UKC09] and the Danish InfoStructureBase [DAN09]. Furthermore, as shown in recent e-government framework reviews [CHA07, GUI07], there exists no infrastructure proposal for constructing, publishing, locating, understanding, and using electronic services by systems or individual users.

In order to take full advantage of the opportunities promised by e-government, a second-generation interoperability frameworks era, launching "systems talking about systems" and addressing issues related to unified governmental service and data models, needs to commence. As presented in the next sections of this chapter, such an interoperability registry infrastructure, should consist of:

- An e-government ontology, able to capture the core elements and their relations, thus representing services, documents, providing organizations, service users, systems, Web services, and so on.
- A metadata schema, extending the e-government ontology and providing various categorization facets for the core elements, so as to cover for information insertion, structuring, and retrieval.

- Formal means for describing the flow of processes, either still manual or electronic, and the structure and semantics of various electronic documents exchanged among public administrations, citizens, and businesses.
- An overall platform integrating data storage, ontology management, enterprise modeling, and XML authoring, data input, and querying mechanisms as well as access control and presentation means.
- The population of the e-government ontology database, with information about administrations, their systems, services, and documents is an important step. Because this task usually involves gathering huge amounts of information, an initial set of data should be considered first: this way, population achieves a critical mass, while automatic knowledge acquisition tools are being developed.

11.3   Defining an E-Government Ontology

The representation means of the proposed system should first capture the core elements of the domain, together with their main relationships. Most existing approaches for e-government ontologies cover neighboring domains, such as public administration knowledge [FRA03, WIM06], argumentation in service provision [DIP04, SEN07], eGovernment projects [DAM01], or types and actors in national governments [CIA02].

As partly depicted in Fig. 11.1, the proposed e-government ontology [CHA08a, SOU08] provides for the representation of the following core elements.

- Services provided in conventional or electronic means by public authorities to citizens and businesses
- Documents, in electronic or printed format, that constitute the inputs or outputs of a service or are involved during their execution
- Information systems that support the service provision and encompass the Web portals as well as the back-office and the legacy systems
- Administrations, nested at infinite hierarchical levels, being ministries, regions, municipalities, organizations, or their divisions and departments
- Web services for the interconnection and the interoperability among information systems during a service execution
- Legal framework that regulates the service provision, documents issuance, and overall operation of the public bodies
- XML schemas and code lists with which the electronically exchanged documents comply and which are exploited in Web services
- Business Process Modeling Notation (BPMN) models for linking services with their workflow models
- Web Services Definition Language (WSDL) descriptions linking Web services with the respective systematic, machine-readable description of their behavior

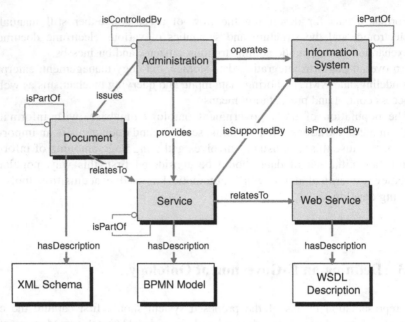

Fig. 11.1 Core elements of the ontology

Additional objects complementing the core ontology elements are citizens (as various types of citizens requesting services), enterprises (both as service recipients but also as contractors for government projects), legal framework elements (that guide services provision), life events and business episodes that may trigger a service request, or technical standards affecting the provision of electronic services.

11.3.1   Metadata Standards for Multifaceted Classification

The e-government ontology is supported by numerous categorization facets and standardized lists of values for systematically structuring database contents during the population phase, including types of services and documents (according to the Government Category List (GCL) categorization).

All the core elements of the e-government ontology have predefined metadata, so that their description, search, and retrieval can be assisted. The implemented metadata structure is based on and extends a number of existing metadata structures in literature and practice, namely:

- Dublin Core Metadata Initiative [DUB07] provides a generic set of attributes for any government resource, be it document or system, including various extensions [TAM05].
- United Kingdom's e-Government Metadata Standard (UK eGMS) [UKC07] lays down the elements, refinements, and encoding schemes to be used by

government officers when creating metadata for their information resources or designing search interfaces for information systems.

- Australian Government Locator Service (AGLS) Metadata Element Set [AUS09] provides a set of metadata elements designed to improve the visibility, accessibility, and interoperability of online information, organizations, and services.
- New Zealand Government Locator Service (NZGLS) Metadata Element Set [STA09] originally designed for use by any governmental agency wishing to make information sources or services more readily discoverable is suitable for more general use.
- IDABC Management Information Resources for E-Government (MIREG) [IDA09] came to supplement MOREQ (Model Requirements for the Management of Electronic Records) results and aimed to develop extensions to the Dublin Core for government information based primarily on the national metadata recommendations of the member states' public administrations.
- CEN/ISSS Workshop on Discovery of and Access to e-Government Resources (CEN/ISSS WS/eGov-Share) [CEN09] presents the ontology for the description of e-government resources (services, process descriptions, standards and interoperability frameworks, requirements, documents) and the metadata schema that is used in its work.

However, such metadata standards and schemes for network resources apply mainly to documents, electronic archives, and public sites or do not cover all the requirements for service-related modeling.

The resulting metadata definitions proposed in this chapter cover all the important facets for classifying and querying the elements of the ontology, so as to provide answers to important questions regarding the status of electronic provision of services, existence and structure of documents, relation of services with public administrations, characteristics of the various governmental information systems, and so on. Table 11.1 shows the metadata definitions for the service element, indicating which of them are represented as lists of values or structured elements themselves [CHA09b, LAM07].

Relevant, extensive metadata description fields exist for documents, administrations, information systems, and Web services, providing an indication of the descriptive power of the ontology. Noncore elements (e.g., legal framework elements, generic governmental resources) may have simpler metadata fields, as shown in Table 11.2.

11.4 Combining Processes and Data

The description of services and documents cannot be complete without formal representation of the services flow and of the documents' internal structure. The importance of formal, combined description of services and document schemas has been properly identified in the current literature [GON06, GUI07].

Business modeling and analysis of the processes and the public documents that take part in their execution, is done using the BPMN notation [OMG06] and the ADONIS modeling tool, provided by BoC International [BOC08].

Table 11.1 Services metadata[a]

General information		
Identifier	Title	Responsible public body
Final service (*)	Addressee (*)	Type (*)
Aggregation (3 level-GCL) (*)	Life event (*)	Business episode (*)
Service in abstract level (*)	Parent service	Service delivery channels (*)
Conventional service provision		
Demand for physical presence in submission (*)	Demand for physical presence in receipt (*)	Conventional authentication method (*)
Electronic service provision		
Website	Electronic service delivery method (*)	Current online sophistication level (*)
Target online sophistication level (*)	Multilingual content (*)	Offline operation (*)
Progress monitoring support (*)	Personal data level (*)	Trust level (*)
Required authentication level (*)	Current authentication mechanism (*)	Registration process (*)
Service significance/importance		
Transactions volume (per year)	Frequency of service requests	Based on European policies (*)
Service delivery information		
Delivery cost	Delivery time	Responsible department
Responsible public servant		
Related announcements	Service preconditions	
Service alternative scenaria information[b]	Related attachments	
Identifier	Title	Conditions
Resources for public administration	Resources for addressee	Total resources
Cost for public administration	Cost for addressee	Total cost
Time for public administration	Time for addressee	Total time

			Mandatory (*)
	Date: published	Date: modified	
Source	State (*)	Language (*)	
Date: valid (from–to)			
Documents list			
Identifier	Title	Position in service (*)	
		Self-appointed call (*)	
Replaces document			
Information systems list			
Legal framework list			
Supporting web services list			
BPMN workflow diagram			

Service tracing

[a] The fields marked with (*) take values from appropriate predefined, controlled lists
[b] It includes computed fields based on the step-by-step calculation of cost, time, and resources, taking into account the possibility of faults

Table 11.2 Legal framework metadata[a]

General information		
Identifier	Title	Official journal identifier
Official journal page numbers	Application field (*)	Application status (*)
Type (*)	Language (*)	Date: issued
Date: signed	Date: valid (from–to)	Relevant attachments
Legal rule details		
Identifier	Title	Description
Legal framework relations details		
Legal framework identifier	Relation type (*)	

[a]The fields marked with (*) take values from appropriate predefined, controlled lists

As shown in Fig. 11.2, e-government processes are modeled using BPMN notation, resulting in easy identification of documents to be exchanged, decisions taken during the service flow by citizens/businesses or administrations, and specific activities or information systems that take part in the overall process execution, in this case the electronic VAT declaration from an enterprise to the Tax Authority.

Design of data schemas involved in the execution of the processes under consideration has been performed with the use of the UN/CEFACT CCTS methodology [UN07], for the creation of common components among the various governmental documents that have been identified through process modeling. Then, following modeling and homogenization of data components, Altova XML authoring tools [ALT09] have been used for defining the final XSD descriptions representing business documents of all types.

Final XSD files [CHA08b] have been linked with the respective governmental documents of the ontology, resulting in a comprehensive and easy to navigate semantic network structure.

11.5 The Interoperability Registry Platform

State of the art in registries and repositories for the public sector typically falls within the jurisdiction of the current European or national e-government interoperability frameworks. In most cases, however, such repositories try to cover the semantic aspect of interoperability with XML schemas for the exchange of specific-context information throughout the public sector within the country borders and do not interfere with service descriptions or Web services deployment. For example in the European Union:

• The United Kingdom has developed the XML Schema Library [UKC07], containing approximately 78 XML schemas.

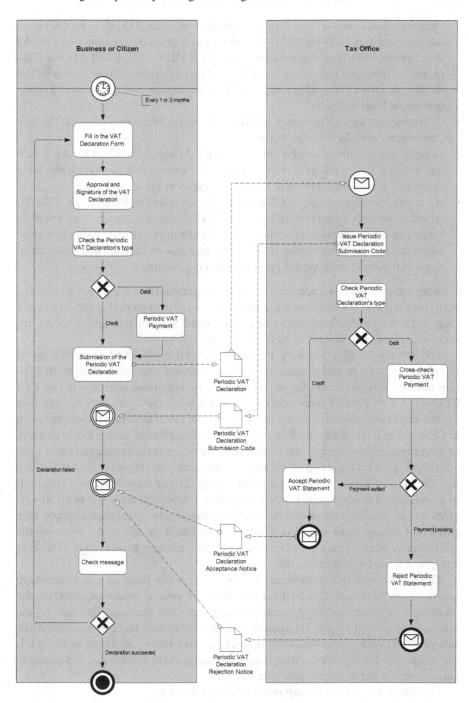

Fig. 11.2 VAT declaration model

- Denmark has designed the InfoStructureBase system [DAN09], including an international standards repository with business process descriptions, data-model descriptions, interface descriptions, complex XML schemas, and schema fragments (information objects) from public and private organizations, and an UDDI (Universal Description, Discovery, and Integration) repository containing information on Web services.
- Germany has the XRepository [BIT09], a central point providing XÖV core components and data models for reuse.
- In Italy, one can find a similar approach in the Arianna project [BAR06], which has defined an ontology for e-government public services and deployed a repository containing service descriptions mainly at the local level.
- At a pan-European level, the European Interoperability Framework [IDA07] which is currently being revised by IDABC [IDA08] is met. As far as the semantic interoperability aspect is concerned, EU-Project SEMIC.EU (Semantic Interoperability Centre Europe) [SEM09] has also been launched in order to support the data exchange for pan-European e-government services.

Gaining knowledge, best practices, and lessons learned from the above similar but partial attempts [PAL08], Greece has deployed an infrastructure that can effectively support the interoperable operation of governmental systems through providing for service composition, discovery, and use in a utility-like way.

The Interoperability Registry Prototype [CHA09a, SOU08] is a Web-based repository of service and document metadata, service process models in BPMN, standardized XML schemas for often-used governmental documents based on UN/CEFACT CCTS (Core Components Technical Specification), as well as code lists for the most common information elements within governmental service provision in Greece. The Interoperability Registry prototype can enhance access to and delivery of governmental knowledge, information, and services to the public and other governmental agencies and bring about improvements in government to operations that may include effectiveness, efficiency, service quality, or transformation. It is built to provide a methodological process modeling framework for e-government services via an ontology-based intelligent Web information system with simple data entry and management and also allows different user groups to be aware of the public sector administration and services provision through a wide range of simple, complicated, and statistical reports.

The architecture that implements the Interoperability Registry comprises three layers: (a) the Web-based and UDDI interfaces for various groups of users, (b) the tools layer including ontology management, process and data modeling, and (c) the information repository for interconnected data elements, process models, XML schemas, and Web services descriptions. These three layers, as shown in Fig. 11.3, are integrated through a relational database management system and the common access control and application engine.

The front-end platform components are the following:

- The registry website found within the Greek eGIF website [GRE08], which publishes the various documents of the e-government framework but also gives access to citizens and businesses for publicly available data.

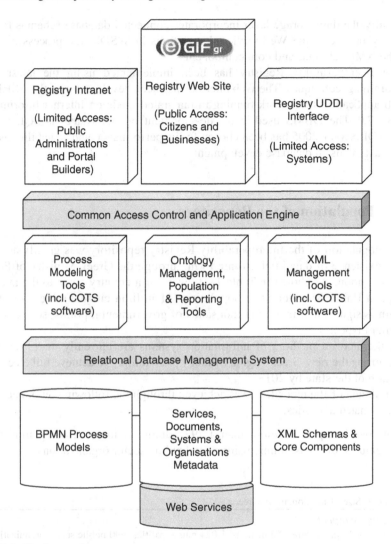

Fig. 11.3 Platform architecture

- The registry intranet, accessible to preselected public administrations and portal builders that gives access to the registry tools (processes, ontology, XML).
- The registry UDDI interface, where administrations publish their Web services or find existing available Web services to use through their information systems, constructing truly interoperable, one-stop services.

The tools layer consists of the process modeling facilities, based on the ADONIS engine, the XML management facilities, based on the ALTOVA XML platform, and the custom-developed ontology management, data entry, and reporting tools that integrate all representations and models.

Finally, the data storage layer incorporates connected database schemas for the ontology instances, the Web service descriptions in WSDL, the process models, and the XML schemas and core components.

The Interoperability Registry has been implemented using the latest Web programming techniques. The Web interface has been developed with the ASP.NET 2 Web application framework running in integrated mode on Internet Information System 7.0. The DBMS used in the development of this system is SQL Server 2005. SQL Server 2005 has been chosen for its performance and scalability as one of the last trends in database development.

11.6 Population of the Repository

Initial population of the Interoperability Registry repository was greatly assisted by the existence of data in electronic form, through the Greek Ministry of Public Administration. As shown in Table 11.3, even for a country close to the average European Union Member State population (11 million citizens), the size of the domain is significant, involving thousands of governmental points, services, and document types.

Furthermore, a plethora of information systems are currently under development, during the new Greek Digital Strategy plan, aiming to achieve full electronic operation of the state by 2013.

Population of the repository was achieved through the following automated and semiautomated activities.

• Automated import of more than 1,797 administrations including ministries, prefectures, districts, municipalities, and public sector organizations

Table 11.3 Size of the domain in Greece

Organizational aspect
18 Ministries, 13 prefectures, 52 districts, 1,024 municipalities, 690 public sector organizations
2,500 Governmental points of service'
Services and data aspect
3,000 Noninteroperable service types (government to citizens and businesses)
4,500 Document types exchanged between administrations
Systems aspect
300 Central government internet portals
1,000 Municipal government internet portals
2,500 Public administration back-office systems
Users aspect
750,000 Enterprises (small, medium and large)
11,000,000 Citizens
18,000,000 Tourists per year
1,000 IT products and services companies

- Automated import of 1,009 public service definitions, with core metadata descriptions and frequency indications, stemming from three million service requests by citizens and businesses during the last year
- Modeling of the core-100 governmental services (including all i2010 services and the services amounting to 85% of the yearly service requests)
- Modeling of the core XML schemas and WSDL for Web services to be developed, an ongoing activity

The resulting platform is now being maintained and further populated with the assistance of engaged public administrations. Already, crucial questions of administrations can be answered, such as the following:

- What is the formal description of the birth certificate issuing service?
- Which services depend on identity card provision?
- What are the most needed services by other services (interoperability request)?
- What are the necessary documents and their XML definitions for issuing a residence permit?
- Which services pertaining to civil registries are already electronic at level 2 or 3?
- What are the existing Web services from the Tax Authorities – Ministry of Finance?

The target audience for the Interoperability Registry Prototype includes the Informatics Development Agency of the Greek Ministry of Interior (as the Registry Authorized Monitor), every public body that provides any type of governmental services, and ultimately citizens and enterprises as beneficiaries of the registered services. The initial users of the Interoperability Registry by the public administration were determined in a three-stage approach: (a) the core team, including the Ministry of Public Administration and the National eGIF team; (b) the main public sector stakeholders, including key ministries, organizations, and local administrations; and (c) e-government project managers and implementation teams, from the public and private sectors. Currently, registry users, with various levels of access, exceed 100.

The acceptance of the Interoperability Registry by the public administration is ensured by the fact that the Greek eGIF is (since January 2009) a national law (Law 3731/2008) in Greece based on which all public IT systems and services must abide by its provisions. According to this law, the competent authority for maintaining the eGIF and the registry (from April 2009) will be the Informatics Development Agency which falls under the jurisdiction of the Greek Ministry of Interior. The prototype has now come into full productivity and is hosted in the infrastructures of the national e-government portal, HERMES.

11.7   Conclusions

The new Greek Interoperability Registry presented in this chapter introduces a new system (not a paper-based specification) that will interact with e-government portals and back-office applications, administration stakeholders, businesses, and citizens, guiding e-government transformation and ensuring interoperability by design, rework, or change.

The implementation addresses a number of key issues, such as the following:

- Definition of an e-government ontology and metadata definitions for all core elements in the e-government domain
- Formal description of governmental services with the use of BPMN models and tools
- Development of unified governmental data models (in the direction of UN/ CEFACT Core Components), with the use of XML authoring platforms [CHA07]
- Integration of models, tools, and repositories in a comprehensive platform, made available to public administrations, businesses, and citizens.
- Specification of truly interoperable, one-stop governmental services.

The initial application of the system, as well as the relevant evolutions from other European eGIFs, are indicating that new perspectives should be taken into consideration in e-government frameworks from now on, analyzed as follows:

- Importance and adequate effort should be put in defining standard, formally described electronic services for businesses and citizens, thus providing clear examples to administrations and service portal developers.
- Paper-based specification should give way to system-based presentation of the framework, incorporating service descriptions, data definitions, unified domain representation ontologies, and metadata in a common repository.
- Organizational interoperability issues should be supported by a more concrete methodology of how to transform traditional services to electronic flows, with the use of decision-making tools. In this direction, the interoperability registry infrastructure presented can be of great assistance as it contains all the necessary information in a comprehensive, well-defined, and connected semantic network.
- The collaboration among European e-government interoperability frameworks is particularly beneficial for the ongoing efforts of individual countries, because it ensures that lessons from the pioneers' experience are learned and that the same mistakes will not be repeated.

Future work concerning the Greek eGIF and the Interoperability Registry includes both organizational and technical tasks, inasmuch as the proper maintenance and usage of the registry is now the crucial issue. As far as the metadata set hindered behind the registry is concerned, further steps include: (a) exploitation in intelligent governmental service front ends that enhance end-users' experience and have recently started to gain momentum at the international research scene, mainly when it comes to provided public services cataloguing and user groups profiling information, and (b) further elicitation in order to take into account service addressees' feedback when creating the service alternative scenarios.

Finally, is has been identified that no system can work without the public servants' engagement: more effort is to be put towards encouraging stakeholders to interact with the registry and among themselves, building synergies across the public sector authorities in a truly interdisciplinary way and, it is hoped, extending the e-participation features of the registry.

References

ALT09   Altova XML-Spy Authorware Tools, www.altova.com

AUS09   Australian Government, National Archives of Australia, AGLS Metadata Standard, Version 1.3, 2009, http://www.naa.gov.au/records-management/publications/AGLS-Element.aspx (2009)

BAR06   Barone A., Di Pietro P.: Semantic of e-Government Processes: A Formal Approach to Service Definition (Arianna), in Proceedings of eGovINTEROP 2006, Bordeaux, France (2006)

BIT09   BIT. XRepository, Retrieved June 12, 2009, from https://www.xrepository.deutschland-online.de/ (2009)

BOC08   BOC International, The ADONIS Modeling Tool, http://www.boc-group.com/ (2008)

CEN09   CEN/ISSS Workshop on Discovery of and Access to e-Government Resources (CEN/ISSS WS/eGov-Share): Sharing e-Government resources: A practical approach for designers and developers, http://www.cen.eu/cenorm/businessdomains/businessdomains/isss/workshops/wsegovshare.asp (2009)

CIA02   CIA World Fact Book, The Government type Ontology, http://reliant.teknowledge.com/DAML/Government.owl (2002)

CHA07   Charalabidis Y., Lampathaki F., Stassis A.: "A Second-Generation e-Government Interoperability Framework" 5th Eastern European e|Gov Days 2007 in Prague, Austrian Computer Society (2007)

CHA08a   Charalabidis, Y., Askounis, D.: Interoperability Registries in e-Government: Developing a Semantically Rich Repository for Electronic Services and Documents of the new Public Administration, in Proceedings of the 41st Hawaiian International Conference of System Sciences, HICCS-08, Hawaii (2008)

CHA08b   Charalabidis, Y., Lampathaki, F., Askounis, D.: "Unified Data Modeling and Document Standardization Using Core Components Technical Specification for Electronic Government Applications", Journal of Theoretical and Applied Electronic Commerce Research, 3(3), 38–51 (2008)

CHA09a   Charalabidis, Y., Lampathaki, F., Psarras, J.: Combination of Interoperability Registries with Process and Data Management Tools for Governmental Services Transformation, in Proceedings of the 42nd Hawaiian International Conference of System Sciences, HICCS-09, Hawaii (2009)

CHA09b   Charalabidis, Y., Lampathaki, F., Askounis, D.: Metadata Sets for e-Government Resources: The Extended e-Government Metadata Schema (eGMS+), Lecture Notes on Computer Science, vol. 5693, pp. 341–352, in Proceedings of 8th EGOV Conference 2009, Linz Austria (2009)

DAM01   DAML, The Government R&D Ontology, http://www.daml.org/projects/integration/projects-20010811 (2001)

DAN09   Danish E-government Project, InfostructureBase, http://isb.oio.dk/info (2009)

DIP04   DIP Project eGovernment Ontology, http://dip.semanticweb.org/documents/D9-3-improved-eGovernment.pdf (2004)

DUB07   Dublin Core Metadata Element Set, Version 1.1, Retrieved January 25, 2007 from http://dublincore.org/documents/dces/ (2007)

EST06   Estonian Government, Estonian Information Society Strategy 2013, ec.europa.eu/idabc/en/document/6811/254 (2006)

EUR07   European Commission, The i2010 eGovernment Action Plan, http://ec.europa.eu/
         idabc/servlets/Doc?id=25286 (2007)
FRA03   Fraser J., Adams N., Macintosh A., Mckay-Hubbard A., Lobo T.P., Pardo P.F., Martinez
         R.C., Vallecillo J.S.: "Knowledge Management Applied to E-Government Services:
         The Use of an Ontology", Knowledge Management In Electronic Government, Lecture
         Notes in Artificial Intelligence, vol. 2645, pp. 116–126, Springer, Berlin (2003)
GON06   Gong R., Li Q., Ning K., Chen Y., O'Sullivan D.: "Business Process Collaboration
         Using Semantic Interoperability: Review and Framework", in Semantic Web – ASWC
         2006 Proceedings, Lecture Notes in Computer Science, Springer, Berlin (2006)
GRE07   Greek Government, The Greek Digital Strategy 2006–2013, http://www.infosoc.gr/
         infosoc/en-UK/sthnellada/committee/default1/top.htm (2007)
GRE08   Greek Government, eGovernment Interoperability Framework, http://www.e-gif.gov.
         gr (2008)
GUI07   Guijarro L.: "Interoperability Frameworks and Enterprise Architectures in
         E-Government Initiatives in Europe and the United States", Government Information
         Quarterly 24(1): 89–101, Elsevier Inc. (2007)
IDA07   IDABC, European Interoperability Framework for pan-European e-Government
         Services, Version 1.0, Retrieved February 5, 2007 from http://europa.eu.int/idabc/en/
         document/3761 (2007)
IDA08   IDABC European Interoperability Framework draft, Version 2.0, http://ec.europa.eu/
         idabc/servlets/Doc?id=31508 (2008)
IDA09   IDABC Management Information Resources for e-Government, http://ec.europa.eu/
         idabc/en/document/3615/5585 (2009)
LAM07   Lampathaki, F., Charalabidis, Y., Sarantis, D., Koussouris, S., Askounis, D.:
         E-Government Services Composition Using Multi-faceted Metadata Classification
         Structures, in Wimmer, M.A., Scholl, H.J., Grönlund, A. (eds.), Proceedings of 6th
         EGOV Conference 2007, Lecture Notes in Computer Science, vol. 4656, Springer,
         Berlin, pp. 116–126 (2007)
OMG06   OMG Business Process Modelling Notation (BPMN) Specification, Final Adopted
         Specification   http://www.bpmn.org/Documents/OMG%20Final%20Adopted%20
         BPMN%201-0%20Spec%2006-02-1.pdf (2006)
PAL08   Palmonari, M., Viscusi, G., Batini, C.: "A Semantic Repository Approach to Improve
         the Government to Business Relationship", Data & Knowledge Engineering, 65:
         485–511 (2008)
SEN07   Seng J.L., Lin W.: "An Ontology-Assisted Analysis in Aligning Business Process with
         E-Commerce Standards", Industrial Management & Data Systems, 107(3–4): 415–437,
         Emerald Group Publishing (2007)
SEM09   SEMIC.EU (Semantic Interoperability Centre Europe), http://www.semic.eu (2009)
SOU08   Sourouni, A.-M., Lampathaki, F., Mouzakitis, S., Charalabidis, Y., Askounis, D.:
         Paving the Way to e-Government Transformation Interoperability Registry
         Infrastructure Development, in Wimmer, M.A., Scholl, H.J., Ferro, E. (eds.),
         Proceedings of 7th EGOV Conference 2008, Lecture Notes in Computer Science, vol.
         5184, Springer, Berlin, pp. 340–351 (2008)
STA09   State Services Commission, NZGLS Metadata Element Set, Version 2.1, http://
         www.e.govt.nz/standards/nzgls/standard/element-set-21/nzgls-element-set-2-1.pdf
TAM05   Tambouris E., Tarabanis K.: "Overview of DC-based E-Driven eGovernment Service
         Architecture", Electronic Government, in Proceedings Lecture Notes in Computer
         Science, 3591: 237–248, Springer, Berlin (2005)
UKC07   UK Cabinet Office – Office of the e-Envoy, e-Government Metadata Standard, Version
         3.1, Retrieved February 5, 2007 from http://www.govtalk.gov.uk/documents/
         eGMS%20version%203_1.pdf (2007)
UKC09   UK Cabinet Office, UK GovTalk Schema Library, http://www.govtalk.gov.uk/sche-
         masstandards/schemalibrary.asp (2009)

UN07   UN/CEFACT Core Components Technical Specification, Part 8 of the ebXML Framework, Version 2.01, Retrieved January 25, 2007 from http://www.unece.org/cefact/ebxml/CCTS_V2-01_Final.pdf (2007)

WIM06   Wimmer, M.: "Implementing a Knowledge Portal for e-Government Based on Semantic Modeling: The e-Government Intelligent Portal (eip.at)", in Proceedings of the 39th Annual Hawaii International Conference on System Sciences (HICSS'06), Track 4, p. 82b (2006)

Chapter 12
Envisioning Advanced User Interfaces for E-Government Applications: A Case Study

Gaëlle Calvary, Audrey Serna, Joëlle Coutaz, Dominique Scapin, Florence Pontico, and Marco Winckler

Abstract The increasing use of the Web as a software platform together with the advance of technology has promoted Web applications as a starting point for improving communication between citizens and administration. Currently, several e-government Web portals propose applications for accessing information regarding healthcare, taxation, registration, housing, agriculture, education, and social services, which otherwise may be difficult to obtain. However, the adoption of services provided to citizens depends upon how such applications comply with the users' needs. Unfortunately, building an e-government website doesn't guarantee that all citizens who come to use it can access its contents. These services need to be accessible to all citizens/customers equally to ensure wider reach and subsequent adoption of the e-government services. User disabilities, computer or language illiteracy (e.g., foreign language), flexibility on information access (e.g., user remotely located in rural areas, homeless, mobile users), and ensuring user privacy on sensitive data are some of the barriers that must be taken into account when designing the User Interface (UI) of e-government applications.

Although several initiatives (such as the W3C WAI) focus on how to promote usability and accessibility of content provided via e-government, many governments are enhancing their technology to make their services compatible with new communication channels available through multiple devices including interactive digital TVs (iTV), personal digital assistants (PDAs), and mobile phones. In this chapter we focus on this latter issue, which means the development of multitarget government services available across several platforms. Hereafter we discuss the major constraints underlining the importance of investment on the UI's design of e-government applications. Moreover, we propose a framework for envisioning advanced UIs where the adaptation to the user's capabilities and available devices as well as physical and social environment will play a major role.

G. Calvary (✉)
Université de Grenoble, CNRS, LIG, 385, Rue de la Bibliothèque,
BP 53, 38041 Grenoble Cedex 9, France
e-mail: Gaelle.Calvary@imag.fr

S. Assar et al. (eds.), *Practical Studies in E-Government: Best Practices from Around the World*, DOI 10.1007/978-1-4419-7533-1_12,
© Springer Science+Business Media, LLC 2011

12.1   Introduction

The large variety of computing systems available nowadays (e.g., low-weight desktop/ notebook computers, cell phones, Smartphones) has created a milestone for cost-effective development and fast delivery of multitarget applications. During the last decade, users have become accustomed to new means of service delivery in the private sector. Today users expect the same level of service availability from the public sector: they want their interactions to be convenient, and they prefer to be online rather than in line [UNI08].

Faced with these expectations, some administrations have started to exploit several channels making it possible for users to consume the services anytime, anywhere, and anyhow. However, the decision of deploying e-government services on new communication channels has to accommodate competing objectives in the e-government domain [EUI04]: to improve the quality of public services and the way they serve the community, and to reduce the costs of providing these services. In this context, the design of the User Interface (UI) of e-government services should acknowledge the following constraints.

- Public administration should ensure multiple access points to e-government applications allowing home access via Internet broadband, computer-based kiosks, as well as mobile platforms.
- Universal access has become one of the major challenges for widespread adoption of many e-services provided to citizens, in particular those suffering from disabilities or literacy barriers (e.g., illiterate users, immigrants seeking information about the country).
- E-government applications present advantages for both front-office users (e.g., citizens, associations, companies) and back-office people (e.g., government employees). Usability for back-office users should not be neglected as usability problems can cause errors and losses of data that compromise the quality of the whole system.

As far as the cost of services is an issue, it must include the adoption rate of services by citizens. A countless number of e-government initiatives worldwide failed due to the low technology adoption levels in their communities [CAR05, TIT06]. Citizens tend to choose the most familiar communication channel available but such a decision is affected by the complexity of tasks involved [PIE07].

This chapter discusses the development process of e-government services for new communication media and in particular, their deployment over many platforms. Designing such applications may turn out to be difficult because of the large variety of tools and methods for developing cross-platform applications.

We propose to use a framework for reasoning about advanced UIs. By "advanced" we mean the UIs' capacity to adapt to the context of use while preserving user-centered properties. The context of use refers to a triplet: user's profile, available platforms, and physical and social environment. A UI capable of a user-centered adaptation is said to be plastic [THE03]. Our work is underlined by two main assumptions:

- By focusing on end-users' requirements we can select the platforms that best suit their needs, thus reducing the risk of rejection.
- By focusing on users' tasks we can measure the complexity of the steps required to accomplish administrative procedures and assess the technical feasibility of deploying tasks on multiple platforms.

The rest of this chapter is organised as follows. Section 12.2 surveys trends on multichannel delivery for e-government services and presents the foundation of plasticity. Section 12.3 elicits the key dimensions of plasticity. A real case study of an e-procurement service is presented in Sect. 12.4 with solutions for delivering plastic UIs. Conclusions and future work are elaborated in Sect. 12.5.

12.2   State of the Art

For promoting government services, transactions, and interactions with citizens, businesses, and other arms of government, administrations have employed a large range of communication channels. The most relevant ones are elicited in this section. Then, the theoretical foundations of plasticity are presented. Switching from one channel to another one is a kind of plasticity.

12.2.1   The World Wide Web Platform

The World Wide Web was the starting point for integrating services available 24/7. E-government services deployed on the Web are smoothly moving from content-based websites to electronic case handling, including connections with all actors involved in the supported process (e.g., central and local government agencies, direct connection between citizens and governments, and connections among stakeholders) [CAP06]. Recently several initiatives have tried to develop guidelines for developing usable and accessible e-government services [UKE03]. Concerned by the ever-growing use of the Web as a common platform, the World Wide Web Consortium [ACA09] has recently started a new interest group for improving access to government through better use of the Web. Among the activities performed by this new W3C group is the recommendation for designing Web applications for delivering content through many communication channels. This interest group is related to previous W3C initiatives on mobile platforms and accessibility. The latter becomes one of the most important references for e-inclusion initiatives undertaken by any democracy in the digital era.

12.2.2   Nontraditional User Interfaces

The huge penetration of mobile technology (about 3.3 billion mobile users around the world) has motivated many public organisations to make e-government services through mobile devices even in developing countries. Mobile technologies have not only been used to enable communication with citizens and organisations but also for delivering advanced services. For example, the BlueTo application [CAR06] deploys a location-based solution for delivering digital content previously distributed by the public administration on traditional media but including located content to citizens and tourists (e.g., basic tourist information, emergency numbers, and events in the city). Mobile technology provides many opportunities but also suffers from lots of drawbacks such as small screen size and resolution limit interactivity. In addition, cell phones can easily be lost or stolen so they are not suitable for storing private data. However, mobile technology has recently become so important that many organisations are deploying huge efforts to find solutions to foster e-government initiatives through mobile technology. These initiatives are often referred to as m-government or mobile government [SON05].[1]

Digital interactive TV (iTV) is a promising communication channel for delivering e-government services. iTV combines television content with some of the interactivity people are now used to on the Internet such as clicking on links. The interactive element comes from the channels having a means whereby the user can send his or her own signals back to the broadcaster [SCH08]. An example of iTV usage in the e-government domain is the VOICE system[2] which has been implemented in India to disseminate information to citizens about government activities. iTV technology is recent but the preliminary results are encouraging [SCH08]. However, there are also various potential problems such as the predominant use of remote control, which is far more restricted than a computer keyboard. Interactive services may also not be suited to the television viewing habits of many users; unlike the Web, TV is a medium often used for recreation or relaxation by several people at once [BER05]. Making sure that iTV contents and devices are flexible enough so that people are able to perceive, understand, and interact with them is an essential requirement for the democratisation of information via TV.

12.2.3   Multichannel Delivery of Services

Most currently available applications are deployed in a single platform but one of the most notable trends is the development of multichannel services. "Looking Local"[3] is a versatile application in the United Kingdom which is accessible at major United Kingdom interactive TV platforms (Sky and Virgin) from mobile phones and on some kiosks. Indeed, many governmental reports strongly recommend that e-government services must be deployed in many different platforms in order to provide better coverage of services and reach users with special needs [ACA09, TAO07]. The study launched by the European Union [EUI04] provides a detailed list of criteria for evaluating multichannel delivery of e-government services (e.g., accessibility and inclusion, speed delivery for time-critical information, etc.) and it points out some best practices. One of the main contributions of such a study is to classify communication channels according to benefits for end-users (i.e., citizens) but also for administrations. The deployment of e-government services through several communication channels can be sought as an ultimate goal for reaching all citizens. However, this diversity offers important challenges such as:

- Producing and maintaining several versions of single applications across multiple devices
- Checking consistency between versions for guaranteeing seamless interaction across multiple devices
- Building into these versions the ability to dynamically respond to changes in the context of use such as network connectivity, user's location, and so on

The availability of several communication channels does not mean that applications convey the same information and services across different platforms. Technical constraints (such as screen size) can prevent the display of large amounts of information. On the other hand, applications can convey information and services via the communication channel that best suits user needs.

12.2.4   Foundation of User Interface Plasticity

The deployment of e-government services with innovative and multicommunication channels faces issues that are addressed in Human–Computer Interaction (HCI). Indeed, with the technological advances and the emergence of ubiquitous computing, interactive systems are constantly evolving. UIs are now increasingly multimodal (e.g., multimodal mobile museum guide [SAN07]), borrowing exotic input and output devices from the environment (e.g., the IO Brush [RYO04]). They can be distributed classically using a PDA as a universal remote controller [REK97]. Finally, they are able to support implicit interaction [SCH00] and to dynamically migrate across a set of possibly heterogeneous platforms [BAL04]. As a result, there is a need for interactive systems to be able to adapt to their context of use. Plasticity refers to this ability of UIs to withstand variations in the context of use while preserving user-centered properties [CAL03]. The context of use is defined as a combination of the user's features, his/her technological platform (i.e., devices), and environmental conditions (e.g., office environment, mobile, etc.). Adaptation consists in remolding and/or redistributing the UI [VAN08].

Remolding denotes any UI reconfiguration that is perceivable by the user and that results from the application of transformations to the UI. Remolding can be intramodal (e.g., from graphics to graphics), intermodal (e.g., from graphics to voice), or multimodal (e.g., combining graphics and voice as in Teresa [BER05]). The first studies on plasticity focused on understanding the abstraction levels at which such adaptations occur [CAL03]. Then, degradation rules for squeezing the UI when migrating from a less-constrained platform to a more-constrained one were investigated [FLO06].

Redistribution denotes the reallocation of the UI components to the interaction resources. For example, the Sedan–Bouillon website [BAL04] that is centralised on a single PC unit can be redistributed across the PC and the PDA via a supra-UI. The supra-UI allows the user to control (i.e., *supervise*) the adaptation process (here to choose the components to redistribute across the interaction resources [COU06, SOT07]). Redistribution is performed along migrations (i.e., UIs transfers from one device to another [BAN04, GRO04]). Migrations can be partial or total. Depending on the discrepancies between the source and the target platforms (e.g., screen resolution, input devices available, etc.), migration may call for remolding [GHI09, UNI08].

Remolding and redistribution have been investigated from different perspectives. The first one is a model-based approach, defining tools and methods for the development (reification, abstraction, translation, or crossing) of UIs adapted to their context of use, such as ArtSudio [THE03], Teresa [BER05], WebRevenge [PAG02], or the UsiXML framework (http://www.usixml.org/). The second approach to mention offers technical tools, such as toolkits (WAHID [JAB03], COMETs [DAA07]) or run-time infrastructures (Ethylene [BAL09]). Finally, Model-Driven Engineering (MDE) seems to be promising inasmuch as it tackles both remolding and redistribution [SOT07].

12.3   Problem Space for Multitarget User Interfaces

One of the trickiest issues when developing multitarget UIs is that the UIs can be adapted according to different kinds of constraints (e.g., screen resolution, interaction techniques, user's archetype) [COU08]. These constraints are taken into account by both multitargeting and plasticity. They both address the diversity of contexts of use by adaptation. However, whereas multitargeting focuses on the technical aspects of adaptation, plasticity requires that the UIs remain usable when adaptation occurs. A large variety of tools, methods, and techniques has been developed to address some aspects of UI plasticity. The problem for designers and developers is to understand which aspects are covered by these contributions, how they are covered, and how they relate to each other. Figure 12.1 presents a classification framework that brings together the different aspects of plasticity into a unified conceptual space, called pStars for Plasticity Stars. pStars is intended to help in reasoning about plasticity. It models a plastic UI as multivariate data in a multidimensional space whose variables are first-class concepts. Interactive systems are studied from the interaction with the end-user perspective. The internal perspectives (i.e., the software developer's point of view) are not taken into account. pStars shapes plastic UIs as stars. The shapes of the stars convey the plasticity features of the UIs. In pStars:

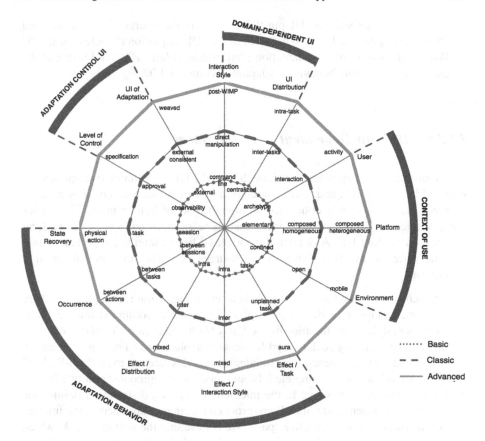

Fig. 12.1 pStars, a plasticity problem space

- A radius (or axis) represents a first-class concept. For example, the first-class concepts "User," "Platform," and "Environment," give rise to three distinct radii. Each radius is divided into three ranked values to denote levels of increasing sophistication: basic, classic, and advanced. For example, the radius "interaction style" is divided into three possible values of increasing sophistication: "command line language," "direct manipulation," and "post-WIMP." The semantics of the origin of a radius depends on the variable it represents. A sector of the diagram denotes a higher-order concept. A higher-order concept groups first-class concepts that are logically related into an overarching more abstract notion. Thus, the "context of use" sector is formed by the radii "User," "Platform," and "Environment" as these dimensions often appear in the literature.
- Star-shapes in this framework can be analyzed individually or they can be grouped into clusters of plastic UIs with similar features. At the two extremes, stars with small footprints denote UIs that support "minimal plasticity," whereas stars with large footprints represent "full-fledged plastic" UIs. The framework is comprised of four high-order concepts that altogether describe the way an

end-user may experience UI plasticity: what is the source-UI to be adapted ("domain-dependent UI")? What does trigger UI adaptation ("context of use")? What is the nature of the adaptation ("adaptation behavior")? And how can the end-user control this behavior ("adaptation control UI")?

12.3.1 Domain-Dependent User Interfaces

The source domain-dependent UI characterises the UI of an interactive application that is likely to be adapted. An interactive application, such as email is a set of services that are logically connected to support a set of human tasks. The UI for these services depends on the domain that these services address, thus the term "domain-dependent UI." A domain-dependent UI has an interaction style and may use the currently available interaction resources according to some distribution granularity.

- Interaction style. An interaction style is a set of interaction techniques that share the same metaphor or design principles, for example, command line language interaction style as exemplified by the UNIX Shell, the classic "WIMP" (Window, Icon, Menu, Pointing device) used for desktop applications (direct manipulation), and the blue sky new generations of interaction styles referred to as "Post-WIMP," such as multimodal UIs, tangible UIs, and mixed and augmented reality UIs.
- UI distribution. Orthogonal to the interaction style, UI distribution defines the way the constituent parts of a UI are grouped together or split across the interaction resources of an interactive space. We believe that the notion of task, which is a human-centered notion, is the appropriate unit for characterising the granularity of UI distribution: in the real world, the accomplishment of a task takes place in a space populated with the appropriate tools and objects. By analogy, a task performed with an interactive application is mapped into a digital space, which in turn is mapped into a set of closely and logically related interactors.

As shown in Fig. 12.1, the basic form of distribution is the absence of distribution (i.e., the UI is centralized). The classic form is intertask distribution where at least two distinct tasks are performed using interaction resources managed by distinct processors. For example, a train schedule is requested by filling out a form on a PDA. The result is displayed on the screen of a nearby workstation and is then browsed using the interaction resources (e.g., the mouse and the screen) of the PC. The task "looking for a particular time schedule" uses the interaction resources of a PDA whereas the task "choosing the appropriate train" is performed with the resources of the PC. With the advanced intratask distribution, the workspace of a task is split across multiple interaction resources. For example, in "choosing the appropriate train," the schedule is displayed on the PC screen, whereas the interactors for navigating from page to page are deployed on the PDA.

12.3.2   Context of Use

Since the early 1960s, the notion of context has been modeled and exploited in many areas of informatics. Quite often, the context is composed by the following triplet.

- User. The user model denotes the attributes and functions that describe the person who is intended to use, or is actually using, an interactive application. Typically, "Preferences" are the basic user models in most interactive applications (archetype). At the classic level, the user model includes interaction idiosyncrasies, that is, observables and functions that synthesise the way users exploit an interactive application (interaction). These are identified from command use frequency as well as from patterns of command sequences. At the advanced level, the user model includes observables and functions that identify current human activity (e.g., reading, writing a paper, etc.) as well as patterns of activities.
- Platform. The platform model describes the computing, sensing, networking, and interaction resources that bind together the physical environment with the digital world. At the basic level, the platform is elementary: from the user's perspective, the platform looks and behaves like a "coherent computing whole" (e.g., a PC, a PDA, a Smartphone). At the classic level, the platform is a cluster of homogeneous computing devices that results from the interconnection of multiple identical elementary platforms (typically, the i-LAND interactive wall [STR01]). At the advanced level, the platform is a cluster of heterogeneous elementary platforms (as in Rekimoto's pick and drop [REK97]).
- Environment. The environment model includes attributes and functions that characterise the physical places along with their social dimension where the interaction is supposed to take place, or is actually taking place. As for the user model, the number of candidate dimensions is quite large. Thus, we have aligned mainstream research in context modeling for ubiquitous computing with our three levels of sophistication. At the basic level, a confined environment denotes a closed place (e.g., a room or an office). At the classic level, the environment is open (e.g., a street or a public space). At the advanced level, a mobile environment refers to a closed space, such as a car, a plane, or a train, which is likely to move in space (and time).

Changes in the context of use (i.e., in any of the user, platform, or environment models) may trigger UI adaptation whose behavior is detailed next.

12.3.3   Adaptation Behavior

A UI adaptation process can be specified according to the different effects on the domain-dependent UI (effects on interaction style and effects on distribution), on the task, and on the occurrence and the recovery state of such an adaptation.

- Effect/Task. The adaptation process can possibly modify the tasks or activities of the user; the procedure of the task can differ after the adaptation (task level), opportunistic tasks can appear (unplanned task), or a more global view of the user's activities can change (aura).
- Effect/Interaction style. Adaptation can affect the interaction style used for the domain-dependent UI (the two dimensions work together): the interaction style can be conserved (intra), changed (inter), or combined (mixed). This dimension can be seen as the characterisation of the remolding mechanism presented previously in Sect. 12.2.4.
- Effect/Distribution. This dimension denotes the reallocation of the UI components of the system according to the distribution granularity of the domain-dependent UI (corresponding to the redistribution mechanism presented previously): the initial distribution is preserved (intra), the different cluster of platforms is used (inter), or the distribution is a combination of existing and new cluster of platforms (mixed).
- Occurrence. The adaptation process is not always triggered at the same time, according to the level of sophistication. The adaptation may occur between sessions (the adaptation process can only occur at the initial state of the system), between tasks (the adaptation process can occur when a task is completed and before starting another one), or between actions (the adaptation process can occur at any time).
- State recovery. The granularity of state recovery characterises the effort that users must apply to carry on their activity after adaptation has occurred. At the session level, all the tasks and actions performed by the user are lost. At the task level, the tasks that have been completed by the user before the adaptation process are preserved but the actions of the interrupted task are lost. Recovery at the physical action level conserves the last action performed by the user before the adaptation process.

12.3.4   Adaptation Control User Interface

The adaptation control UI refers to the supra-UI that makes it possible for the end-user to observe, control, or configure the different operations performed during the adaptation process.

- Level of control. This dimension characterises the level of control that the user has on the adaptation process. The dimension origin corresponds to the absence of control; the adaptation process is fully autonomous and transparent for the user. The adaptation process is observable when the user is aware of its state, but cannot intervene. Approbation is the next level of control; the user can accept or reject the proposition of adaptation. Finally, in the specification level, the user fully controls the outcome of the process.
- UI of adaptation. This dimension describes the properties of the supra-UI regarding to the domain-dependent UI. The dimension origin corresponds to the

absence of supra-UI: the user cannot interact with the adaptation process. The next levels of complexity mean that there is a UI of adaptation. This last one can be external to the interactive system, and at a higher level consistent with the domain-dependent UI, in other words the supra-UI is developed with the same paradigm and looks like the domain-dependent UI. Finally, advanced systems might offer a supra-UI woven into the domain-dependent UI.

12.4   Case Study

In order to illustrate how the constraints for delivering services in different communication channels and how the plasticity framework can help in reasoning on these issues, we present a case study issued from the Regional French Administration Midi-Pyrénées[4] (RMP), one of the partners of the MyCitizSpace[5] consortium. Due to some privacy issues, some internal aspects have been voluntarily removed. We introduce all actors involved and their interactions along the process, which is enough for our purpose. Our focus is on end-users' requirements for adapting the UI according to different contexts of use.

12.4.1   Informal Description

Vocational high schools offer hands-on training to students and prepare them for careers in fields such as information technology, marketing, business, engineering, and the medical professions. However, to attend some technical programs such as plumbing, electricity, or cooking, students need to bring their own equipment to classes (e.g., purchase of knives, aprons, and suits for inn students). BRPE (French acronym for "Regional Scholarship for First Equipment") is a program of RMP, which provides students with a scholarship for buying such equipment. A student can only apply for this scholarship once whilst attending a specific technical program in a vocational high school. However, a second application is allowed if students change to a different technical program. The high schools' principals are in charge of advising students about the calendar and procedures and helping them to prepare applications. BRPE applicants get forms from high school principals. For students under the age of majority, their parents or legal tutor are the ones allowed to fill in the form. The forms and required documents (e.g., bank account statement) are given back to high school principals who are in charge of controlling the completeness of forms and sending the complete ones to RMP. On receipt, RMP agents treat BRPE applications. If the application is accepted by RMP, the accounts department (a state institution distinct from RMP) pays the BRPE scholarship through a bank transfer to the bank account of the student (or his parents).

12.4.2 Users' Tasks Analysis

The general procedure required of a BRPE application is summarised by the 11 steps depicted in Fig. 12.2.

Like many other governmental programs, BRPE is a complex program that integrates actors with diverse juridical status such as citizens (i.e., students/parents), units

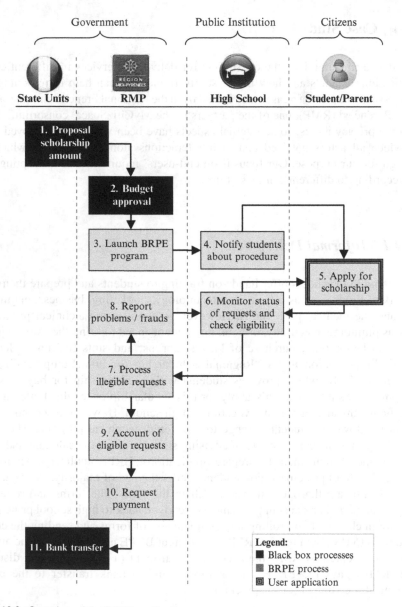

Fig. 12.2 Overview of the BRPE application

of the regional governmental (i.e., RMP), state governmental (i.e., accounts department), and educational units (i.e., high schools). Educational units are controlled by education offices (i.e., "rectorat" in the French system), which discuss BRPE scholarships amounts with RMP once a year. For the sake of simplicity, education offices, accounts departments, and national banks are considered here as "state units."

Figure 12.2 presents how the BRPE process (i.e., gray boxes) is connected to outside processes represented by black boxes. From an administrative point of view, the procedure starts with the annual definition of money allocation for a scholarship which varies according to the technical program (cf. Step 1). Scholarships are subject to the annual budget approval from the RMP's council (Step 2). Citizens do not request a BRPE scholarship directly from RMP: the process is mediated by the high school's principal who notifies students (Step 4) and explains how they should fill in the form (Step 5). Principals are also responsible for checking the completeness (i.e., no information is missing) and correctness of requests (e.g., attest that students are regularly attending a vocational high school) (Step 6). RMP receives student's applications and verifies their correctness and eligibility (Step 8). Problems (e.g., fraud, missing information) are reported to high school principals (Step 7) who monitor (Step 6) the status of student applications. Eligible applications are recorded, letters of credits are sent to beneficiaries (Step 9), and payment requests (Step 10) are sent to the accounts department (Step 11).

For citizens, the most important task is "Apply for scholarship" (Step 5). This task should be decomposed into a set of subtasks that are required to accomplish the procedure as follows shown by Fig. 12.3. Due to some administrative constraints, the administration requests paper-based certificates, so that the subtask "Provide certificates" (i.e., B2) is not supported by the system.

12.4.3 Users' Requirements

Much of the success or failure of information technology implementation programs such as BRPE relies on the adoption rate of the applications by the end-users. However, it is clear that some actors involved might have conflicting requirements. For example, citizens would like to have close contact with stakeholders which might delay the treatment of requests. Table 12.1 presents some main requirements

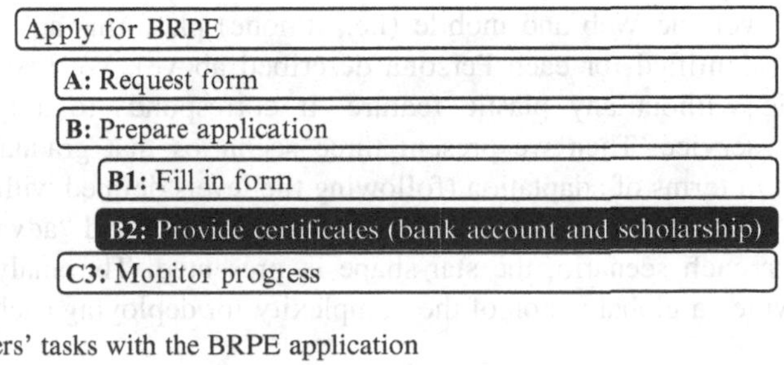

Apply for BRPE

A: Request form

B: Prepare application

B1: Fill in form

B2: Provide certificates (bank account and scholarship)

C3: Monitor progress

Fig. 12.3 Users' tasks with the BRPE application

Table 12.1 Some requirements affecting adoption of the BRPE

Users	Criteria
RMP stakeholders	Costs/prevent frauds/time for checking eligible applications/ traceability of applications
High school principals	Visibility of students applying for the scholarship in his or her institution/time for checking eligible applications (e.g., no required information is missing)/time for assisting students in filling in the forms/pedagogical value of procedures in daily life
Citizens	Ensure eligibility of application/time for filling in the forms/time for obtaining the scholarship/full transparency

for the three main actors of BRPE. Some requirements such as "ensure eligibility of applications" (that can be supported by automated tools for checking if no required information is missing) can be a common motivation to both stakeholders and citizens.

Hereafter we only focus on a particular category of users, that is, citizens. Inside this community, we identify three main user groups: parents, students under the age of majority, and young adults. To capture special user needs, we have created user archetypes using the "Persona" technique [COO99]. A Persona is a description of a user archetype that is mainly used to communicate requirements with the development team during the design process. An archetype can be synthesised from a series of field activities such as interviews and work observations resulting in a representation of an individual that embodies the characteristics of a target user population [GRE03]. User archetypes are named after a fictional character to help designers to talk about a specific user profile without having to describe all their attributes. Table 12.2 shows user profiles used in our case study.

12.4.4 Plasticity Analysis

The functions provided by the BRPE are described in such a way that they should be available to all citizens and they do not imply any particular communication channel. Moreover, we must ensure that implementations of BRPE will fulfill specific users' requirements. From this point, several implementations of an electronic version of the BRPE are possible.

Hereafter we present some scenarios that illustrate how the BRPE application could evolve over the Web and mobile (i.e., iPhone) platforms according to the user's needs (identified for each Persona described above). We first present the basic scenario without any plastic feature. It corresponds to a typical basic e-government service. Then we present three scenarios that gradually increase sophistication in terms of adaptation (following the levels defined within the problem space): "basic multiplatform," "classic multiplatform," and "advanced multiplatform." For each scenario, the star-shape is presented. The analysis of their footprint provides a global vision of the complexity for deploying each solution.

Table 12.2 Three personas: Rémi, Sarah, and Iban

First name	Rémi, the nature boy	Sarah, the blogger girl	Iban, the artist
Age (years)	16	17	18
Nationality	French	Lebanese	French
Family status	Single, living with his parents in a farm	Single, living with her uncle who is her legal tutor in France. Her parents still live in Lebam	Single. Part-time job in a restaurant. Sharing an apartment with friends. Parents live in another city
Education	Repeating first year at the vocational high school on veterinary technical program after failing a first year in a traditional high school	Second year of cooking program in the vocational high school George Sands	First year of vocational program in arts at the high school Matisse after 2 years attending plumbing program at the same high school
Information technology skills	He prefers to use the Internet at school due to the low bandwidth in the rural area where he lives. There is a poor mobile network on the farm	She has created her own website and she maintains a regular blog	In the top five students in informatics. He is very skilled with drawing programs
Motivation for using new information technologies	He does not have any specific motivation but he knows how to use a computer to check his assignments at the electronic kiosk available at the school	She makes good use of IT for communicating with her parents and friends staying in Lebam. She recently started to use an iPhone for surfing on the Web and reading emails	He likes innovative IT solutions and he is very keen to try new devices. He was a first adopter of the iPhone, using it to show his paintings everywhere he goes
Professional projects	To finish high school and go back to the farm to work with his father	She plans to open her own restaurant	Work in the game industry

Basic scenario. Rémi is notified that the procedure for the BRPE scholarship application is now opened. He goes to the library, which is equipped with computers and Internet access. He launches the Web application e-BRPE and opens a session. He first has to enter his student number and select a password. Once registered, he fills in his personal data and selects a scholar program. The next part of the form has to be filled in by his parents as he is under the age of majority. Rémi saves his session. Once back home, with the help of his mother, he finishes the procedure and submits it. The system indicates that his application has been submitted to the high school principal. Rémi now has to provide the principal with specific physical documents that he can print from the application. One week later, Rémi is interested in knowing the state of his application. He logs on to e-BRPE. The system indicates that his application is complete and that it will be sent to the RMP. One month later, Rémi receives a physical letter telling him that his request will be funded. Figure 12.4 shows the UI for this scenario. The UI remains basic in that it is form-based and centralised in a unique desktop. There is no process of adaptation.

Basic multiplatform scenario. At this level of sophistication, the application is available over several platforms. The scenario was conceived to fulfill the requirements of the archetype Sarah (cf. Table 12.2). The application runs over the Web but can also be accessed via a cell phone. Figure 12.5 presents an adapted version of the application to be displayed on an iPhone. Notice that the form is presented in several screens (Fig. 12.5.2 a–c). The limited number of form fields per screen reduces the need of scrolling whilst keeping the text legible, however, the system can record the information filled in across the pages so that Sarah does not have to start from the beginning if she is interrupted by a phone call. This scenario illustrates adaptation to the platform with effects on interaction style (from direct manipulation to Post-WIMP) and on the task procedure. The granularity of the UI distribution remains the same. There is neither adaptation to the user nor to the environment. The adaptation is performed when the user launches the application. The state recovery is the user's session. Figure 12.6 characterises the adaptation.

Classic multiplatform scenario. In this case users can not only decide which platform to use to access the service (the Web or cell phone) but also can interrupt a task on a platform (e.g., fill in an application form over the Web) and resume it on another one (e.g., monitor progress on a cell phone). The archetype used in this scenario is the student Iban. Iban is informed about the availability of the BRPE at the school. On his way back home he starts using his iPhone to apply for a scholarship (cf. Figs. 12.7.1 and 12.7.2). Arriving home, Iban decides to resume the BRPE using the Web version because his computer desktop provides him with a larger screen and access to a printer (cf. Fig. 12.7.3a, b). Iban can use his iPhone to monitor the application progress (cf. Fig. 12.7.4). In this scenario, the application was conceived to support changes according to the composition of heterogeneous platforms (PC and iPhone) with effects on the UI distribution; the user controls the adaptation process (via a supra-UI) by selecting the migrating platform (interdistribution effect). The interaction is continuous because it occurs at the task level. Figure 12.8 characterises the adaptation.

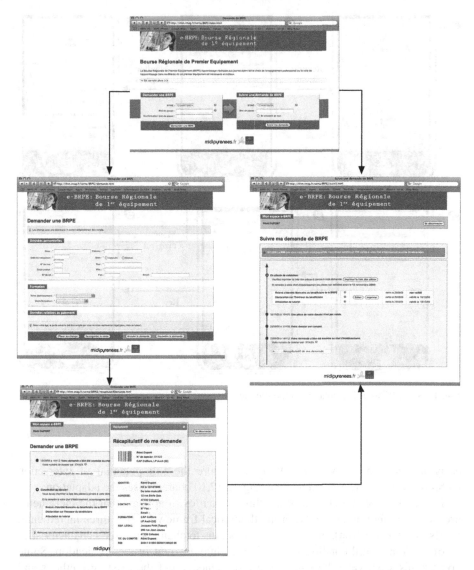

Fig. 12.4 BRPE as it is available on the Web

Advanced multiplatform scenario. Using pStars we can envision improvements of the previous scenarios. Figure 12.9 shows a continuous interaction across these adaptations: in a multidistributed version of e-BRPE, the student can choose to detach a section of the form from his iPhone in order to migrate it onto the living room PC (cf. Fig. 12.9.2b, c). In this case, the application becomes distributed onto several devices, with different interaction styles. The adaptation specifications are woven into the UI and the user is able to specify the distribution organisation. This scenario focuses on

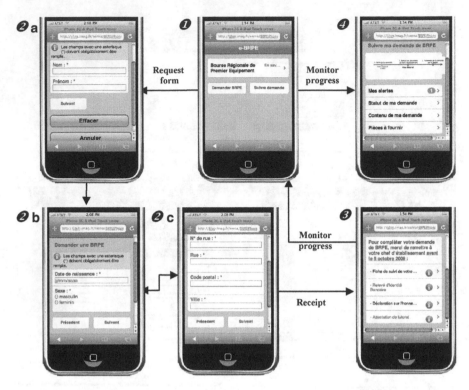

Fig. 12.5 BRPE as it is available on the iPhone

early adopter's needs who are keen to explore the full potential of interaction techniques and devices, such as Iban. Figure 12.10 characterises the adaptation.

Looking at the star shapes of the three scenarios, it appears that the increments are not as perfect as presented in the theoretical framework (the three incremental levels of sophistication). For example, adaptation to changes of user's characteristics or of environmental conditions is not taken into account in the application. Some compromises between the study case requirements and the existing methods and techniques for adaptation have been taken while designing the application.

12.5 Conclusion and Future Work

In this chapter we have presented a case study describing user needs and technical constraints related to the development of multitarget UIs for e-government. Moreover, we propose a framework to characterise the plasticity of the UI when services are deployed on many communication channels and platforms.

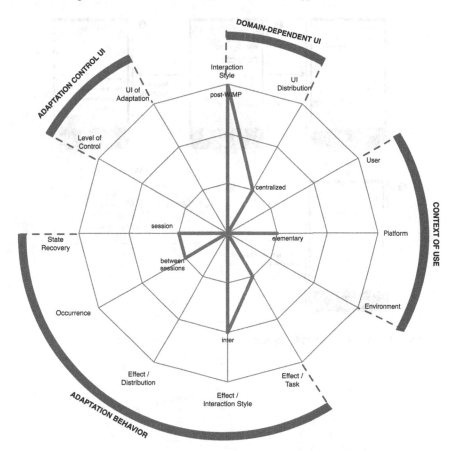

Fig. 12.6 Star of the basic multiplatform scenario

As we show, deploying services on multiple communication channels is not just a matter of technological concern. It requires a deeper understanding of user needs to propose convenient solutions and thus have a better chance to get adopted by the community. On the other hand, there are many platforms available and the best UI depends on the adaptation of services according to platform constraints. Currently there is no single answer to questions such as, "Which is the best UI?" or "Which is the best communication channel for deploying e-government services?" So, we exposed the use of a multidimensional space for supporting decision making when designing advanced UIs. End-user requirements and usability criteria are useful for grounding decisions but they certainly should be considered in a larger picture than presented here. However, UI is a key aspect that is worth study in its own dimension before being aligned with business processes constraints, political/social wills, and so on.

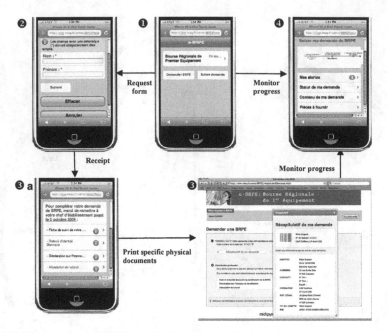

Fig. 12.7 UI migration in BRPPE application

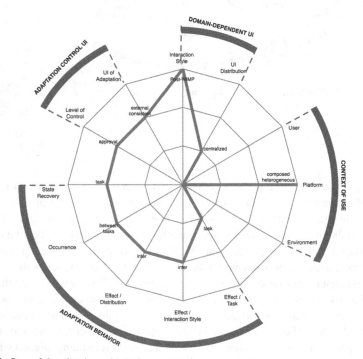

Fig. 12.8 Star of the classic multiplatform scenario

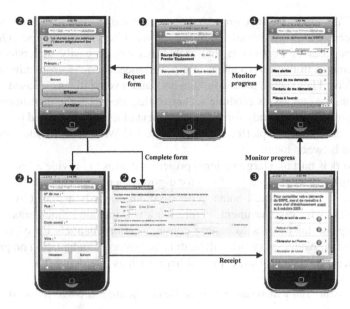

Fig. 12.9 Continuous interaction across devices

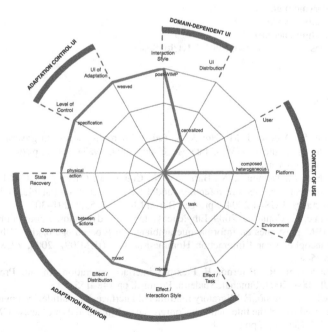

Fig. 12.10 Star of the advanced multiplatform scenario

In MyCitizSpace, we have grounded our research on a deep review of end-users' requirements, which are formalised by the means of Persona archetypes. One of the main advantages of Persona is that archetypes can be easily understood by all people involved in the development of e-government services, from administrative stakeholders, IT experts, decision makers, and even citizens. Based on such descriptions we can assess credible scenarios that are worth the investment in new development. The case study for the development of the BRPE has led to successful implementations on two platforms (i.e., mobile and Web) and provides continuous interaction between them.

This work is part of a large national project that aims to provide a framework for developing the next generation of UIs for e-government applications. Based on this experience we have started some generalisations towards a plasticity space for multitarget UIs for e-government. Future work will include refinements of criteria for helping administrations to choose communication channels for e-government services better. Additional work will be done to explore UI adaptation on promising communication channels (not exploited here) such as interactive TV.

Acknowledgment This work is supported by the French MyCitizSpace project (ANR 2007–2010).

Notes

¹http://www.mgovernment.org/.
²http://www.ourvmc.org/.
³http://www.digitv.gov.uk/.
⁴http://www.midipyrenees.fr/.
⁵http://genibeans.com/cgi-bin/twiki/view/MyCitizSpace/.

References

ACA09   Acar, S., Alonso, J. M., Novak, K. (eds.), Improving access to government through better use of the web (W3C Interest Group), 2009, Available at http://www.w3.org/TR/egov-improving/

BAL04   Balme, L., Demeure, A., Barralon, N., Coutaz, J., Calvary, G. CAMELEON-RT: A software architecture reference model for distributed, migratable, and plastic user interfaces. EUSAI 2004, Springer, Berlin LNCS 3295, pp 291–302.

BAL09   Balme, L., Coutaz, J. 2009, Ethylene: Composants dynamiques pour la mise en œuvre d'IHM plastiques en informatique ambiante. In Proceedings of the 21th Conférence Francophone sur l'Interaction Homme-Machine (IHM'09), 2009, ACM, Newyork, pp 75–84.

BAN04   Bandelloni, R., Paterno, F. Flexible interface migration. In the Proceedings of IUI'2004, 2004, Funchal, Madeira, Portugal, pp 148–155.

BER05   Berti, S., Paternò, F. Migratory multimodal interfaces in multidevice environments. In Proceedings of the International Conference on Multimodal Interfaces, ICMI'05, 2005, ACM, Newyork, pp 92–99.

CAL03   Calvary, G., Coutaz, J., Thevenin, D., Limbourg, Q., Bouillon, L., Vanderdonckt, J. A unifying reference framework for multi-target user interfaces. Journal of Interacting With Computer, Elsevier Science B.V, June 2003, vol. 15, no. 3, pp 289–308.

CAP06   Capgemini Report, Online availability of public services: How is europe progressing? Web Based Survey on Electronic Public Services Report of the 6th Measurement, June 2006, Available at: http://www.epractice.eu/files/media/media_854.pdf

CAR06   Carcillo, F., Marcellin, L., Tringale, A. BlueTo: A location-based service for M-government solutions. In Proceedings of the EURO mGOV, 2006, pp 51–60.

CAR05   Carter, L., Bélanger, F. The utilization of e-government services: Citizen trust, innovation and acceptance factors. Info Systems Journal, 2005, vol. 15, no. 1, pp 5–25.

COO99   Cooper, A. The inmates are running the asylum. Sams (eds.) 1st edition, 1999, p 288.

COU06   Coutaz, J. Meta-user interfaces for ambient spaces. Invited speaker, In Proceedings of TAMODIA 2006, Hasselt, Belgium, Oct. 2006, Springer LNCS 4385, pp 1–15.

COU08   Coutaz, J., Calvary, G. HCI and software engineering: Designing for user interface plasticity. In The human–computer interaction handbook: Fundamentals, evolving technologies, and emerging applications, 2008, Taylor & Francis Press, pp 1107–1125.

DAA07   Dâassi, O. Les comets: Une nouvelle génération d'interacteurs pour la plasticité des Interfaces Homme-Machine. Thèse de l'Université Joseph Fourier, Grenoble I, Janvier 2007.

EUI04   EU IDA Programme Report, Multi-channel delivery of eGovernment services, June 2004, At: http://ec.europa.eu/idabc/servlets/Doc?id=16867.

FLO06   Florins, M. Graceful degradation. A method for designing multiplatform graphical user interfaces. PhD Université catholique de Louvain, Belgique, 2006.

GHI09   Ghiani, G., Paternò, F., Spano, L. D. Cicero designer: An environment for end-user development of multi-device museum guides, IS-EUD, 2009, pp 265–274.

GRE03   Greaney, J., Riordan, M. The use of statistically derived personas in modelling mobile user populations. In Human-computer interaction with mobile devices and services, 2003, Springer LNCS 2795, pp 476–480.

GRO04   Grolaux, D., Van Roy, P., Vanderdonckt, J. Migratable user interfaces: Beyond migratory interfaces. In the First Annual International Conference on Mobile and Ubiquitous Systems: Networking and Services (MobiQuitous'04), August 2004, pp 422–430.

JAB03   Jabarin, B., Graham, T. C. N. Architectures for widget-based plasticity. In Proceedings of DSV-IS 2003, Springer LNCS, 2003, pp 124–138.

PAG02   Paganelli, L., Paternò, F. Automatic reconstruction of the underlying interaction design of web applications. In Proceedings of 14th International Conference on Software Engineering and Knowledge Engineering, ACM Press, July 2002, pp 439–445.

PIE07   Pieterson, W., van Dijk, J. Channel choice determinants: An exploration of the factors that determine the choice of a service channel in citizen initiated contacts. In Proceedings of the 8th Annual International Digital Government Research Conference, 2007, pp 173–182.

REK97   Rekimoto, J. Pick-and-drop: A direct manipulation technique for multiple computer environments. In Proceedings of UIST'97, 1997, ACM Press, pp 31–39.

RYO04   Ryokai, K., Marti, S., Ishii, H. I/O Brush: Drawing with everyday objects as ink. In Proceedings of ACM CHI'04, Vienna, Austria, April 24–29 2004, pp 303–310.

SAN07   Santoro, C., Paternò, F., Ricci, G., Leporini, B. A multimodal mobile museum guide for all. In Mobile Interaction with the Real World (MIRW 2007), 2007.

SCH08   Schibelsky, L., Piccolo, G., Cecília, M., Baranauskas, C. Understanding iDTV in a developing country and designing a T-gov application prototype. In Proceedings of ACM DIS'08, Cape Town, South Africa, February 25–27, 2008, ACM, New York, pp 379–385.

SCH00   Schmidt, A. Implicit human computer interaction through context. Personal Technologies, vol. 4, no. 2&3, 2000, pp 191–199.

SON05   Song, G. Transcending e-Government: A case of mobile government in Beijing. The
         First European Conference on Mobile Government, Sussex, July 2005.
SOT07   Sottet, J. S., Calvary, G., Coutaz, J., Favre, J. M. A model-driven engineering
         approach for the usability of plastic user interfaces. In Proceedings of Engineering
         Interactive Systems (EHCI-HCSE-DSVIS 2007), Salamanca, Spain, 2007, Springer
         LNCS 4940, pp 140–157.
STR01   Streitz, N. A., Tandler, P., Müller-Tomfelde, C., Konomi, S. Roomware: Towards the
         next generation of human-computer interaction based on an integrated design of real
         and virtual worlds. In J. A. Carroll (ed.), Human-computer interaction in the new mil-
         lennium, 2001, Addison Wesley, New York, pp 553–578.
TAO07   Taoufik, I., Kabaili, H., Kettani, D. Designing an e-government portal accessible to
         illiterate citizens. In Proceedings of ICEGOV, Macao, China, December 10–13 2007,
         ACM, New York, vol. 232, pp 327–336.
THE03   Thevenin, D., Coutaz, J., Calvary, G. A Reference Framework for the Development of
         Plastic User Interfaces, in Multiple User Interfaces: Cross-Platform Applications and
         Context-Aware Interfaces (eds A. Seffah and H. Javahery), John Wiley & Sons, Ltd,
         2005, Chichester, UK. doi: 10.1002/0470091703.ch3.
TIT06   Titah, R., Barki, H. E-government adoption and acceptance: A literature review.
         International Journal of Electronic Government Research, vol. 2, no. 3, 2006, pp
         23–57.
UKE03   UK e-Government Unit. Quality framework for UK government website design:
         Usability issues for government websites, 2003, Available at: http://archive.cabinetof-
         fice.gov.uk/e-government/docs/qualityframework/pdf/quality.pdf
UNI08   United Nations, e-Government Survey 2008: From e-Government to Connected
         Governance, 2008, United Nations publication, New York, ISBN 978-92-1-123174-8.
VAN08   Vanderdonckt, J., Coutaz, J., Calvary, G., Stanciulescu, A. Multimodality for plastic
         user interfaces: Models, methods, and principles. In D. Tzovaras (ed.), Multimodal
         user interfaces: Signals and communication technology. Lecture Notes in Electrical
         Engineering, 2008, Springer, Berlin, pp 61–84.

Chapter 13
Practices to Develop Spatial Data Infrastructures: Exploring the Contribution to E-Government

Joep Crompvoets, Glenn Vancauwenberghe, Geert Bouckaert, and Danny Vandenbroucke

Abstract The main objectives of this chapter are to introduce Spatial Data Infrastructures (SDIs), and to explore their potential contribution to good e-government. In order to understand the possible strengths of SDIs for good e-government, the concept, components, governance, and the cost–benefit analyses regarding the implementation of these infrastructures are first explained and presented followed by a short presentation of four existing SDIs in practice (Europe, Catalonia, Flanders, and Leiedal). These practices clearly show the dynamic, integrated, and multiple natures of SDIs. The main reason to invest in SDIs is that they facilitate the sharing of spatial data in a way that the management and use of these spatial resources happens more efficiently and effectively. This concept of sharing resources from multiple sources is not common practice in e-government research and implementation. However, it is very likely that ICTs will play a key role in improving the sharing of public resources in order to have a more efficient and effective management and use of these resources. Therefore, the lessons learnt from the existing SDI-practices and understanding of the nature of SDIs could be useful support in developing good e-governments.

13.1 Introduction

We live in an information age. One important type of information is geographic information referring to the descriptions of locations on the surface of the Earth. Geographic information can be stored digitally, allowing it to be processed by computers. Geographic information can consist of addresses, market research data, census data, health data, data on the environment and natural resources, descriptions

J. Crompvoets (✉)
Public Management Institute, Katholieke Universiteit Leuven, Parkstraat 45,
B-3000, Leuven, Belgium
e-mail: joep.crompvoets@soc.kuleuven.be

S. Assar et al. (eds.), *Practical Studies in E-Government: Best Practices from Around the World*, DOI 10.1007/978-1-4419-7533-1_13,
© Springer Science+Business Media, LLC 2011

of transportation and utility networks on flows of goods, cadastral and land registration data, as well as data obtained by remote sensing from satellites in space [MAS07]. The simplest way of presenting geographical information is the map. Maps are widely used, because everything that happens, happens somewhere, and knowing where something happens can be important (e.g., in case of an emergency planning and response). Spatially related questions (such as: Where is it? How far is it? How can I get there?) can be answered by the use of Geographic Information Systems (GIS). GIS can be defined as computer systems for capturing, managing, integrating, manipulating, analysing, and displaying data that are spatially referenced to the Earth [MAS07].

Geographic information in particular is one of the critical elements underpinning decision making for many disciplines [CLI94, GOR98, LON99, MOR04, WIL03]. Over the last decades, many governments and the private sector have invested tens of billions of euros in the development of geographic information, largely to serve specific communities (forestry, agriculture, urban/rural planning, land records management, military, security service, health care, development aid, emergency services, retail, etc.), within a local, regional, national, international, and even global context [CRO06]. At present, an estimated 90% of all information used by any (national) government has spatial characteristics.

Geographic information can be derived from spatial datasets, which are thematic collections of data. Examples of spatial datasets are: cadastral, topographical, land use, and soil. These spatial datasets are often very expensive to produce, produced more than once, stored in numerous different places, and unavailable for public access for various reasons (e.g., privacy, intellectual property rights). In order to search for, exchange, manage, or use spatial datasets, the use of metadata might be very helpful. Metadata can be defined as "data about data" [LON99]. From a spatial context, it describes, for example, the characteristics of a dataset in terms of spatial extent, scale, quality, ownership, and user conditions

Regarding the developments in the domain of geographic information, the focus is increasingly shifting to the challenges associated with integrating broadly sourced geographic information, so as to create a manageable framework. This has led to the creation of the Spatial Data Infrastructure (SDI). This infrastructure facilitates access to the spatial data and services [FEE03]. Moreover, it facilitates (and coordinates) the exchange and sharing of spatial data between stakeholders within the geo-information (GI) community. In this way, it saves users resources, time, and effort when trying to acquire new data by avoiding duplication of the very high expenses associated with the generation and maintenance of data and their integration with other data.

The main objectives of this chapter are to introduce spatial data infrastructures, and to explore their potential contribution to good e-government. In the next section the concept, components, benefits, and costs of spatial data infrastructures are introduced in more detail followed by some SDIs in practice; Europe, Catalonia, Flanders, and Leiedal. The chapter concludes with some remarks on how spatial data infrastructures could contribute to e-government developments.

13.2 Spatial Data Infrastructures

13.2.1 Introduction

An SDI can be defined as the means to assemble geographic information that describes the arrangement and attributes of features and phenomena on the Earth. The infrastructure includes the materials, technology, and people necessary to acquire, process, and distribute such information to meet a wide variety of needs [NAT93].

The overriding SDI objective is to facilitate access to geographic information assets that are held by a wide range of stakeholders in both the public and private sectors with a view to maximising overall usage. This objective requires coordinated action by governments. Therefore, SDIs are about the facilitation and coordination of the exchange and sharing of spatial data between stakeholders in the spatial data community. This means that SDIs must also be user-driven, as their primary purpose is to provide access to spatial data they need. SDI implementation involves a wide range of activities. These include not only technical matters such as data, technologies, standards, and delivery mechanisms but also institutional matters related to organisational responsibilities, overall information policies, and the availability of financial and human resources [MAS07].

From the early 1990s onward, many countries are developing SDIs to manage and use their spatial data assets more efficiently and effectively [CRO06]. These countries found it necessary to develop SDIs to assist in decision-making that has an important impact within their national boundaries [WIL03]. This need has also been intensified recently by new technologies such as GPS, satellite navigation systems for cars, and a new generation of mobile phone services that can also display map-based information. In addition, new Web-based geographic information services such as Google Earth make it possible for users to view different parts of the world at the click of a mouse. These developments mean that the majority of people, either knowingly or unknowingly, are now users of geographic information [MAS07].

Since the term "spatial data infrastructure" was first used in 1991, more than 120 countries in the world have embarked on some form of an SDI initiative [CRO06]. Given these circumstances the term "SDI phenomenon" as introduced by Ian Masser [MAS07] seems to be a reasonable description of what has happened in this field over the last 15 years. The original SDI leaders were relatively wealthy countries such as Australia, Canada, The Netherlands, Portugal, and the United States, but SDIs are now being developed in all parts of the world. There are considerable differences among countries in terms of both the approach and the content of these initiatives [CRO06, MAS99, MAS05].

SDIs are under construction at different levels of government. Their ultimate objectives are typically to promote economic development, stimulate better government, and foster environmental sustainability at these levels [MAS05, MAS07, WIL03]. The notion of better government can be interpreted in several different ways. In rapidly developing countries such as Malaysia, it means better strategic planning and resource development. Planning, in the sense of a better state of readiness to deal with emergencies brought about by natural hazards, was also an important driving force in the establishment of the Japanese national SDI after the Kobe earthquake. In Portugal, on the other hand, the National SDI has played an important part in modernising central, regional, and local administration (e.g., simplification of administrative procedures, and better availability of information) [MAS07].

The most known National SDI (NSDI) is the one set up in the United States by Executive Order from President Clinton on April 11, 1994: "Coordinating geographic data acquisition and access to the National Spatial Data Infrastructure" [CLI94]. This directive set forth the main tasks to be carried out and defined time limits for each of the initial stages of the NSDI. It strengthened the powers of interagency coordination of the Federal Geographic Data Committee (FGDC), whose membership includes representatives from all the major federal departments with an interest in geographic information and the collection and management of such information. The Executive Order also required the creation of a national digital spatial data framework of the most frequently used data and the establishment of a national spatial data clearinghouse to increase user awareness of what data are available and facilitate access to these data. The FGDC clearinghouse has been one of the most obvious SDI success stories. The FGDC Clearinghouse Registry, for example, lists more than 500 registered nodes within its network from the United States and other countries [CRO06, MAS07, NEB04, WIL03]. These facilities have been augmented since 2002 by the creation of the Geospatial One-Stop portal to support President Bush's e-government Initiative (see http://www.geodata.gov).

Alongside these developments, a number of organizations at international, regional, and global levels have been set up to promote capacity building and raise awareness of the need for governments to promote the creation of SDIs. Examples of such organizations are the European Umbrella Organization for Geographic Information (EUROGI) and the Global Spatial Data Infrastructure Association (GSDI).

13.2.2 SDI Components

The process of SDI development and implementation consists of several key components. Rajabifard et al. [RAJ02] distinguish five SDI components – access network, standards, policy, people, and spatial data – to clarify the SDI concept in more operational terms (Fig. 13.1).

The access network component of an SDI is critical from a technical perspective to facilitate the use of data by people. This component seeks to facilitate access to relevant data sources and spatial information services by anyone, anywhere. It includes access and distribution networks, Web services for cataloguing, viewing, downloading spatial data, data warehouses, and so on. The component standards

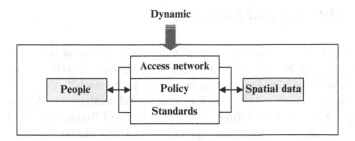

Fig. 13.1 Nature of and relations among SDI components (adopted from [RAJ02])

ensures interoperability amongst the data and access mechanisms defined. Standards can be applied at many different levels within an SDI. In terms of data, Australia's former national mapping organization, the Australian Land Information Group [AUS01] identified that standards are required "in reference systems, data models, data dictionaries, data quality, data transfer, and metadata." Interoperability is a key consideration of both the standards and data components. Component spatial data refers to core datasets to be shared and exchanged between stakeholders. Examples of core datasets are cadastral, topographical, administrative, and land use. These datasets should be compatible in terms of format, reference system, projection, resolution, and quality. The policy component is critical for the construction, maintenance, access, and application of standards and datasets for SDI implementation. In general, policies are required for SDI that incorporate: spatial data access, pricing and licensing, funding, privacy, spatial data transfers, custodianship, metadata, and standards. "Component people" refers to all the data and service users, providers, and value-added resellers who can be employed by public authorities or private companies. Through increased use and awareness of spatial information, dramatic growth has occurred in the user base. With the proliferation of online Web services, and navigation/direction information, an increasing number of people are using spatial data; this is obviously of importance in the development of an SDI to facilitate spatial data activities.

Rajabifard et al. [RAJ02] suggested that different categories of the SDI components could be formed based on the different nature of their interactions within the SDI. Considering the important and fundamental role between people and data as one category, a second can be considered consisting of the main technical components: the access networks, policy, and standards. The nature of both categories is very dynamic due to the changes occurring in communities (people) and their needs, as well as their ongoing requirements for different sets of data. In addition, with the rapidity with which technology develops, the need for the mediation of rights, restrictions, and responsibilities between people and data are also constantly subject to change (Fig. 13.1). This suggests an integrated SDI cannot be composed of spatial data, value-added services, and end-users alone, but instead involves other important issues regarding interoperability, policies, and networks. This in turn reflects the dynamic nature of the whole SDI concept.

13.2.3   SDI Costs and Benefits

The costs and benefits associated with SDI development cannot be easily estimated with any precision. Nevertheless, it is clear that the tasks of SDI coordination and governance are relatively inexpensive in relation to the overall expenditure on geographic information, whereas the task of core digital database development is relatively expensive. The U.S. Office of Management and Budget has estimated that U.S. federal agencies alone already spend at least US$4 billion annually to collect and manage domestic data, whereas the cost of FGDC and its work are less than 1% of this amount [MAS05, MAS07].

As mentioned before, SDIs have economic, social, and environmental benefits. The most important SDI benefit is the promotion of economic growth as a result of an expanding market for geographic information products (e.g., navigation systems) both locally and internationally. A PIRA International study conducted in 2000 for the European Commission [PIR00] gives some indication of the value of public-sector information in the tightly constrained European market of that time. The findings showed that over half the economic value of public sector information in 1999 (€68 billion) came directly from geographic information sources. This is equivalent to about 1% of the European gross domestic product. The findings showed that the economic value of public geographic information resources in the less constrained U.S. market was €750 billion. With the easing of constraints through the development of SDIs, it might be expected that the size of the European market will move toward that of the U.S. market over time. Estimates of the growth of the commercial geographic information market are more readily available and have been on the order of 15–20% per year in recent years [GEO09]. The impact of an expanding market of this size on job creation is also considerable. Other economic benefits of SDIs include increased efficiency and lower operating costs for both public and private sector organisations due to wider access to geographic information and information-based services [CRA03, DUF04, GAR08, LON08, MAS07].

The most important social benefit of SDIs is the extent to which they create more efficient and more transparent governments at all levels as a result of the increasing availability of authoritative data to policy and decision makers. Another important social benefit stems from the opportunities that SDI data-sharing creates for citizens to actively participate in the democratic process [MAS07, WIL03]. Because they bring together data from many diverse sources, SDIs are also likely to lead to better security arrangements and more effective systems for emergency planning and response. There are also many operational benefits for social services, public health, education, and public safety from the more effective targeting of areas and groups with special needs.

SDIs can have many environmental benefits, and they have an important role to play in promoting sustainable development throughout the world. At different government levels they provide the data required for effective management and monitoring of natural resources [CRA03, EUR07]. They are particularly useful in coastal zones because of the extent to which they can integrate maritime and terrestrial data [VAE09].

So far, the number of existing studies that systematically analyses the costs and benefits of SDI implementations is still very low. The benefits can be examined from different viewpoints, such as the impact of a different SDI project, impact on an agency, impact on users, or impact on a wider community or section of society. Significant benefits may accumulate for a wide community or section of society, however, such benefits are very difficult to quantify in financial terms. If implementation of an SDI supports other projects or infrastructures, how can one accurately assign a portion of the total financial or societal benefit derived from that project or initiative to the SDI. Funding agencies worry about double accounting for such benefits, claiming the benefits as accruing to both the SDI and the project or infrastructure supported by the SDI. Longhorn and Blakemore [LON08] made an extensive overview of existing cost–benefit SDI studies. Table 13.1 shows the key studies and their results in terms of benefit:cost ratio. The results indicate that the SDI benefits are generally (much) higher than the costs.

The dearth of cost–benefit studies in the field of SDIs (but also of e-government) may be rather surprising considering the large number of SDI initiatives taking place worldwide, but may be explained by the changing nature of SDI. The first SDI implementations were largely driven by public sector mapping agencies from

Table 13.1 Some benefit–cost study results (adapted from [LON08])

Year	Organisation	Country	Type of study	Benefit:Cost
2003	Environment agency U.K. and University of Sheffield	EU-wide	Contribution to the extended impact assessment for INSPIRE	4.4:1 to 8.9:1
2004	European Commission INSPIRE	EU-wide	Extended impact assessment for INSPIRE	5.4:1 to 12.4:1
2004	Twijnstra and Gudde	The Netherlands	Cost–benefit analysis for Dutch Innovation SDI-Programme 'Space for Geo-Information'	10:1
2007	Information society department of the regional ministry of universities, research and information society	Spain	Socioeconomic impact of the SDI of Catalonia	8:1

the United States, Canada, and Australia with an emphasis on specific products such as the creation or completion of a spatial database, the diversification in multiple products, the creation of metadata as part of the production process, the development of clearinghouses, the emergence of view services, and so on. Multiple projects took place through dedicated project funding often internal to an organisation or part of existing operational practices. If estimations of costs and benefits were made, particularly to access grants or other types of funding, they appear not to have been published or validated in the light of postproject experience. There is a definitional aspect here: we consider all of these projects under the SDI umbrella but it is a fragmented type of SDI, leading to multiple interpretations of what an SDI is, and difficulty in developing meaningful comparisons. Nevertheless, as the diffusion of SDI has gathered momentum and social networks of SDI practitioners have contributed to greater shared understanding and exchange of practice the internal/project characteristics of earlier developments have moved toward wider coordinated efforts among multiple stakeholders. This opening of SDIs to external partners may be now contributing to greater demands for cost–benefit analyses, exposing the dearth of existing studies more clearly [CRA06].

13.3 SDI Practices

The next SDI practices at different administrative levels show examples of SDI in practice, the application of the SDI components, and their impact on society. The following four SDIs are briefly described: European, Catalonian, Flemish, and Leiedal. For each SDI practice, the objective, the state of implementation, and the impacts are briefly presented. This information forms the basis for the systematic analysis of the four SDI practices that results in a summary table presented at the end of this section (Table 13.2).

13.3.1 Europe

Environmental policy is one of the key policy areas in Europe, and it has certainly gained importance over the last decades. Environmental policy aims at preserving our environment and therefore the need to monitor and report on the status in different sectors such as water, biodiversity, air quality, land use, climate change, and so on. It involves all levels of government: from global to European, national, subnational, and even the local level. But environmental policy also requires a cross-border approach to tackle phenomena that do not stop at national borders. Think about flooding alone. In addition, also other policy sectors need to consider environmental aspects including agriculture, transport, health, and regional policy. In order to prepare, monitor, and evaluate measures to protect our environment, all stakeholders involved should readily have access to a lot of data: statistical and scientific information, in situ measurements, and spatial data. The latter are critical to assess the status of the environment in a well-balanced way.

Therefore, the Directive 2007/2/EC of the Council and the European Parliament is established as the legal framework for setting up and operating an Infrastructure for Spatial Information in Europe (INSPIRE) based on SDIs established and operated by Member States [EUR07]. The main objectives of this European SDI are to support the formulation, implementation, monitoring, and evaluation of community environmental policies, and to overcome major barriers still affecting the availability and accessibility of spatial data. These barriers include the following:

1. Inconsistencies in spatial data collection (spatial data are often missing or incomplete or alternatively the same data are collected twice by different organisations).
2. Lacking documentation (description of available spatial data is often incomplete).
3. Spatial datasets not compatible (spatial datasets often cannot be combined with other spatial datasets).
4. Incompatible geographic information initiatives (the infrastructures to find, access, and use spatial data often function only in isolation)
5. Barriers to data sharing (cultural, institutional, financial, and legal barriers prevent or delay the sharing of existing data).

The key elements of the INSPIRE directive to overcome the above-mentioned barriers include: metadata to describe existing information resources so that they can be more easily found and accessed; harmonisation of key spatial data themes needed to support environmental policies in the European Union (EU); agreements on network services and technologies to allow discovery, viewing, download of information resources, and access to related services; policy agreements on sharing and access, including licensing and charging; coordination and monitoring mechanisms; and implementation process and procedures.

A key milestone was 15th May 2009 at which stage all Member States should have passed national legislation transposing the INSPIRE Directive, and established their SDI. Another milestone will be the establishment of the INSPIRE Geoportal that provides the means to search for spatial datasets and spatial data services, and subject to access restrictions, view and download spatial datasets from the EU Member States within the framework of INSPIRE. The current version is a prototype (http://www.inspire-geoportal.eu/) and allows for discovery and viewing of spatial datasets and services. Its aim is to identify issues related to its implementation and accessing distributed INSPIRE services, to help toward the development of the operational geoportal. This prototype currently accesses a limited number of discovery and view services and therefore only a few metadata for spatial datasets and services can be found and viewed. These will increase as more services become available from the EU Member States.

An extended impact assessment of INSPIRE was carried out during 2003. This analysis found that the overall costs of data harmonisation; the development of metadata services; and the coordination of EU and national, regional, and local organisations over the first 10 years might be somewhere between €200 and €300 million per annum [CRA03]. These costs would be borne largely by the public sector, and they would be incurred mainly at regional and local levels. Estimating the likely benefits was more difficult, but even partial assessment indicated that they would amount to somewhere between €1.2 and €1.8 billion a year. The main benefits were considered: more cost-effective expenditure on environmental protection, reduced duplication of spatial data collection, improved delivery of risk prevention policies, and improved delivery of health and environmental policies were envisioned. A later study estimated the INSPIRE costs were between €92 and €137 million and the estimated benefits between €770 and €1150 million [DUF04]. These lower estimates are the consequences of the scope of INSPIRE being reduced as well as the number of priority data to be shared.

13.3.2 Catalonia

Catalonia is one of the 17 autonomous communities of Spain. It comprises four provinces and 942 municipalities.

The Catalan SDI, known as IDEC (Infraestructura Dades Especials de Catalunya), started in 2002 as a collaboration among the Cartographic Institute of Catalonia, the two departments of regional government, the Department of Land Policy and Public Works, and the Secretary of the Information and Telecommunication Society of the Department Universities, Research and the Information Society. The objective of IDEC is to promote the use of geographic information by making data more easily available to public and private sector users, and ordinary citizens. Its main function is to develop an enabling platform to promote the dissemination of information and encourage contacts between data providers and users [GUI06].

The IDEC Geoportal gives access in three languages (Catalan, Spanish, and English) to the data catalogue service and Web map service (http://www.geoportal-idec.cat/geoportal/cat/). The catalogue contains some 15,000 metadata records for datasets, and some 200 records for services provided by 17 organisations. The geoservices provided include view, downloading, geocoding, and coordinate transformations. There are also thematic applications addressed to local authorities and universities, including customisable viewers and editors for local authorities which are used as mash-ups in many public and private sector Web pages (e.g., Web tourist routes, industrial company registers). Currently, 250 municipalities have published in their Web pages their customized viewers, which receive more than 30,000 visits monthly. The geoportal is accessed by another 20,000 visitors monthly, to consult the catalogue service and Web map service. Most of the visitors come from the public sector, but private users also represent a significant percentage. Many other public and private end-user applications use the Web map service to access reference and thematic data.

A socioeconomic impact assessment study was undertaken in 2007 [GAR08]. The key findings were categorised into costs and benefits. The total costs of establishing and operating the IDEC over a five-year period (2002–2006) was €1.5 million of which €325,000 for each of the first 2 years (2002–2003) was necessary to launch the SDI, and €283,000 per annum to operate and develop the infrastructure in the three subsequent years. Human resources represented 76% of the costs during the launch period, and 91% during operation. The costs include the following: metadata creation and maintenance, development of geoservices (including geoportal, catalogue, Web Map Service client), preparation of data for publication, applications, hardware and software, and management. The evidence collected shows clearly that the main benefits of the IDEC accrue at the level of local public administration through internal efficiency benefits (time saved in internal queries by technical staff, time saved in attending queries by the public, time saved in internal processes) and effectiveness benefits (time saved by the public and by companies in dealing with public administration). The study estimated that the internal efficiency benefits account for over 500 hours per month. Using an hourly rate of €30 for technical staff in local government, these savings exceed €2.6 million per year. Effectiveness savings are just as great at another 500 hours per month. The study indicated that the total investment to set up the IDEC and develop it over a 4-year period (2002–2005) is recovered in just over 6 months. Wider socioeconomic benefits were also identified but not quantified. In particular, the study indicated that Web-based spatial services allow smaller local authorities to narrow the digital divide with the larger ones in the provision of services to citizens and companies.

13.3.3 Flanders

Flanders has historically been a region overlapping parts of modern Belgium, France, and The Netherlands. Today, Flanders designates either the Flemish Region, a territorial circumscription, or the Flemish Community, which indicates the cultural community of Dutch-speaking Belgians, including Dutch-speaking residents of the Brussels–Capital Region. The parliament and government govern both the Community and the Region, even though they are not entirely coextensive. The Flemish Region consists of 308 municipalities and it is divided into five provinces.

Flanders started in 1995 to set up a framework for cooperation to develop and implement a sound communication and management system for geographical information: GIS-Flanders. Many stakeholders have taken part in the development of GIS-Flanders including all the departments of the Flemish government, the Flemish public agencies (e.g., environmental agency, land agency, institute for nature conservation, etc.), the provincial authorities, and the municipalities. The agency for Geo-Information Flanders (Agentschap voor Geografische Informatie Vlaanderen), which used to be the Support Centre of GIS-Vlaanderen, is the secretariat and executive body responsible for the coordination, organisation, and provision of services of and to the GIS-Vlaanderen partnership. It operates as the central point for anyone wishing to access GI in Flanders.

The key results of GIS-Flanders are the adoption of interoperability standards, and the supply of data and services. One of the key objectives of GIS-Flanders is to distribute spatial data in a vendor-independent context, and therefore to support systematically the most frequently used data formats. More than 50 full coverage datasets are available, including: street network, Flemish hydrographical atlas, orthophotos, cadastral parcels, digital elevation models, Flemish ecological network areas, land cover, addresses, and soil maps. In addition, several services have been developed. The following are some examples.

• Geo-Flanders (http://geo-vlaanderen.agiv.be): Application for visualisation and querying tools as well as an ISO-standardised catalogue service. One example is the visualisation and querying tool on the various rights of pre-emption (nature conservation, reallotments, social housing) integrated in a single application. This application facilitates notaries and public authorities who are dealing with real estate sales, and enables the identification of the potential rights of pre-emption on specific cadastral parcels.
• GIRAF (http://giraf.agiv.be/): Application for spatial data tailoring, ordering, and downloading.
• FLEPOS (http://www.flepos.be): Flemish Positioning Service (network of groundstations for GPS measurements). This application is so successful that it is used by all topographers and land surveyors in Flanders.
• CRAB (http://www.agiv.be/gis/projecten//?catid=34): Central Reference Address dataBase. Through this service, the municipalities become the starting point for its maintenance according to specifications for the exchange of address information.
• KLIP (http://www.klip.be): Centralised plan request module for digging and excavation requests works to prevent damage to subsurface utility lines. The KLIP application (Cables and Pipeline Registration Portal) enables utilities and constructors to identify (underground) cables or pipes situated in an area where they intend to start to do some work. Automatic forms are generated which can be sent to other companies active in the same area to check whether economy of scale can be reached by profiting from the fact that a certain road segment will be opened. Another benefit is the avoidance of damage to others' cables and pipes by requesting detailed plans [VAN08].

The increasing number of Web services/applications and their usage figures shows the rising popularity for all these new Web facilities in Flanders. As an example, the Cables and Pipelines Registration Portal KLIP featured, after the first year of operation, more than 300 utility companies and more than 200 stakeholders registered, with more than 40,000 plan requests processed for digging and excavation requests.

Along with the development of GIS-Flanders, several results have been obtained thanks to coordination efforts, including: important reduction of scattered initiatives; coordination amongst provinces has become the default practice; multiusage has become the default perspective for new data collection initiatives (orthoimagery, CRAB, etc.); and much earlier warning on new initiatives, resulting in better coordination and avoidance of unnecessary duplication.

The harmonisation efforts have resulted in the acceptance and use of the data sources made available through GIS-Flanders as the single reference source for new data throughout Flemish public authorities. The common usage of agreed specifications, services, and recommendations makes, for example, the technical exchange of spatial planning data and address information also feasible.

13.3.4   Leiedal

Intercommunale Leiedal is a co-operative of 13 municipalities in the province of West-Flanders, Belgium. This SDI practice is a good example of ICT and geo-information used for regional cooperation and common service provision to promote local development. Local governments play an important role in providing services that enhance the environment for local business. These better services to local businesses can be achieved by better information exchange between governments. Therefore, the objective of the Leidal SDI is to promote local development by powerful Web services. This initiative was funded by Log-IN project 'Building Better Business Services Through E-Government' (http://www.login-project.net).

This local SDI started to be developed in 2004 and is strongly based on Web services and open standards (e.g., XML, GML), so that data and information in different formats can be easily exchanged with other governments and partners. The Leiedal SDI enables local authorities to build powerful Web services using only a Web browser. The Leiedal SDI allows local authorities to manage and publish their spatial data online, to link their data and services with others, and where needed extract, transform, and load the data automatically. In this way, an open environment is created for the local authorities to exchange their spatial data (address, buildings, sewerage, etc.), to build Web services and to promote the use of spatial data in electronic service delivery. It is Leiedal's ultimate ambition to build one Web service by just one local authority that can be reused by others [MEU09]. Examples of developed local services are: location of schools and services, child care, waste water, and roadworks (see http://www.leiedal.be/e-government/geo-informatie).

The Leiedal SDI has proven to be added value for the local authorities by linking their back offices and providing information-rich services. Through this initiative, the local authorities got access to powerful tools usually only available to central governments, and became a "big player" so that they got the attention of larger ICT consortia who usually do not work for these customers. In addition, the SDI resulted in a change of perception of the business community to the local governments. Finally, this infrastructure has already saved €0.5 million, and a calculated saving of five employees. The business benefits include an improvement in effectiveness of up to 50%, as well as up-to-date and more accurate data available at all times for sharing [MEU09].

13.3.5   Summary of the SDI Practices

Table 13.2 systematically summarizes the four SDI practices on the basis of the
following characteristics: the year of initiative, the reasons to start the initiative, the
key objectives, the key components, the stakeholder groups, and the results of
cost–benefit analysis.

13.3.6   Discussion

These four practices show clearly that the current SDIs at different levels are
dynamic, integrated, and multiple in nature, dynamic in the sense that SDIs are an
evolving target with changing demands. These changes and the evolution of SDI
are only possible because people play a key role in the SDI concept. Referring to
Rajabifard's SDI conceptual model (see Fig. 13.1) it has to be stressed that people
are not limited to one side of the diagram as a separate component, but are rather
an integral part of all other components, especially access networks, policy, and
standards. The human factor plays a key role in shaping those components: people
develop the technology behind access network facilities; policies on SDI are solely
created and obeyed by people; standards can only be developed and applied successfully if people reach agreement.

Integrated in the sense of regional, system, and digital sense integration, each
of the practices presents a process in which jurisdictions enter into a regional
agreement in order to enhance regional cooperation through regional institutions
and rules. Its objectives could range from economic to political although it likely
becomes a political economy initiative where commercial purposes are the
means to achieve broader sociopolitical and security objectives. All the practices
also show aspects of system integration, the bringing together of the SDI-
component subsystems (access network, standards, policy, people, and spatial
data) into one system and ensuring that the subsystems function together as a
system. Finally, all the practices focus on the idea that data or information of any
given electronic device can be read or manipulated by another device using a
standard format.

The practices also clearly show the multiple natures of SDIs. This refers to the
multiple SDI reasons to start, multiple objectives, the multiple approaches to
achieve the objectives, the multiple key components, the multiple scales, the multiple stakeholders, multiple perspectives, and the multi-impacts.

Viewing the impact of the four practices, it appears that the benefits are generally higher than the costs. Of the four practices only Europe and Catalonia have
undertaken an impact study by means of a detailed cost–benefit analysis. The other
two practices have expressed qualitative assessments of the benefits. Although the
qualitative benefits should not be underestimated, it is crucial to quantify the benefits
and their relationship with the investment made to maintain political support and

Table 13.2 Summary of the four SDI practices

SDI practice	Europe	Catalonia	Flanders	Leiedal
Year of initiative	2001	2002	1995	2004
Reasons to start the initiative	Inconsistencies in spatial data collection Lacking documentation Spatial data not compatible Incompatible geo-information initiatives Barriers to data sharing	Limited dissemination of spatial data Poor contacts between data providers and users	Lack of cooperation No support for public authorities to manage their geographic information	Poor exchange of spatial data Weak provision of services (for local businesses)
Initial objective	To support the formulation, imple-mentation, monitoring, and evaluation of environmental policies To overcome major barriers still affecting the availability and accessibility of spatial data	To promote the use of geographic information by making data more easily available to public and private users and ordinary citizens	To develop and implement a sound communication and management system for geographic information To distribute spatial data in a vendor-independent context	To create an open environment to exchange spatial data, to build Web services, to promote the use of spatial data in electronic service delivery for promoting local development
Key components[a]	Metadata Harmonisation of key spatial data themes Agreements on network services and technologies Policy agreements on sharing and access Coordination and monitoring mechanisms	Metadata Network services (catalogue service/Web map service) Policy agreements on sharing and access Coordination mechanisms	Harmonisation of spatial data and services Policy agreements on sharing and access Coordination mechanisms	Network services Harmonisation of spatial data and services

(continued)

Table 13.2 (continued)

SDI practice	Europe	Catalonia	Flanders	Leiedal
Stakeholder groups	All public authorities in the European Union	Public authorities, private sector agencies, and citizens	All the departments of the Flemish government, the Flemish Public Agencies, the provincial authorities, and the municipalities	Local authorities, private sector agencies and citizens
Cost–benefit analysis	5.4:1 to 12.1:1	8:1	No cost–benefit analysis performed	No cost–benefit analysis performed

[a] A more detailed description of the most important components on which the SDI-practice is focusing

user engagement. In this sense the Catalonia study not only provides good evidence of how quickly the investments made can be recovered, but also points in the direction SDIs should take, that is, toward those applications/services that are routine, and that save time and money, even in small quantities, for a large number of users among citizens, businesses, and the public sector. In this sense, it is interesting to see how all the practices presented are making a real effort to engage local authorities, which are closer to the citizens in providing essential services. This bodes well for achieving positive impacts.

13.4   Spatial Data Infrastructures and E-Government

This chapter introduced the concept and current practices of spatial data infrastructures. This final section explores the potential contribution of these infrastructures to e-government.

Being aware that certain developments are happening, e-government is still mainly considered as simply placing governmental services and products online. In other words, it is the front office that gets the full attention. However, it is likely that the key e-government benefits are located in the back-office environments. For example, ICTs can be implemented within organisations to streamline internal processes. They can also be implemented to streamline interorganisational processes to improve the sharing of existing available public data.

The SDI concept of sharing resources from multiple sources is not well applied in e-government research and practice. Until now, the vast majority of governmental bodies focus upon the use of ICTs within individual organisations. Increasingly, ICTs also have a role to play in improving efficiency, effectiveness, and competitive advantage between (public) organisations. With regard to ICTs, there is clearly considerable scope for developing interorganisational exchange of data and information. Organisations need to share data to avoid duplication of expenses, associated with the generation and maintenance of data and their integration with other data. Progress in developing interorganisational sharing of data in the past has been hampered considerably by the variety of proprietary formats in which such data have been traditionally held and, to some degree, by difficulties in transmitting large data volumes via slow networks. The move toward interoperable ICTs and (open) standards, and the ever-increasing bandwidths of communications, however, are rapidly lessening the technological difficulties associated with sharing data between organisations. During the next few years there will certainly be a considerable growth in interorganisational exchange and use of data, although it should be observed that sharing data between organisations raises a host of interorganisational issues, which are only now beginning to be explored.

If organisational issues are often barriers to successful ICT implementations within individual organisations, what problems will there be when attempting to share data between organisations? When data are shared between two or more organisations, whose definitions of the meanings of the data will be adopted? Who will have the right to update the data? Who is responsible for quality and who for errors? If company A takes action on data supplied by company B, who is legally responsible? And finally, what are the best coordination structures? In order to partly answer these questions, the lessons learnt from the existing SDI practices could be a useful support. For example, awareness of the dynamic, integrated, and multiple nature of SDIs could have a positive impact on good e-government. The knowledge and experiences about the changing demands of the stakeholders, the strengthening of the regional, system, and digital integration, the multiobjectives of multistakeholders at multiscale levels, and the multiple approaches to achieve these multiobjectives could contribute somehow to the development of successful e-government practices.

On the basis of potential SDI support, it is strongly recommended to integrate SDI research with e-government research (although the gap between these two perspectives is still very wide [DEV07]) and to perform multidisciplinary SDI research necessary to improve future SDIs. To date, the SDIs have been mainly analysed from a technological point of view, taking the nontechnological issues such as the institutional framework, funding mechanisms, and human resources as stable, immobile factors. However, it appears that SDIs often fail due to these nontechnological issues [BOU06]. Therefore, it is necessary also to analyse the nontechnological issues. This need of a multidisciplinary approach is strongly in line with the multiple perspective to e-government as described by Bekkers [BEK05].

Another reason of SDI importance to contribute to good e-government is the critical role of geographic information underpinning the decision-making process in many domains. Moreover, the high percentage of geographical information used by governments to perform their public tasks (as presented in the introduction) confirms the need to focus on SDIs as a support to e-government. Only then the full potential of the application of geographical information can be used, and so e-government.

References

AUS01   AUSLIG, Australian Spatial Data Infrastructure. Australian Land Information Group, 2001.
BEK05   Bekkers, V.J.J.M., Van Duivenboden, H.P.M., Lips, A.M.B., "Van e-government naar e-governance", A.M.B. Lips, V.J.J.M. Bekkers and A. Zuurmond (Eds.), ICT en openbaar bestuur, Implicaties en uitdagingen van technologische toepassingen voor de overheid, Utrecht, Uitgeverij Lemma, 2005, p. 419–440 (in Dutch).
BOU06   Bouckaert, G., Van Orshoven, J., Dumortier, J., Van Hootegem, G., Macharis, C., Spatial Data Infrastructures and Public Sector Innovation, SBO Project Proposal, Leuven/Brussels, Belgium, 2006.
CLI94   Clinton, W., Coordinating geographic data acquisition and access to the National Spatial Data Infrastructure, Executive Order 12096, Federal Register 59, Washington DC, US, 17671–4, 1994.

CRA03   Craglia, M, Contribution to the extended impact assessment of INSPIRE, Environment
          Agency for England and Wales, 2003, http://inspire.jrc.ec.europa.eu/reports/fds_
          report_sept2003.pdf, (last access 17 November 2009).
CRA06   Craglia, M, Novak, J., Report of International Workshop on Spatial Data Infrastructures'
          Cost-Benefit/Return on Investment, Luxembourg, OPOCE, 2006.
CRO06   Crompvoets J., National Spatial Data Clearinghouses: Worldwide development and
          impact, PhD-thesis, Wageningen, The Netherlands, 2006, http://library.wur.nl/wda/
          dissertations/dis3894.pdf, (last access 17 November 2009).
DEV07   De Vries, W., "eGov and SDI: The common grounds and missing links", Proceedings
          of the 8th annual international conference on Digital government research: bridging
          disciplines & domains, Philadelphia, Pennsylvania, May 20–23, 2007.
DUF04   Dufourmont, H., Extended impact assessment of INSPIRE Based on revised scope,
          European Commission, DG Eurostat, Luxemburg, 2004.
EUR07   European Commission, Directive 2007/2/EC of the European Parliament and of the
          Council of 14 March 2007 establishing an Infrastructure for Spatial Information in the
          European Community (INSPIRE), 2007.
FEE03   Feeney, M.-E.F., "SDIs and Decision Support", I.P. Williamson, A. Rajabifard and
          M.E. Feeney (Eds.), Developing Spatial Data Infrastructures: From Concept to Reality,
          London, Taylor & Francis, 2003, p. 195–210.
GEO09   GEO-Business Nederland, Geo-sector in kaart, Marktmonitor Nederlandse geo-
          informatiesector 2008/2009, 2009.
GAR08   Garcia Almirall, P., Moix Bergadá, M., Queraltó Ros, P., Craglia, M., The socio-
          economic impact of the spatial data infrastructure of Catalonia. JRC Scientific and
          technical reports, 2008.
GOR98   Gore, A., "The Digital Earth: understanding our planet in the 21st century", The
          Australian Surveyor, Vol. 43 no. 2, 1998, p. 89–91.
GUI06   Guimet, J., "From theory to practice: the SDI platform and its application to public and
          private sectors in Catalonia", Proceedings INSPIRE Workshop. Ispra, Italy, 2006.
LON08   Longhorn, R.A., Blakemore, M., Geographic information, value, pricing, production,
          and consumption, CRC Press, Taylor & Francis Group, New-York, USA, 2008.
LON99   Longley, P.A., Goodchild, M.F., Maguire D.J., Rhind, D.W. (Eds.), Geographic
          Information Systems, Second Edition, New York, John Wiley & Sons, 1999.
MAS99   Masser, I., "All shapes and sizes: the first generation of National Spatial Infrastructures",
          International Journal of Geographical Information Science, vol. 13, 1999, p. 67–84.
MAS05   Masser, I., GIS Worlds, Creating Spatial Data Infrastructures, Redlands, California,
          ESRI Press, 2005.
MAS07   Masser, I., Building European Spatial Data Infrastructures, Redlands, California, ESRI
          Press, 2007.
MEU09   Meuris, F., GovMaps.eu (LoG-IN Generic Information Infrastructure), Intercommunale
          Leiedal (B), 2009.
MOR04   Morales, J., Model-driven Design of Geo-information Services, ITC, Enschede, 2004.
NAT93   National Research Council, Towards a Coordinated Spatial Data Infrastructure for the
          Nation, Mapping Science Committee, Washington DC, National Academy Press,
          1993.
NEB04   Nebert, D.D. (Ed.), Developing spatial data infrastructures: the SDI cookbook, Global
          Spatial Data Infrastructure association, Version 2.0, 2004, http://www.gsdi.org/
          docs2004/Cookbook/cookbookV2.0.pdf (last access 17 November 2009).
PIR00   Pira International Ltd, Commercial Exploitation of Europe's Public Sector Information,
          Luxemburg, 2000.
RAJ02   Rajabifard, A., Feeney, M-E.F., Williamson, I.P., "Future directions for SDI
          Development", International Journal of Applied Earth Observation and Geoinformation,
          vol. 4, no. 1, 2002, p. 11–22.

VAE09   Vaez, S, Rajabifard, A., Williamson I.P., "Seamless SDI Model – Bridging the Gap
        between Land and Marine Environments", B. Van Loenen, J.W.J. Besemer and J.A.
        Zevenbergen (Eds.), SDI Convergence, Nederlandse Commissie voor Geodesie, 48,
        2009, p. 239–252.
VAN08   Vandenbroucke, D., Janssen, K., Spatial Data Infrastructures in Belgium: State of Play
        2007, Country report by the Spatial Applications Division, K.U. Leuven R&D, 2008.
WIL03   Williamson, I.P., Rajabifard, A., Feeney, M-E.F. (Eds.), Developing Spatial Data
        Infrastructures: From Concept to Reality, London, Taylor & Francis, 2003.

Index